Poetic Encores

Poetic Encores

FRANK DE CANIO

Library of Congress Control Number: 2020924280

ISBN:	Hardcover	978-1-6641-4645-7
	Softcover	978-1-6641-4644-0
	eBook	978-1-6641-4643-3

Print information available on the last page.

Rev. date: 12/10/2020

To order additional copies of this book, contact:
Xlibris
844-714-8691
www.Xlibris.com
Orders@Xlibris.com
822396

Contents

To His Cruel Mistress

To give up love for power,
to forfeit the sacred grail's
redeeming quest, or an hour
of happiness, just to rail
senselessly against the world's
injustice, were crime enough,
where Time forgets the unfurled
standard flying in the dust.
But how much worse, thoughtless girl,
to bind me to your bower
and let Love's secrets unfurl,
not like the perfumed flower,
rich with nectar for the lips,
but like a war-torn banner
blowing on the battleship
of cold, wind-whipped surrender.
How merciless of you, dear friend,
to lure me to this bitter end.

PUBLISHED in PLEIADES 1992

Macho Chic

I need a girl who toughs it in a gym;
whose body's fitness constitutes her pride.
She's not concerned with sexes, her or him,
as long as both of them are satisfied.
She doesn't show off necklaces or pearls
that lend a glow to lewd décolletage,
or style her hair in bangs or dangling curls.
Guys see her naked mostly to massage
her muscled sinews flashing jewels of sweat.
The laces of her gloves hang from her wrists
like frills in rings where she's an even bet
to lay opponents out with pounding fists.
A stand-up gal, she throws a solid jab
to compensate for being weak on gab.

Published in Nuthouse, winter '06

Ode to Footwear

No gorgeous garments tailors sew
from front to back and head to toe

that grace the contours lovers woo
are so well fashioned as a shoe,

which I could fondle in my hand
without the slightest reprimand

from tight-laced gals who'd think it rude
if similarly I'd intrude

on clinging vestments half as sweet
as those receptacles for feet.

They never make demands on me
to toe the line unhappily

when otherwise I rue in bed
(as one half of the pair I'd wed -

which other half puts her foot down)
that polished shoes don't wear a frown,

nor step-wise age into a shrew
like well-heeled ladies sometimes do.

Previously Published in Nuthouse, winter 2006

Upset

I couldn't help it if your lack of skills
in sparring couldn't stay my taunting jabs.
Your pleated mini-skirt and blouse's frills
seemed more stiff than your upper lip and abs.
I flicked a left and with presumptive right
I barbed a little, snickering for sport.
Because I was a pro and you seemed slight
for such a beef, I'd hoped to make it short.
How quickly you adjusted to my speed
and glancing blows once you got under way.
You bobbed and weaved as wisecracks made me bleed,
then followed up with heated repartee,
whose swift, relentless flurry sealed my loss.
How fast I moved to reinstate the rules,
afraid you'd throw a consummate right cross
to crown my glory as the king of fools.
Now I was left - who'd clearly had enough -
a standing witness to your stiff rebuff.

Published in "Love's Chance" -Fall/Winter '05

Jail Bait

She wasn't the attractive date I'd sought.
But like a matron collaring a thief,
her perfume mollified my being caught
and turned her imposition to relief.
And in the sultry prison of her arms,
I found a shelter without rent to pay
to denizens less smitten by her charms.
Though this arrest cause freer men dismay,
I opted to play shackled racketeer.
For with my loss of face, I lost the need
to do more at the portal of her ear
than feign resistance to what she decreed.
And when she fixed my sentence with a kiss,
I marveled that confinement fueled such bliss.

Published in Love's Chance Fall/winter '05

Black Widow

Her cold, cosmetic visage decomposed
in the flush of amorous prostration,
she rises - an accusatory ghost -
swishing sheets that boast her defloration.
Gathering up the silk, brocaded dress,
pumps and lace chemise lying on the floor
like scattered ash of courtship's politesse,
she makes abortive efforts to restore
the shattered vestige of her virgin pride.
But plundered loins, jeweled with sweat, quicken
with the fervor of shame's vindictive stride,
as she contemplates her passion-stricken
consort. And, riding tides that in him ebb,
she binds him like a spider to its web.

Now rendering the conqueror's largess,
she wipes the perspiration from his head,
as if aloof compassion could redress
her shameful violation in his bed.
And thus she mounts him, legs astride his chest;
alighting on his efflorescent lips,
the pollinating forage of her breast,

as if for nectar that its nipple sips.
And seeing him trussed-up, she half resists
the thought that satin sheets are the trousseau -
augmented with a love knot on the wrists -
of death-in-waiting's soon enravished beau.
And thus, she seals a kiss on his dismay,
as when a father gives the bride away.

Published in Red Owl, Autumn 2005

Prisoner of Sex

Hung over from his binge the night before,
he sits against the backboard of his bed
as his fond lover enters through the door
with breakfast - coffee, scrambled eggs and bread.
Despite a pompous sense of royal ease,
he feels in some unsettling way remiss
as she unloads her burden on his knees,
and then bends over with a sideling kiss.
Unable to maneuver her to bed,
he plays a foppish king on borrowed throne
who takes base tribute from her lips instead
of her subjection to his sceptered bone.
This stiffens like a trophy in her keep
as she sets off to work and he to sleep.

Published in Red Owl, Autumn 2005

Regressive Variations on a Waitress

How fast you fetch that free carafe of wine
for me as if to heed the stern behest
of majesty before which you're supine.
And I imagine that you're as obsessed
with feting me as I'm disposed to shine.
Yet you just grant my stammering request,
like you're a nanny able to divine
my childish avarice and think it best
to bare the bosom toward which I incline.
Still, I indulge the fancy that I'm blest
with service that's maternally benign.
But, pouting lips, you sullenly divest
me of the sense my nursemaid has no spine,
and that I'm pampered tyke or royal guest
whose interests you're afraid to undermine.
For now it's obvious you're overstressed
and utilize the wine as anodyne
to quiet me so you could get some rest.

Published in Quothade '05/spring '06

“You’re shorter than I thought,”

I said. “I know it. But let’s not go there,”
she countered. For I’d reassessed her size
as quantified by amplifying eyes
which focused on the tresses of the hair
she’d loosened to ingratiate my stare.
So can’t I ask what makes the muffin rise,
or penetrate a fugitive’s disguise?
Must I be hostage to a hollow dare
or taken in by some false Santa’s beard
without my questioning its shabby work
to make sure Nick’s not shrewdly engineered
by promo whiz or literary clerk?
And no man puffs up woman till she’s feared,
unless to serve her like a soda jerk.

Published in Hazmat (date uncertain)

Till Death Do They Part

She wasn't much concerned to take her bath
today; to brush her teeth or daub perfume
behind her ear. She didn't think a bloom
on bludgeoned cheeks a fitting match for wrath
which scoffed at polish in the aftermath
of his beatings. A gun supplants the plume
that once adorned her hat. Her ersatz womb
turns cold, metallic, off the beaten track
in the dank trunk of her car. There her bad
dream ends, hog-tied in the nightclothes he'd been
wearing. Now, like the submissive consort
he'd longed for, she supports his limp body
on her stiffened back without a retort
groaned from him. "A remnant of his shoddy
lovemaking", she muses. "The ground spinning."
Cocking her head, she feels his still grinning
lips cavorting with her ear like he's glad
to nuzzle her in lieu of turning in.

Previously Published in Hazmat, date uncertain

Horticulture

Refusing my scholastic skill as means
to help her grow a garden in her yard,
she utilized the muscles she made hard
by breaking ground when, in a shirt and jeans,
she cultivated oranges and greens.
Her sheer skill sowing pruned my self-regard.
For it seemed like her planting prowess sparred
with my book smarts. Indeed. She spilled the beans
when she began to seed her fecund brain.
As though she sensed her academic flaw
engendered a compensatory gain
in me, she gleaned from physics, math and law
until I felt my efflorescence wane
and yielded to her husbandry with awe.

Published in Thick with Conviction, Spring 2006

Tennis Racquet

She flaunts her gender with subversive pride
by flashing dangling earrings on the court.
Not happy just to take a smash in stride,
she lobs returns to guys whose reach falls short.
Much more than forward femme with backhand force
who happens to sport tresses and a skirt,
she's someone who can drive meek men off course.
Past channeling her prowess into flirt
who shows off beads of sweat like pendant pearls,
she marshals male desires with her game
which makes the strongest sportsmen reel like girls.
Indeed. Her strokes' precision stoke their flame.
And though her curves might make their senses vault
her swift serves startle them to double fault.

Published in Thick with Conviction, Spring '06

Wages of Age

How nice when I had money still to spare.
Big deal if I passed up a meal or two.
A more nutritious dish was always there.
I wore drab clothes. Nor did I need a new
wardrobe every spring. Now, with diminished
funds, I've developed an impulse to buy
items that I'd not previously wished
for. Approaching financial ruin, I sigh
for days when there were still dozens of doors
to open, packages to be unwrapped.
Appliances had graced the shelves of stores
in shopping districts which I'd hardly mapped
amidst the bustling crossroads of my mind.
Now tawdry goods sit marked-up in a mall
that with the best directions I won't find,
despite the fact that I now want it all.
And trapped in backroads of my penury,
I seek less sustenance than shopping spree.

Published in POETZ Spring '06

School Daze

Beware the girl you've taken for a fool.
For even while you think you're in control,
this neophyte is taking you to school,
preparing you for the apprentice role.
And while you teach her lessons from a book
that she makes you believe she's never read,
she supersedes the courses that you took
so that it seems like you're the knucklehead.
At last, so baffled by her arcane text,
you cast aside the wisdom that you've learned
to find you're under skilled and oversexed,
just as the crucial session's been adjourned.
Thus, you're left mumbling phonemes in her ear
which she seems too preoccupied to hear.

Published in Blue Unicorn, Oct '07

Misfire

Although adorned in Sunday clothes
she ties her hair into a bun
and, with the disaffected pose
of frazzled people on the run,
she guzzles down her glass of beer.
As such, she greets his puzzled stare
with an insinuating leer
that glazes over into glare.
Small holes in lobes of dainty ears,
disowning studs that she'd once worn,
become subversive souvenirs
of affability forsworn.
And even as she starts to rise
he hastens to apologize.

Published in "Ship of Fools", Spring 2006

Purple Heart

I mobilized love's legions for a girl
whose arch retreat made both flanks sorely pressed.
Besieged, I thought it best to huff and hurl
my battery of balls at lust's behest.
At once her tresses started to unfurl
like warlike banners from their ribboned crest.
Still quartered soldiers scattered in a whirl,
as regimental fingers clutched her breast,
but more to supplicate than to aggress.
For crack battalions won't more deftly dress
down armored strength than she whose earlobe's pearl
arrested sundered senses in their swirl.
My vaunted weapon - slipped into her sheath -
parlayed its horny edge to wilted wreath.

Published in Love's Chance, Fall/Winter '06

Blissful Bondage

I peer through chambers of my captive heart
to ponder innocents who wander free.
But they walk walls of grey who live apart
from you, exempted from love's stern decree.
Recidivist offender on the run
I've grown averse to skies that flash their blue
like badges presaging a stun-gun sun.
Not fighting extradition back to you,
I glean warm glints of daylight from your eyes
of ashen grey before my stiff arrest.
Divestment mocks my fugitive's disguise.
As such you bind your bounty to your breast,
not like a servant saddled with a chore,
but as a soldier bearing spoils of war.

Published in Contemporary Rhyme June '06

Casing the Bag

I always wonder what's inside her bag.
Though not the most desired thing she owns,
she bears it on her shoulder like a flag
carrying soldier in a battle zone.
She's mustn't think her money makes me want
the pocketbook she carries in her arms,
then covers, even as she seems to flaunt,
her real or fancied currency of charms.
She fosters the impression that she's rich,
until, seduced to take a second look,
I'm overcome by carnal tension which
exposes me as profligate and crook.
No matter if the lady is a hag,
I'm thief and pervert fixed upon the bag.

Though some push baby strollers like they're tanks
on combative city streets, and others
with a mocking grin, manage to outflank
our gross brotherhood of ill-bred bothers,
the slick sophisticates play deaf and dumb.
Some, trapped in crowded elevators,
begin their conversations with an "um",
that works better than incinerators
at pulverizing bums. If studs dine near,

they slam their glasses down on table tops,
or shove a tuft of hair behind their ear.
This "sticks it" with more flair than calling cops
to usher out a dissipated bum,
who'll never hear the words that follow "um".

I realize that I'm sensitive to slights,
and try to suffer insults with a grin,
but Nature holds me helpless in her might,
and coupled with a rebuff, I begin
to wonder what it is I want to steal
when sitting near a wary, nubile chick.
I only know her antics make me feel
a quickening within that makes me sick
enough to undermine my self-esteem.
Guilt-ridden, I then hastily retreat
into my private sanctum, and redeem
my chastened self in ways that aren't meet.
And even as my gonads start to sag,
I still don't know what's in that frigging bag!

Published in Backstreet Quarterly
August 2006 #7

Changing Positions

Although my passion posted as its goal
Kathleen, whose line of scrimmage was the bar,
the waitress Angelina took control,
preventing me from getting very far.
Her pulse now racing, she secured the ball
then rushed to touch down on my end zone heart.
And though deterred by my defensive wall -
whose tight end compromised her running start -
she scrimmaged with a fullback's body mass.
Her strong arm tactics helped her muscle through
sufficiently until I took the pass
as rash receiver in this rendezvous.
Indeed, she made the pass with such a spin
I knew that this was one game she would win.

Published in Red Owl Magazine Sept '06

Hitting Her Target

Of course a bull's eye might perplex
her boyfriend, skilled in archery,
and vex his pride. But since her sex,
transgressing strictures with esprit,
its arrow's now a fledgling lark
which takes her fellow on the wing
until the missile hits its mark.
For once in youth his shot fell short
and landed in the target's butt,
at which the wench he'd hoped to court
rebuffed him with dismissive strut.
Now riding on the buzzing shaft
his fail-safe girlfriend put in flight
in demonstration of her craft,
he finds reparative delight
rejoicing in her afterglow,
as though she'd handled Cupid's bow.

Published in Red Owl, September '06

Shakira Unplugged
(singing Ciego, Sordomudo)

I hear the call of her melodic voice
charge slackened measures marching at her word.
Her vocals are supply lines to rejoice
at; military transports as they're heard
in whistling stops along the winding track.
Rat-a-tat drumbeats follow in their train
as, riffs recruited, spearhead an attack
of finger-strummed projectiles from her brain,
and rapid fire mop-up raps break through.
Conscripting ragged melismas from the sweep,
she marshals them like soldiers in review
where, uniformed in 16th notes, they leap
around resounding chambers in her ear
to march in quick time with this grenadier.

Published in Art Magazine, November 2006

Right Attire

It's not the coats, but how they fit
that most affects our happiness.
Adopting duds whose seams are split
or which we don't take time to press,
can downgrade even costly clothes.
And dated wardrobes take up space
that's needed for the guy who grows
beyond them at a normal pace.
But if well-tailored garb is best,
the worst is raiment loafers comb
from discards which they once possessed
when they were young and lived at home.
For outfits drawn from duffel bags,
though new, are worn like motley rags.

Published in Iambs and Trochees, Fall Winter '06

Telltale Sign

Though one stuffed toy cannot portend
that this affair had hit a snag -
or that I'd lost a female friend -
just after I began to brag
about the poetry I'd penned,
and left our table to zigzag
to the commode, I'd apprehend,
implicitly, just what a drag
I was whom you'd tried to commend
your welfare to. For, as a gag,
you'd coyly managed to upend
the amply antlered stuffed toy stag -
I'd bought that afternoon to send
as Christmas present - in my bag,
headfirst! Indeed! My deer, rear end
extended, made my passion flag.

Published in Poetalk/winter/spring 2007

Poetic Mimic

The cuckoo imitates the sparrow hawk
not just to gain protection from that bird,
but on the wings of its deceit to stalk
small cocks until they leave their nests. My word,
with equal craft deceived by mis-en-scene,
no longer feathered literary nest
with metaphor and sublimated pen,
but at the fledgling parasites' behest
began to feed subversive appetites
that compromised my true, neglected brood.
The filchers egged me on to parlous flights
of fancy to secure essential food.
Seduced by ends perceived to be my own,
I served their needs till they were fully grown.

Published online in *True Poet* August 2006
and printed in *Magnolia Quarterly* Winter 2010

Repetition Compulsion

I thought I had a hold on you
whose eyes suggested "rendezvous
with some exotic ingénue
in distant lands, like Timbuktu."
Such happiness I never knew
beyond the bliss which I outgrew.

Imagine my surprise when you
repelled my dreamt of rendezvous,
not like some clueless ingénue,
but more the busy mother who,
though feeling for me, through and through,
had more compelling things to do.

Published in Words of Wisdom, March '06

Boarded

I cast my passion's anchor leagues behind
you. Vain presumption of noblesse oblige!
How fast you flagged me down to state of siege,
then commandeered my arms till they entwined
your waist. Seductive scent would soon remind
me you held sovereign sway, and my prestige
was just what you accorded me as liege
lord of a love-sick vassal stricken blind.
I navigated tresses of your hair
to breach the portal of your ear with lips
that fished with desperation to declare
surrender. Salty smells would soon eclipse
the perfumed fragrances you'd harbored there
to snare lost sailors on their lovelorn trips.

Published in The Lyric summer '06, v. 86

Courtly Joust

I didn't need to read "The Lovelorn Heart"
or see the tapestry where Lancelot
is shamelessly transported in a cart
to rescue Guinevere to know the knot
uniting lovers is a chafing one
whose loose ends lie within a woman's hand.
Albeit Guinevere became a nun,
for starters melting looks were her command.
Thus, notwithstanding cuirass, shield and lance,
I found the treasure of my manor sacked
while chivalrously focused on romance.
For my subversive ladylove attacked
the stronghold of my masculine estate
while I stood in attendance at her gate.

Published in The Well-Tempered Sonnet i
and in Blue Unicorn '13

Love's Child

If you had wielded lethal force,
I would have fought you tooth and nail.
And if mere kindness fixed my course,
I'd swiftly scurry from your jail.
If you had threatened me to test
my resolution next to yours
I'd muster countless means to wrest
out victory despite your roars.
But how can I presume to beat
a savvy foe who saps my will
with sweets? Your wheedling tones entreat
me to indulge the shameless thrill
of ceding to you spoils of war
you'll neither fight for nor restore.

Published in Westward Quarterly

Miss Firecracker

He felt their war games getting out of hand.
Though slight, the smell of liquor on her breath
when frisking him put steel in her command.
But as she marched him to pretended death,
while pleas for mercy importuned her side,
his regiment's surrender sealed the peace
that stopped the exercise. Although untied,
he hardly would enjoy an abject lease
on life. For she soon trumpeted the claim
that his becoming prisoner of war
enhanced her rank. The unextinguished flame
of love let him assess her pluck with awe.
And when she helped remove his captain's suit,
he sheepishly held forth a stiff salute.

Published in Mad Poets, '06, v. 20

Renewal

If only I could pop out of the grave
as though delivered from my mother's womb.
The first two steps I'd take would be to shave
and seek baptism with some chic perfume.
I'd feel a growing springiness in joints
as years accrued subtracted from my lot
arthritic pains and swellings God appoints
disease-afflicted muscles sprung from rot.
I'd celebrate my eighties in pre-school,
at 65 leave college for my job
where decades hence I'd recommence as fool
to some shrew who'd soon make my senses throb.
And consummating bliss between her thighs
I'd follow it to where conception lies.

Published in Irish Stew/Summer '07

Bitter Fruit

I labored years to cultivate the soil.
Yet I was young and muscular enough
to buy into the future with my toil.
Though never lucky, when the winds grew rough,
I lost the scanty harvest gleaned till then.
And now with my small fallow gone to seed,
I must begin the enterprise again.
Indeed, I first need to uproot the weed.
But with both plow and plower compromised
by bitter weather and the toll of time,
I find that, faced with this unfertilized
estate, I've neither will nor way to prime
it. Drawn before my once auspicious field,
I wallow in whatever it will yield.

Published in Irish Stew, summer, '07

Yuko Does Prokofiev

(Minuet from Romeo and Juliet)

Absorbed, she seesaws, bow in hand,
with two chords stroked in counterpoint
to brass and winds which take command,
like roughnecks breaking up the joint
with their grotesque, melodic thrust.
But they don't compromise her cool
or otherwise make her adjust
relentless measures of the rule
her bow imposes on her strings.
in fact, her cocksure passage struts
as if the brass's blusterings
were echoed in her cello's guts.
And while she swaggers – unaware
of importuning saxophones,
or too preoccupied to care –
her pulse stays stalwart as her tones.
Thus, fellow cellists in her tow,
she marches forward with her bow.

Published in ***Free Lunch*** Autumn 2006

Moral Abstractions

When I see how God's sentinels admit
injustice; how conspirators hatch plots
until their venom manages to hit
unwitting objects; how lawful crack shots
miss targets righteous ends depend upon;
when I see seedlings dropping off from life
before they have a chance to blossom on
its greening branch and stem the winds of strife;
I challenge God to bear us His intent.
And He responds: "I pity men like you,
imagining there's something provident
or moral in the canvases they view.
Notwithstanding scrawls of moral feinting
Life is just a Jackson Pollack painting."

Previously Published in Rockford Writer's Guild

String Theory

It's always music when you're young.
Adversity's a cello bow.
Dashed hopes are melodies that flow
from violin strings tautly strung.
Life's burdens are guitars we've slung
around our necks so tunes can grow
from the discordances of woe.
And even sniffling sighs are sung
in measures that let singers crow
their triumph over loves that stung
their senses. What do lovers know
of sobs when bellows fill each lung?
And so I wish as gale winds blow
that age possessed a honeyed tongue.

Published in Thick with Conviction '07

Winter Harvest

I garner branches in a sheaf
who once plucked pear and nectarine.
And daffodils that gave relief
to me are nowhere to be seen.
My nights are spent in threadbare grief,
and balmy days, wherein I'd glean
sweet happiness, however brief,
have vanished with the season's green
in shades of autumn, like a thief.
Now once abundant trees are lean
and russet has become the chief
estate of hues that intervene
to lighten up the grey motif
that seals my fate with harsh routine.

Published online in Thick with Conviction

Grand Hotel

We come into this world to pass on genes,
and all the rest is just a shadow play.
The richness of its wrought tapestry means
nothing, beyond the season of our stay.
Nor do its rooms include amenities
if we remain longer. In any case,
age will bend to smoldering memories
before they turn the lights off in a place
emptied of the remnants of desire.
There'll be little to do but sit and wait.
No kindled flame and nothing to aspire
to. Just some leftovers for a late
night snack, while waiting for that bugaboo
before which life keeps passing in review.

Published in Art Times, June 2008

No Reprieve

When I was young, an inmate doomed to die
reminded us we too were on death row.
I snickered at his self-consoling lie;
and in my high-rise cell presumed to sow
the seeds of liberty that might defy
my jailers. Thus, I cultivated mind
and body in a vain attempt to buy
myself more time against Life's fatal bind.
And later, on a television show,
a killjoy meets the felon she'd betrayed.
He lets her weary brain enjoy the flow
of warmth inside the prison that she'd made
for herself, then kills her. Just so, some god
sends us a cornucopia of years
that pass like haunted ghosts. And thus, we plod
our way in chains. Sweet recollection sears
amidst the shadows and advancing gloom
that mark our plaintive journey to the tomb.

Published online in Contemporary Rhyme '07
and Thick with Conviction '09

Pastoral

On the whole, the singing for obvious
reasons is confined to the rural walk.
There, my uplifted soul's oblivious
to the insistent tone of idle talk
that grated on my brain in the little
cottage where my wife's mother still remains.
Here, acrimony finds brief acquittal
in the woodland voices that entertain
among fresh meadows and the rustling trees.
Enchantment's full-throated chirping of birds
commingle with the murmuring of bees,
until the crow's cackling caw echoes words
heard in tears; and as I briskly withdraw,
begins to sound like my mother-in-law.

Previously published online in Contemporary Rhyme 2007

The Murderer's Dirge

We offer prayers for the man who murdered,
breaking the bonds of love and trust.
Taking arms against his brother,
he stands with bloodied hands, accursed.

Paying in kind the one who murdered,
in likeness to his mindless lust,
we bear a kindred guilt, like brothers,
and grind salvation in the dust.

We mourn again, now two men murdered,
with incense rising from the dust.
Arm in arm, they ascend like brothers.
Newly born, may they mourn for us.

Previously published in Pleiades 1991

Gossamer Dreams

When I was young, I loved Odette,
the forlorn cygnet from Swan Lake.
Her pasty cheeks and pirouette
seduced me. I was on the make!
I scarcely asked how upraised arms
positioned for an arabesque
could radiate balletic charms
on subways and not look grotesque.
And why the dickens would I want
a satin-slippered fiancée
who'd frequent restaurants en pointe
and peck my cheek en relevé?
But since it never dawned on me
that ballerinas hardly fuss
offstage with choreography,
I'd dream we'd pas de deux the bus,
if my swan diva wouldn't frown
to don a tutu on the town.

Published online: Language & Culture
2008

Fractured

How hard it seems for broken bones to heal
in best of circumstances. Even young
philanderers must find it hard to steal
into their lover's bedroom while they're hung
up worrying how best to manage arm
or foot. The older that we are, of course,
creates a greater reason for alarm.
Thus, lacking the rejuvenating source
to draw upon, I've taken to my bed.
Since nothing can reverse a ticking clock
or heal the damage, I'm consumed with dread
at not redeeming joys I had to hock.
The cast is set and here I must remain,
a prisoner of memory and pain.

Published in Raintown Review
September 2007

Poem

I conceived an idea.
It gestated in my brain,
grew to full-term
and developed to maturity
as a hale and hearty poem.

They asked me how long I took
to make the little fella.
What an impertinent question
to ask! No longer than
necessary, of course. I labored
with enough love so he'd be cradled
in meaning, without smothering him
in verbose layers of clothing,
just to show him off.
He didn't wear wooly words,
like mittens in summer, or syllabic
scarves. Nor did I constrict him
in a playpen stuffed with punctuations
when he could walk on metrical feet.

And when they ask me how much
I spent on my child, I tell them:
not a word less than he needed.
I gave him the best formula
to keep him strong
against the blowing wind of criticism.
Anyway, thin is in, and shows
tailored clothes to better stead.

And I dressed him in the best
outfit language could buy. If being fitted
for a sonnet, I gave him a quatrain
for a hat, iambics for a shirt
cut from the same fabric,
and a pair of pants to match.
And for shoes I gave him
a polished couplet
buttressing his metric shanks
so he could dance.

Previously published in Pegasus, winter '08

Elegy for an Abused Child

Thirty-year old John Franklin grew enraged
because his spaghetti was overcooked
by the woman to whom he was engaged.
Perhaps in his unconscious mind he took
her for his mother, and her two-year old
son for himself. Or does it matter why
he put the child in a pot on the stove,
turned up the heat, and then began to cry?
Could be, confused by trauma from his past,
John accused his own mother of torture
for withholding the succor of her breast.
The scalded boy was placed in foster care.
Now Franklin festers in a country cell,
assailed by felons of his private hell.

Published by Pegasus, Summer '07

Actor

I've played it well, the studied part
assigned to me - in strict design
and meter. How can glib ad-libs
or scripts espousing freedom wrest
a measure from the dancing stride
of tide and season? How to stay
the wonted ways informing rhyme
and reason? Stage and scene's been set.
Cast members let me play my part,
which I assayed with diligence
and heart. And thus, I tender them -
and future stars that seasons Life's
revolving stage - their pending start,
before I cede my craft and art.

Published in Pegasus

Tilling the Soil

"How dare you look at me?!" you might have said
with that harsh glare, before I took my seat.
So with a mix of anger, pride and dread
I felt it wiser not to brave defeat.
For I'd conjectured that a woman's scorn
not only served to punish man's misdeeds,
but targeted those actions yet unborn.
As it turned out your scowls were meant as seeds
that you perversely took the pains to sow,
as much to leave me wallowing in weeds
as to allow my passion fruit to grow
amidst your garden's cultivated needs.
For just as soon as your rebuke took root
you darted off like some wind-scattered shoot.

Published in Poesia summer '07

Time

Time seems wasted, time seems long,
in the Spring when we are young.
But time goes on as we grow old,
and autumn nights, turn brisk, then cold.
Till now we face a wintry gray,
bemoaning days we've thrown away,
and all the work we might have done
before the setting of the sun.

previously published online in Long Story Short Aug. 2010

Post-Mortem Thought

The only difference between death and a tv suddenly turned off is that, in the case of the latter, you miss an interesting program while you're doing something else. In the case of the former you don't miss a thing.

Previously Published in Black Book Press '08

Passive Pleasures

The only thing that he'd conclude
when she decidedly subdued –
with sass – a fellow who was rude,
was that the want of turpitude
in his own life would not preclude
or dampen pleasure's plenitude.
For though he lacked the aptitude
for manliness or fortitude
should life's exigencies intrude,
she'd be sufficiently imbued
with overbearing attitude
to satisfy this pliant prude
who, without feeling coarse or lewd,
could still succeed in getting screwed
in all the senses thus construed.

First Published in Genie 5

Failed Diplomacy

As if you were a sovereign state
with right to occupy my land,
you managed both to isolate
me from the friends I had at hand
and put them under your command.
I never launched a verbal raid
that might have justified grandstand
gestures. But friends were my brigade
against nefarious designs
that you had on my civil rights.
Thus, you advanced beyond my lines
in order to direct your sights
on one who neither fought nor ran
but seethes, a scorned, embittered man.

First published in Ship of Fools, winter, '07/'08

Nicole Eulogy

(for Anna Nicole Smith)

At 39, the woman's dead.
Forget the barbs and mordant jokes
of heartless, heavy-footed folks
who, loth to pity, stomp instead
sacred ground. She whom Nature bred
to suffer nurture's brutal yokes
has sloughed off those oppressive spokes
around the wheel that makes us tread
with labored footsteps to the grave.
Thus, she's been freed of further grief
from those survivors who won't waive
the judgment spared them by belief
in Jesus - predisposed to save
both Magdalen and hanging thief.

First Published in Thick with Conviction

Approaching Age

Until fleet-footed passion
paused at the crossroads
of my stride
and lost its rage;
until the staff of Life
became for me
in tottering age, a cane,
I walked like a man
who hides his wealth
behind apparent dearth of means.
I didn't need
to brag or swagger
like a bucking stag,
but bottled up youth's season
in a bunch of rags.
Weighed down with gold,
I didn't need to show my stuff
or strut with peacock pride;
my cache was bona fide.
Now like the empty hull
of an ancient ship,
I fly my banner high;
bright, silken threads
around the sodden deck inside.

Published in Thick with Conviction

Bad Harvest

Averse to find relief from dread
of dealing with what's close at hand,
this poet plays with words instead,
beguiled by prompts to understand
a problem lying far afield.
In this way he can cultivate
its topsoil for a fecund yield
and still preserve his proud estate.
Or so he thinks who doesn't heed
the plowshare hacking at his chest
or feel disseminated seed
that's germinating in his breast.
And thus, he's both the plundered plain
and gleaner of ill-gotten gain.

Published in Ceremony

Fall Forage

How beautiful those bee-stung lips
which open like a perfumed rose
before the honeybee that sips
the golden nectar with his nose.
Had I that tube which God equips
him with to suck what I'd transpose
as honey to my ladyship's
boudoir to sugarcoat her woes!
But I'm too languorous for dips
beyond the vestments that enclose
such saffron-dappled landing strips.
And yet, what treasure troves for those
not weighed down by the fate that clips
off wings when old man winter blows.

Previously Published in Ceremony

Fool's Gold

The woman must have thought it odd
that I appraised her with a leer
as if she wore a priceless gaud
around her neck or in her ear.
I scrutinized her profiled face
as only diamond dealers do
when they decide what price to place
on jewelry that they review.
But flashing smiles in lieu of pearl -
whose luster might have well beguiled
men lusting for a moneyed girl -
she must have thought I was a child
confusing pyrite with the gold
which shrewder men might wish she sold.

Published in Love's Chance, Spring, Summer '08

Basic Instinct

No academic skill or boarding schools
inform the know-how that she brings to work.
But she applies more elemental tools,
from petulance to self-complacent smirk.
This gal possesses just a thin veneer
to cover up raw nature's native thrust.
Convention's niceties she doesn't hear
or have inherent tendencies to trust.
Thus what good is a drawbridge to her heart
or smart words in a syntax she can't speak?
She reigns beyond our language and our art.
And man's hands-on approaches merely tweak
her tresses like a child upon her lap
precipitously rising from its nap.

Published in Love's Chance '08

Snow

The last time I went to my sister's on Xmas Eve
it was snowing. The last time I went to my sister's,
soft flakes were covering grimy roads on the way
to Nutley, New Jersey. Soot and slime, the asphalt,
all of it lightly covered with snowflakes. It was beautiful
the last time I went to my sister's on Xmas Eve. The past is
always beautiful through tinted windows. Rhapsodic
monograms of hope fell with those flakes. A blessing for tired
eyes. That was several years ago. That light layer of snow has
long since vanished beneath tires and hard-nosed seasons.
There's no glow this year to drape the dismal roads leading to
Nutley. No bright, glistening mantle of promise. Oh, it's
snowed many times since. Snow that clogs up roads with
cracked crystals that a thousand feet have trampled on; grey
slush making treks through city streets difficult. Snow that
impedes traffic and causes cancellations on the latest stop to
the suburbs. It was snowing last Xmas Eve. But not this time.
There's nothing covering the asphalt on this latest of my
journeys. Just roads, endless roads. And rain in the forecast.

Published in Moon Journal Volume 13. Issue 2

Her Big Nose

She need not strike a macho pose
or fashion muscles she can flex.
For here's some part of her that rose
above the strictures of her sex.
Its marked dimensional conceit
adds measure to her mushy lips,
constricted contours of her feet
and passive fullness of her hips.
Here's matter that has all the strength
of tone and bone that men can boast
without the compromise in length
that makes them feel they're uppermost
in woman's eyes, Nor should they dread
inadequacy in her bed.

First Published in Pearl (39) 2008

Giving Voice

Free will's a concept for the birds!
Not even blank verse poets roam
freely. But if you're hooked on words,
consider how I write this poem.
Since sonnets are my chosen form,
as soon as sounding my first line
I'm apt to conjure up a storm
till rhyme permits the sun to shine.
Of course I've yet another verse.
If I can't make bad weather nice,
I'll try to let it not get worse.
And though enticed to turn to ice
while bound to laws of sonneteers,
with skill and luck, a light appears.

Published in R B's Poet's Viewpoint, Sept '07

Blue Penciling

Whoever said the second sex was fair
have never been induced by them to write
a script. They keep the project well in sight,
then greet completed efforts with a glare.
If that won't work their probity's a snare
inviting us to fix our studied sight
beyond desire to be erudite.
We thus end up unlettered in her air,
until she feels resurgent might by dint
of using marking pens with nylon tips.
Though sensing censorship, men would abort
her slanted work before it goes to print,
he first must tackle smug, presumptive quips,
and falling short is taken by the sport.

Published in RB's Poet's Viewpoint
Sept '07

Crossfire

Once left to burrow in our brain,
the parasite makes perfect sense.
And we believe it's for our gain
that we defend its battlements.
For when conscripted for a war
whose theater lies inside the mind,
the battle lines are hard to draw,
and enemies are hard to find.
They don the outfits that we wear,
co-opting us for an attack
on senses that we have to bear
with fortitude until we crack.
And as the hurt insurgents moan,
we tend them like they were our own.

Published online in Illogical Muse Fall 2008

Crossroads

No longer do you whine and cry
when battered by my snide remarks.
But marshalling your inner guy,
your tongue's as sharp as streetwise sharks.
And I who face this stringent hitch
to my preferred ill-mannered role,
bemoan that I am forced to switch
to watching you assume control.
Thus, hovering between attack
and rankling fancies of defeat,
I start maneuvering my lack
along a track that's bittersweet.
And ceding fight for compromise,
I rise beneath my stifled sighs.

First Published in Freefall 2008

Sex and the Maiden

Consuming still another pint of beer,
he brushes back her hair as if to coo
inside the soft confection of her ear.

His eyes dilate while he begins to leer
with murmurings of all he'd like to do
with her, as he consumes another beer.

She senses that his thinking isn't clear.
But so convinced that patience can subdue
the guy who's now cavorting with her ear,

she lets him talk as if enthralled to hear
how he'll soon consummate their rendezvous.
As he consumes another pint of beer

her mock demeanor's blend of love and fear
assures him she just needs a talking to
inside the whorled confection of her ear.

Now she begins to play as cavalier
with him who still insists he'll follow through,
when, loaded with another pint of beer,
he falls asleep cavorting with her ear.

Previously published in Freefall magazine, Spring 2008

In Good Standing

Although the pretty girl gave me her seat
because she saw the cake between my hands,
the role reversal made me as discreet
as some small child in thrall to her commands.
For by her kindness she'd put me in debt.
Constrained by her, I watched my p's and q's,
and polished up on needed etiquette.
Indeed, I felt I had to pay my dues.
When finally I exited the bus,
my glee at wresting free from her was brief,
since I believed she still could make a fuss
if I failed to turn over that new leaf.
Thus she who had the gumption to be nice,
became my ruthless keeper in a trice.

Previously published in the Funny Paper '07 with $100 prize

Suds

It's not the beer that constitutes the binge.
It simply breaks down barriers to drink.
This opening of channels will impinge
impending navigation till I sink.
For though at first the leeward sea seems calm
I never know what lies around the bend.
And once a sailor casts out fear and qualm
he's subject to what distant trade winds send.
So though it seems like such a balmy day
and I just want to take a peaceful cruise
behind the placid waters of the bay,
a siren lurks beyond whose singing woos
bewildered tars - who'd otherwise take stock -
to ply the deep till scuttled on a rock.

Previously Published in Writer's Journal
Nov-Dec., 2007

Hard Currency

I loathe that ostentatious kiss
that narcissists put on display
to demonstrate what singles miss
by lacking ways of making hay.
Imagine should the moneyed flash,
in celebration of their means,
a mortifying wad of cash
that mock our envy with its green.
You'd never see such showing-off
of moolah in the well-to-do
without a countermanding cough
from the less fortunate, in lieu
of stealing it. Yet lovers flaunt
their much beloved currency
at us. It seems they want to taunt
impoverished peers. For penury
encourages the poor to brook
the guilt of a potential crook.

First Published in Contemporary Rhyme,
Jan/Feb. '08

Pregnant Lament

Frustration isn't what my grief's about.
As my taut heartstrings throb their threnody,
the echoed past gives her soft voice the clout
of smitten Tristan's plaintive melody.
She functions in the rendezvous I missed -
because I heeded self-defeating qualms -
for all those who from fear I never kissed,
or lacked the pluck to cradle in my arms.
Indeed. She stood to temper life's rebuff,
reverse the scourge of Time, and soothe those wounds
which cut so deep that mere love's not enough
to sate the hunger that my fate lampoons.
She would have salvaged all the ground I'd lost
to surging tides. I failed to chart a course
across those seas of longing where I've tossed
upon the troughs and crests of deep remorse.
Thus washed ashore, I carry on my back
the weight of all I had to sublimate
to shoulder what's become a shabby sack.
And midst the darkness of my stark estate,
she would have served as a sustaining link
to liquid dreams beneath which now I sink.

Published in the winter issue of
The lyric as Lament

Accomplice

I hear an inner voice
compose a line or two
till, feeling I've no choice,
I add another few.
These bolster the conceit
that's mesmerizing me
to walk on metric feet
in rapt captivity.
And thus I serve my time,
constrained by metaphor,
pentameter and rhyme
to finish what I swore
I wouldn't start again
till locked inside my pen.

Published in Write on!,
then in Foliate Oak, October '12

Sound Rebuttal

He bellowed with a resonating trill,
in order to add power to his voice.
Though waxing proud, he should have waited till
she gave her shrewd rejoinder to rejoice.
For like the mother getting on her knees
in order to constrain her naughty child,
and make him sense resources she could seize
upon should he try an aggressive ploy,
she changed her alto to a baritone.
This not just trumped the vocal hand he held,
but bagged the bluster that he might have shown
to ride its thrust. Thus, managing to geld
his manhood just by dropping her voice down,
she turned his zoot suit into dressing gown.

Published in RB'S Poet's Viewpoint
Jan '08

Botched Robbery

The lass observes my oldster's unarmed heist
but browses through the store with mock aplomb.
She seems more piqued that goods are overpriced
than troubled as to where I'm coming from.
No patronizing smiles to mask her fear
or keep me busy while she makes a dash
to her beloved should the coast be clear.
Enriched by passion's sureties of cash,
she doesn't even try to call police
who earnestly patrol the street beside
the candy counter. Neither does she cease
to look at sweets as other patrons bide
my raid on bankrupt hearts. For nothing's won
from pricey stores without a loaded gun.

Published in: Westview:
Jrnl of Western Oklahoma: Fall, Winter '07

For Miss Robyn

No sappy poem for you, Christine,
to take back to your sunny Isle.
A valediction in-between
a sad demeanor and a smile
epitomizes what I feel
on seeing you depart for home.
I'm happy that though Time must steal
your presence like the trail of foam
behind a sailing schooner, birds
return as harbingers of spring
to harmonize these plainsong words.
And yet I'm sad that on the wing
you'll be too busy warbling notes
in bliss to miss old winter's coats.

Published on Westward Quarterly, winter 2008

Ill-Suited

It's not the poem that stirs desire's bent
but fantasies that hang upon the poem,
as though it were a clothing hook to vent
their hung-up fascinations in my home.
Forget that most of them are stained with grease
picked up from stamping grounds they've slouched about.
When salvaged from my closet, every crease
in syntax or conceit needs ironing out.
With such soiled garments, rogue ideas soon prick
my sensibilities with shards in sleeve
or fabric's weave. I bleed till I get sick
transforming rags to dresses I conceive
amidst duress. And then another flood
of verse and images to stanch the blood.

Published in Ellipsis/winter '08 #44

Misalliance

Her sparring with me - not a scratch
to mar her sense of agency -
afforded me a safety catch
from speaking with such flagrancy.
This perky phone rep brooked my bile
before she'd stem the rising tide
deriding her. Her laid-back style
required flak to get in stride
before she mustered an offense.
But when she did, I all but flinched.
She gave her name for reference,
which she repeated, while I clinched,
as if to trumpet her display
of prowess with a signed bouquet.

Previously Published in Art Times

Corrective Measures

Emerging from the hideout of my pride
I felt like I'd surrendered firearms
while foolishly submitting to be tied
to trumped-up charges of your trying charms.
Indeed, once you had taken me in tow,
I felt perverse sensations of release
from fears of being subject to the blow
I'd hazard if resistance didn't cease.
What piquant mix of being on parole
from more exacting time I'd have to serve
and feeling subject to the strict control
of goings-on you hawkishly observe!
But those were the conditions I agreed
upon for privileges I'm bound to cede.

Previously Published in Writer's Journal

A Mother's Love
(on the death of her infant son)

Because she would not weep,
nor bend beneath the grave allure
of sorrow's dread relief,
still the child survives,
nursed in the arms of his mother's grief.
Nor would it wither
like the winnowed flower
wasted on its wintered leaf;
but blossomed forth
in the coldest hour,
in the night-light glow
of its bedded gloom,
to plant a row of roses
on his perfumed sleep,
which perseverance keeps
apart from the forgotten tomb,
secret in her sheltered womb,
beside her beating heart.

Published in the Penwood Review
2008

Strong Moves

Like parasites who prick a host
in order to fulfill their needs,
or Hamlet's dad who used a ghost
to instigate vindictive deeds,
I thrive on that je ne sais quoi
in dancers as a saving grace.
A ballerina's port de bras
suggests a strength that can replace
faux pas I make in my heart's quest
that I'm just scarcely conscious of.
How fast she's able to arrest
my stepwise foraging for love
and sustenance to thus provide
for footing I keep cramped inside.

Published in slightly different version in:
Hazmat Review Spring 2010

Shopping Stall

“Come here for Dead Sea soap you’ll want to buy,”
she chimes. “Tel Aviv! You speak Hebrew,” I
ask? ‘Ken ve lo’, she tutors with a smile,
emboldened by her power to beguile
me. “Ken means ‘yes’, ve ‘and’, lo, ‘no’, she chants,
as if she were a Siren wearing pants.
“That means I’m telling every gal I flirt
with, ‘ken ve lo’, I tell her who’s as pert
as she’s seductive. “No. You’re gonna tell
them ‘ken’. Just so to me and what I sell
you.” Though I’m thinking “lo”, I’m saying “ken”,
regardless of whatever I might spend,
if just to guarantee a steady flow
of banter from this perky dynamo.

Previously Published in:
Sunken Lines & The Taylor Trust

Vernal Equinox

I trudge across the drab, dismantled earth,
crucified by hammering winter storms.
There seems to be no sprinkling of rebirth
and icy branches lean, as if for warmth,
against the top-coat grayness of the sky.
Neither monkish buds, cowled in sepal stripes,
nor lily-togaed prophets testify,
as trumpeting winds muffle shepherds' pipes,
and fell fields freeze in furrowed disrepair.
The earth wears tattered garments, stained like sin,
while April's linen dress is worse for wear.
I pray Life's resurrection now begin
to usher in its eager, faithful flock
past darkness toward the crowing of the cock.

Published in SUNKEN LINES Spring '08

Moving Parts

Life's like a huge conveyer belt.
And after passing workmen's hands,
a few of us come off it svelte,
others stocky. We fill demands
for varied types of merchandise.
All are painted in diverse hues.
The gals exude sugar and spice
until prized accessories fuse
them with upgraded circuitry.
Men are made of pup or ducktails,
buzz cuts, snaps, caps and coquetry.
The lot of us endure travails.
And thus on the assembly line
we move until we're boxed in pine.

Published in Sunken Lines, Spring '08

To His Leading Lady

Two ways to win an actor's heart.
The first six drafts extol his worth,
the seventh brings him down to earth
where you show him he's not as smart
as you are with dramatic art.
You give the guy a smaller berth
to ply his craft till, left with dearth,
he relishes the starring part
you've seized from what was once his play.
Make sure you get the crucial lines
and he's got nothing much to say
beyond what your auteur assigns
him. Pending the climactic fray,
he wallows in the wings and whines.

Published in Sunken Lines, Spring 2008

Smart Bus Driver

How artlessly she manages the wheel
that's whirled with cavalier, commanding mien
as shafts and grinding axels whine and squeal
amidst the hot exhaust from gasoline
her transit thrusts into the atmosphere.
And my heart races, driven by the charge
of watching this brunette engage each gear
and exercise control of such a large
unwieldy vehicle. The stand-up guys
beseech her mirrored eyes or, sitting down,
relax, content to bask in her reprise
of motherly excursions into town.
Yet I, thus galvanized, commence to yearn
while spinning wheels whose rubber starts to burn.

Published in Freefall/winter '08

How Not To Drown

Well drowning's not the problem.
It's trying to swim where you shouldn't
be in the first place.
It's treading murky, turbulent seas;
lying on a rocky slope
at the water's edge
where you know you're going to
to lose your balance
and plummet in its depths.
With bold, futile strokes you race
against the tide
after just having a hearty meal.

Drowning's not the problem,
but its fatal consequence;
the issue that ensues
when troubling still waters,
wading waist-deep
on a breezy day
when you know the undertow
might pull you from the shore.
It's getting wet in the first place;
flirting with an element
that only those with flippers
and the will and way are wise to navigate.

Published in Black Book Press #38

Card Shark

I rode upon a winning streak
till hearing her affirm, "I will –
find what I'm looking for." "What cheek,"
I thought, while pondering the thrill
of being trumped by her pursuit.
But I lost confidence to play
the minute she seemed resolute
enough to call my bluff and lay
a wager. Cool till then, with cards
covertly held in front of me,
my poker face broke into shards
of glassy-eyed transparency.
And being challenged made me stand
behind my compromising hand.

Previously Published in Art times Jan/Feb '10

Horsing Around

Some females jockey for whatever chance
us men afford them while they sit astride
our saddles. Primed with spurs that prick the hide
they wheedle us to gallop or to prance
past obstacles upon the happenstance
that they'll decide to take us for a ride.
Forget that once dismounting us they chide
while changing from their jodhpurs into pants.
We're happy after hurdles just to graze
while they wheel baby carriages with deft
maneuvers just beyond our bristling neighs.
And after grooming, when they loom bereft
of youth and looks, some bridled child obeys
the "whoa!" of any riding skills they've left.

Published in Lucid Rhythms '07

Wired

Not everybody has a chatty friend
to chew the cud with on a cellular;
a disembodied person to attend
to, while they wonder how the hell you are.
So why not hang a Bluetooth on your ear
and make believe you're in a hot exchange
while walking pass the have-nots with a sneer,
suggesting they're infected with the mange.
Now you can show them that you have a life
that doesn't have the time for him or her.
What matter that your glare cuts like a knife
when they're bedeviled by your raconteur.
The center of the world is in your cell
and all the rest of us can go to hell.

Published in Freefall

Gymnast

(performing her Olympic floor exercise)

Jackhammer in a spangled leotard.
Raised arm shouldered like a bit in its chuck,
her perfunctory salute stalls the hard
incisiveness of piston-driven pluck.
It perks us up, in lieu of that glancing
smile which evaporates beneath the heat
of youth's primed purpose. Her antic dancing,
accompanied by an acidic beat
of guitars shrouded in sinuous brass,
propels her dash from the gangstering grip
of gravity. She hurls her tumbling pass
at its floored carcass. Double-back, front flip-
flop, handsprings, somersaults piked with full twist!
She lands unscathed with chin cocked on her wrist.

Published in The Poet's Art, Issue #39 June 2011

Shell Shock

How I internalize the battlefield
and then disguise the kindling state of war,
so that, instead of bayonet, I wield
an equally pernicious metaphor
against the occupier in my breast.
Nor does it matter if I'm one remove
from combat in my self-destructive quest.
For Kamikaze pilots can't improve
upon the brutal thrust of a conceit
that rides on wings of fantasy. Brigades
of tanks can't pound positions like a fleet
of words against collapsing barricades.
For I who ceded first lines of defense,
betrayed myself with fatal consequence.

Bereft of forward marching flanks,
it's hard to engineer a sound attack.
For how decide to fight or join the ranks;
to rush in opposition or pull back?
The measures I'm compelled to activate
assail my senses such to give me pause
that maybe I've betrayed my native state
instead of fighting for a noble cause.

And once I take a metaphor in stride
it's camouflaged in verse and metric feet
that make me think it's marching on my side.
The form it uses fosters the conceit
I've been enlisted for a noble end,
until I rue the very words I penned.

By stirring up confusion at the front
subversive fancies make me serve a foe
who instigates some discontented grunt
to deal my harried heart a crushing blow.
My forces, mobilized at his behest,
do everything to dress and integrate
the enemy to serve a common quest
whose dubious success just seals my fate.
I'm growing weary of this tug of war
between combative factions in my breast,
where inspiration questions martial law
and puts my constitution to the test.
For tropes, which infiltration undermines,
break ranks before I boost defensive lines.

Published in Poe Talk, Bay Area Poets

Anonymous Package

The world is like a secret gift.
Since nothing's conjured out of air,
it gives us all a moral lift.
Some see it as a cause for prayer.
The atheist is quick to think
the parcel dropped down from the sky.
The monotheist doesn't shrink
from postulating reasons why
the benefactor grants him life.
The Wiccan thinks the present is
from some symbolic man and wife.
The deist posits "its" or "his".
Since I'm not sure who put it there
I see the giver everywhere.

Published in Feelings of the Heart

Juxtapose Rose

I get a kick when women whine
and castigate the men they love
for plucking them from off the vine
to suck the succulence thereof.
Forget the buds on Kate's bouquet
while she decides which one to pick,
in lieu of those she casts away
to ponder that some flowers prick.
When planted seeds fulfill her ends
of cultivating ardent needs
the rest of them are pruned to friends
she rakes aside like rampant weeds.
But woe to us if what she sows
with fertile weeping never grows.

Published in Freexpression Oct '08

Shifting Perspectives

They say that age is just an attitude.
It's true when I was 35 years old -
comparing myself with a younger dude -
I felt I'd never fit into his mold,
and promptly fell into a mental rut.
But since advancing years have settled in
along with sagging chin and bloated gut
in those who brook the label "stout", how thin
I feel when I assay to weigh my age
against the many incremental mounds
of flesh that heavies bring upon the stage.
I gauge my years in weight against their pounds.
And pudgy as I feel beside young folk
I seem here more an acorn than an oak

Published in Freexpression, October '08

Ode to Music

A serenade does much more than the arm
a mother puts around her forlorn child.
More than religious talisman or charm
which leaves us less disburdened than beguiled.
A Mahler symphony or Mozart string quartet
puts absolution on a new plateau.
We need not purge an ex we can't forget
because we gave up beaux arts for the beau.
A Chopin etude or the Bach chaconne
imparts a benediction to my heart.
And what was once Love's goddess on a throne
becomes a fallen angel, half as smart
as those with mystic measures on a staff
transcribing Heaven to a sonic graph.

PUBLISHED IN FREEXPRESSION '08
and again in SOUL FOUNTAIN

Love's Charge

No felon hunted down by burly cops
could so resign himself to his arrest
before a gun barrage that never stops,
as I, who cede before your ardent quest
to send me to the prison of your arms.
A bruiser threatening the use of force,
could not intimidate me like your charms,
to follow you along your chosen course.
And I who fought opponents with more might
than you - when honor made me stand my ground -
delight imagining my taking flight
to emphasize the ties that leave me bound.
Yet, weary from pursuit of love's constraint
I waive my civil rights without complaint.

Previously Published in Freexpression, Oct '08

Four Seasons

It's always springtime when we're young,
despite old threadbare winter's chill.
For some lone blossom may have sprung
inside our breast. Love warms us till
the harvest of our years portend
a gathering of autumn leaves.
Still, Nature's brown-stemmed children bend,
and taking in earth's ripened sheaves
we ward off hoar-frost limbs of age.
But stalked by summer's sultry breath,
when sunlight shaves snow's bearded sage
from off the trees, bequeathing death
a comforter of teeming meads,
then I bewail my garden's weeds.

Previously published in Poet's Art, 2010

Salesmanship

If that smart suit's her business dress,
I pity men whose debts outweigh
their revenue and can't defray
expenses but through her largess.
They're petrified she'll repossess
appliances they didn't pay
in full or which were put on lay-
away. How fast they reassess
her while they're standing in arrears
before her assets, good as gold.
Prodded by the opal in her eyes,
that pitch like ruthless marketeers,
they swallow wholesale goods she's sold
them, while their rates of interest rise.

Published in Fighting Chance 2009

Grand Hotel

We come into this world to pass on genes,
and all the rest is just a shadow play.
The richness of its wrought tapestry means
nothing, beyond the season of our stay.
Nor do its rooms include amenities
if we remain longer. In any case,
age will bend to smoldering memories
before they turn the lights off in a place
emptied of the remnants of desire.
There'll be little to do but sit and wait.
No kindled flame and nothing to aspire
to. Just some leftovers for a late
night snack, while waiting for that bugaboo
before which life keeps passing in review.

Published in Art Times, June 2008

To His Leading Lady

Two ways to win an actor's heart.
The first six drafts extol his worth,
the seventh brings him down to earth
where you show him he's not as smart
as you are with dramatic art.
You give the guy a smaller berth
to ply his craft till, left with dearth,
he relishes the starring part
you've seized from what was once his play.
Make sure you get the crucial lines
and he's got nothing much to say
beyond what your auteur assigns
him. Pending the climactic fray,
he wallows in the wings and whines.

Published in Sunken Lines

Grim Reaper

Death always gets the bum rap. But this time -
a youngster, burnt over 90%
of her body! How well the horrid crime
fit his modus operandi. Intent
on tearing the old buzzard limb from limb,
I sifted through the mounds of smoking ruins.
But nothing found was grounds for holding him.
As pity for her torment made me swoon,
I grew more fixed on tendering relief
than collaring the cruel and ghoulish goon.
Then, through the burning cauldron of my grief,
I saw the murder scene; flowers strewn
across an open coffin, where they laid
the child beside grim mourners as they prayed.

He followed her last journey to the grave
with baleful steps, ungainly and suspect.
Despite the fact that he seemed more a slave
to her than she to him, I'd soon project
upon the derelict my kindled rage.
But there was more of sympathetic pain
in this contempt than legalistic sage.

For he'd left neither fingerprints nor stain
among the ones that sealed his victim's fate,
but merely fudged its tragic consequence.
He might have been a marriage magistrate,
or father; mulling with ambivalence,
the giving up his youngest child, as bride,
to night's nuptial mysteries, bleary-eyed.

Published in Autumn Leaves, 2009

Requiem for a Cat

The flourish in my furnished room is dead;
his purring fur, now stiffened by disease,
who otherwise would burrow with his head
inside my lap or stretch across my knees.
He'd scratch outside my door, until I let
his lordship wander in to do just as
he pleased. Perhaps I'd be allowed to pet
him as he lumbered in with arch pizzazz
beneath my stumbling feet. At times I'd kneel
in thralldom on the floor, petitioning
disdainful majesty to take his meal,
while he preferred to lick his paws. My king,
I'm pledged to consecrate him on the chair
where he, enthroned, left talismanic hair.

Published in PKA's Advocate Aug/Sept '16

Ballerina

Although I make believe I'm non-chalant
while watching arabesques at the ballet,
my pulse so quickens when a girl's en pointe,

I feel just like a giggling debutante
who's carried (metaphorically) away.
Although I act as if I'm nonchalant,

I'm titillated if the girl should flaunt
her pirouettes and sassy relevés.
As my pulse quickens when the girl's en pointe,
her attitude, with foot croisée devant,
unfolds the leg to suave développé.
And though I make believe I'm nonchalant,

my lungs expand with her grand battement
and blissfully expel with the plié.
Oh God! My heart's set on pied a pointe

to distraction. What matter that I can't
do more than just adore the fleet bourées
of dancing feet while I seem nonchalant?
My pulse still quickens when a girl's en pointe.

Published online: Barefoot Muse

On Bach's "Well-Tempered Clavier"

How perfect the cathedral that resounds
to make one feel Elysium on earth.
Gay 32nd notes turn stalwart grounds
to architectures of transcendent mirth.
No glib pronouncements of an afterlife
with foursquare hymns or dissonance in hell.
Just upright tones that echo joy and strife
which left-hand sermons bolster or repel.
Nor do you need a priest or arcane key
to enter in this citadel of sound.
Just tempered scales to bridge polyphony
and keep the homily on solid ground
upon which we, the faithful, safely trod.
And cynics say they don't believe in God!

PUBLISHED IN: NOMAD'S CHOIR '09

Butterfly

She pressed me in the book I tendered her.
Expostulating Cio-Cio-San's sad fate
in music I pulled every stop to stir
emotions in her that would cultivate
her sensibilities and leave her ripe
for me to pluck like some exotic fruit.
I waxed rhapsodic till compelled to wipe
my tears. They grouped like dew upon the shoot
that had extended from the seeds I'd sown
within her breast. For passion watered them.
And when the flower of my love had grown,
dismissively, she plucked it from its stem;
a sign the burgeoning chrysanthemum
in me was sentiment she'd overcome.

Previously Published in Eclectic Muse

Captured Fancy

"You know you want me to win it,"
she boasts, referring to the prize.
She senses I've my heart in it
that she succeed, but clarifies
it just in case she needs to show
me that my luck is tied to hers.
And since the gal has me in tow
her cheek's a strategy that stirs
my yen to render her my arms.
"So just give it to me," she smiles
with the assurance that her charms
suffice to bend me to her wiles.
I hope she wins, but barring that,
I'm taken by her caveat.

Previously Published in a slightly different version in Eclectic Muse v.14, Christmas 2008

Love's Bluff

How cunningly you played your winning hand
to make me put more money in the pot.
Since you concealed your suit, I'd understand -
regarding what seemed my propitious lot -
that I could confidently raise the stakes
without possessing more than paltry pairs.
Of course the player who's the shrewdest rakes
the dollars in amidst the loser's glares.
And with my huge investment in the game
I had to play you with a lesser hand,
if only to win back the chips I came
in with. But even as I bleakly fanned
my cards - which clearly weren't good enough -
the gamester in me stoically hung tough.

Published in Daybreak Press

Goodbye and All That

Forty-five years from now, my dear,
when roots of your bleached hair turn gray,
no one will care that you were here
churning my passion to dismay.
Then you who led me by the nose
will crumple like a withered rose
upon the ground beneath which I,
insensate to all pain, will lie.
And if perchance you recognize
amidst chilled voices in the wind,
one, broken-hearted and chagrined,
don't dally to apologize
for canceling another tryst,
since that appointment won't be missed.

Published in ASCENT PUBLICATIONS

Wireless

Does woman really need to add a cell
phone to her amatory arsenal?
As if she can't already give us hell,
she now can spurn us and get personal
with people on the mobile's other end.
She keeps the thing cemented to her ear
till it becomes her auditory friend.
Though dial tones may be all that she can hear,
can charm or fetish serve a better turn
idolatrizing contact with the world?
Such access makes the disconnected yearn
for less self-centered women to be curled
beside them on the bed with nuptial band -
instead of sterile cellular - in hand.

Previously Published in Illogical Muse

Inflammation

No autocrat would move so fast
to put an insurrection down;
with arteries and joints aghast
as white cells occupy their town
to squash suggestions of revolt.
Militias infiltrate a web
of nerves and ligaments that jolt
receptors quartering the ebb
and flow of mercenary germs.
But what reward internal peace
affords! Its salutary terms
give shell-shocked corpuscles release
into a salutary state
where internecine wars abate.

previously published in Blue Unicorn

Twilight Meditation

Once I used to see autumnal dusk
as a cozy backdrop, a waiting room
leading into the darkness, safe keeper
of seasonal pleasures, mixing cold
with warmth and holiday bright
decorations sparkling like snake eyes
not too far in the distance.
Sunset would lift the stopper off a bottle of scotch.
Even the carved pumpkin had airs
of transgression about it. Tonight twilight's
a moral indictment, a smothering blanket,
a shade cutting off quotidian day, foreclosing
a house teeming with possibilities,
hope and renewal, swallowing up my dreams
in a suffocating dust storm; a lid
on the coffin of days that have passed
away with only me at the wake.

First published in Thick with Conviction '09

Goodbye Love

Enough of Mona! I won't play the fool
to trappings of her borrowed majesty,
or bend my strength to her tyrannic rule.
For what imparts the dint of her decree
if it be not me? Whence ensues her might
to pillage golden gleanings from love's field,
except it serve my worming heart's delight
to wallow in the muck that ups its yield?
I'd merely plow my paltry plot of land
while paying tribute to her potent arms.
Despite my need, I'll balk to lend the hand
that bolsters her indoctrinating charms.
For she must know the dreaded season's near
which hurls its curse on patriot and foe.
It cuts off lagging forces in the rear,
and stays advances with its freezing snow.
So let her play the arbitrary liege
till rebel Time's incendiary siege.

Previously Published in Autumn Leaves, online

Guerilla Girl

She sits sedately in the subway car
with Smart phone set at ease upon her lap.
For wanting male pedestrians to spar
with it's the time to meditate or nap.
But soon as she gets to her subway stop
and walks into what's deemed a combat zone
of male combatants that she needs to mop
up, she maneuvers from her coat the phone,
as though it were an unpinned hand grenade
she keeps at hand for contumacious guys.
And though not every man's a renegade,
should some dude fill the bill of her surmise,
her Smart phone is positioned right in front
of her to neutralize the noxious grunt.

Previously published in Homestead Review

Jungle Fever

Imagination stalks me in my room.
It's tough pretending he does not exist
when odors from him trumps the best perfume
I use to counter smells that still persist.
He can't accompany me on a date
with someone who could be my future wife.
For even ingénues won't tolerate
the extra baggage in their married life.
Indeed. How mix the civil with the wild?
I find it troublesome to go outside
because this hungry beast I've domiciled
beside me makes me bide his bristling hide.
And since it's hard to let my fancy roam
I groom the animal while staying home.

Previously published in Timber Creek Review

Demure Waitress

If spleen's an act to shield a coward's heart
I'm heedless of combative gals whose ranks
betray a regiment that's torn apart
and musters bluster to protect its flanks.
But what strong infrastructure does she boast
who posts no soldiers at her borders' gates
but plays with flair the diplomatic host.
She's dauntless as my armed invader baits
her to assess her readiness for war.
She needs no battery of ragtag men
to make me wonder if I should withdraw
the forces that I've mobilized to pen
her sensibilities. Her smile affirms
she's won unchallenged peace on favored terms.

Previously Published online in: The Jrnl of Formal Poetry, Spring '09

Child Beguiled

She burgeons from behind the seat
where I sit scribbling on a bus
some hasty notes. I fill the sheet
with inky swirls. Positioned thus,
she cross-examines what I do
with such disarming earnestness
I drawl: "I'm trying to review
a movie I just saw." I stress
my meaning to abstracted eyes.
For she's more focused on her quest
than with my ponderous replies.
Beguiled by such a sweet behest
I make an effort to persuade
my mentor that I made the grade.

Can I at 60 feel so young
when being questioned by a child?
For since she's studied in her tongue,
her fluency leaves me beguiled.
I start to measure every word
that I begin to speak to her,
afraid that I'm not being heard

or that my words are Greek to her.
Beseechingly, I fix my gaze
upon her mother, on the seat
beside her, with a paraphrase
of thoughts I fear were incomplete.
The mother smiles from ear to ear,
assuring me my meaning's clear.

Published in Freexpression April '09

Bipolar Beethoven

(Beethoven's Piano Concerto No. 1 in C Major)

How playfully he modulates his voice
in those discursive moments of the first
and rondo movements where it looms a choice.
Yet though he's fundamentally well-versed
in those urbane exchanges where the bass
keeps alternating with the treble keys -
like beefy bodies slipping into lace
and back - this call and answer game's a tease
before his virtuosic muscle's flexed.
If musty listeners are still in doubt,
suggestive trills will leave them more perplexed.
And though his first cadenza crows with clout,
he opts to close its macho sounding board
assault with a disrobing seventh chord.

Published in Freexpression in April '09

That Old, Sad Tune
(Die Alte Weise)

The thought of you looms like Isolde's sail
to Tristan pining near the ocean's blue
expanse. My former pale complexion's hale
at thoughts of our impending rendezvous.
Alas! Your dreamed arrival's a mirage
of my romanticized delirium.
Loss quickly triggers memory's montage
of life's frustrating spectacle, wherefrom
I draw the source of my obsessive needs.
For since my youth I've nursed a dire quest
for something that the far horizon breeds
from longings of my incubating breast.
And you're its proxy riding on the foam
of undulating seas that call me home.

Published in FREE XPRESSIONS April 2009

Barbadian Ode

Barbados sizzles like an omelet
of charmed calypso beats. Spiced potpourri,
its seasoning's the hot sauce of regret

for passing flavors palates can't forget.
Well-done by sun and garnished by the sea,
Barbados sizzles like an omelet

sautéed by waves sirenic winds beget
beside enchanted sands. Rapt reverie,
whose seasoning's the hot sauce of regret,

hears Lisa, Jonlin, Donna and Suzette
midst soft-sell sounds of vendors by the quay.
Barbados sizzles like an omelet

served up with smiles of student and soubrette
suffused in hues of cream and ebony
whose seasoning's the hot sauce of regret

at far-off faces framed in silhouette.
For when its sun has set into the sea,
Barbados sizzles like an omelet
whose seasoning's the hot sauce of regret.

Published in Freexpression April '09

Bracer

He'd scarcely find a sweeter nurse.
The tippler stood beside the bus
when he began to wail and curse,
continuing to make a fuss
as some young lady lent a hand
to try to help him stand upright.
She softly issued a command
enforced by pluck instead of might,
to clasp her shoulder for support
so she could steer him to a chair.
She then proceeded to escort
him on the bus like some au pair
positioning a naughty child
whom she'd decidedly beguiled.

Tucked opposite her facing seat,
he'd be invited next to her -
as if he wouldn't fret she'd treat
him with indulgent force majeure!
At length they had a friendly chat
where she revealed her tender age
of 19 years accomplished that
which smoothly managed to assuage
tense passengers. Her wispy tone

of voice belied her spunky style.
She cautioned that he'd be alone
the next time, as she freed the aisle
for his return trek home. He thanked
her, feeling blissfully outflanked.

No sooner was her charge dispatched
then she took on a forlorn look.
For scrappy as she was outmatched,
no brawler left a donnybrook
with such a self-effacing sigh
at wishing she had shown more game.
Her sad mien seemed to query why
she didn't spark a bigger flame
behind her effort to engage
the guy. For he did not leave cell
phone number nor take hers. Her wage
for fixing him beneath the spell
of her imposed society
was speeding his sobriety.

Published as double sonnet
in Free Xpressions 4/09

Holding Cell

I feel just like a baby in your arm,
for all that I'm constrained in my intent,
by virtue of the cell phone in your palm.
I slyly eyeball you for your consent
to let me move as freely as I please.
But since I see you focused on your cell,
content to casually shoot the breeze,
I swallow pride, beseeching you to quell
concerns I have that you seem too aloof
to monitor where I'll be moving next.
Thus, beckoning you for that glancing look,
I tender you the privilege to be vexed
that figuratively I ensnared your hair,
were eyes your locks and pulling them my glare.

Published in Freexpression 4/09
and again in The Poet's Art 2011

Barren Death

No wonder people say this reaper's grim
and picture him in mortuary black.
For prospects he has harvesting are dim,
and those who sow the seeds don't cut him slack.
Considering the unrewarding task
he has of gathering life's fallen leaves
it's not surprising that he wears a mask
and glares in silence when the planter grieves
at desiccated branches of his tree.
For time allotted growing season's fleet.
And what can he put in his granary
except the chaff from the survivors' wheat.
Thus dew on tombstones are the tears he weeps
for all the fruitless produce that he reaps.

Published in Free Expressions, April '09

Corrective Medicine

"Money can't buy you happiness", they say.
Perhaps that's true for those dyed-in-the-wool
blue, who won't use their revenue to play.
But the rest run best on a tank that's full.
"Money can't buy you love", poor pundits muse.
But neither can poverty. Nothing lasts.
And women, having options to refuse,
choose to use them less with the richer castes.
Affluence doesn't guarantee good health.
We know that a store of riches can't buy
longevity, and that wisdom is wealth.
But would bromides help? Rich and poor must die.
But it's more fun going to the grave
enjoying money, than having to save.

Published in Writer's Journal, May/June '09

Sea Drift

Possessions are flotsam in the sea
of memory. Excessive ballast can sink
a ship. The gale's too rough to cast anchor,
and it's late. Amidst storm waves, I abandon
my vessel and swim to nearby islands.
Efflorescent shores suggest safe harbor.
There, I'll practice novel skills, adapt old
habits to fresh environs. But drift wood
plays havoc with the coastline.
Remembrance is a hazard for old navigators
who, like me, ply new routes. Castoffs
from the past cling to my knees; tarnished
prospects that remind me of distances
traveled, and far-off harbors long since closed.
Tides recede, as I listen to the foghorn
bellowing in the encroaching darkness.

Published in Yasou Engine

Old Routes

Sometimes obstacles are blessings in disguise.
Accustomed to the safety of familiar roads,
I coasted. Oh! I've been forced to drive
along narrow lanes. The sea on one side,
cliffs on the other - I hugged the well-trod shoulder.
My windshield - spattered with mud from past journeys -
guaranteed I'd take the self-same course.
I drove with drunken consistency,
if only to avert disasters of the newly wakened.
Neither could I see what lay ahead. But trodden paths
breed laziness. And so I ply a different course.
Habits disappear like slabs of rock
before my four-wheel drive. I hear new sounds.
Radio stations are satellites of discovery.
Beneath the rustling autumn leaves
strange paths now unfold before me. In the darkness,
I map my moves, wary of sleeping policemen.

Previously Published in Yasou Engine

Midwife

These streets are so pregnant with memories,
I'd be happier bringing them to term
than terminating them. I loathe forlorn
wards of convalescence while physicians
mull the workings of my brain. And I've borne
hope too long for a stillbirth that might prove
dangerous. But the labor of regret's
just as searing, and at this advanced stage
it seems more providential to abort
than bear this load to no productive end.
I should have listened to obstetricians
whispering that the path I'm taking leads
to ruin. Life cannot survive in such harsh
environments as I've been forced to brook.
In these unsavory quarters forceps
aren't sterilized even if they're used.
I'm desperate for a still elusive nurse.
And the balloons I fancied gracing rooms
in hospitals of hospitality
have burst with noxious vapors of remorse.

Previously Published in Yasou Engine

For Kindling Stars Who Die

I wonder why some people make a fuss
when fans commemorate the young who've died?
For lamentation comforts all of us

who in the dark must cross that nebulous
divide where misty yearnings still abide.
I wonder why some people scoff and fuss

at them who mourn a starling's terminus
while she provided all the gods provide?
The lamentation is for all of us

who wing it toward the sun like Icarus,
or, being forced to swim against the tide,
must wonder why some people make a fuss

beneath oppressive skies, when luminous
performers, flying high and starry-eyed,
die. Lamentation comforts all of us

who worship idly by, while posthumous
celebrities attempt to hitch a ride
on sighs of those who make a fuss
till lamentation comforts all of us.

Previously Published in Creosote

A Lover's Complaint

I love this girl who gives me pain.
The further I'm from happiness,
the more it is I think I gain.

Though surely I would be insane
to covet bliss and then confess
I love this girl who gives me pain;

it's love I glean from her disdain.
Since she is such a sorceress,
the more it is I think I gain

when I have reason to complain
that of the girls I might possess,
I love this girl who gives me pain.

So for as long as I remain
enraptured by her haughtiness,
the more it is I think I gain,

according to my love-sick brain
that's keeping score. Since nonetheless,
I love this girl who gives me pain,
the more it is I think I gain.

Previously Published in Poet's Espresso

Dreamscape

I've taken my mother to the airport.
God only knows how. I don't own a car,
and if I did, I wouldn't know how
to drive it. Anyway, I'm there, reading
The New York Times. She tells me I'm tired.
Of course I'm tired. 7 am is not a good hour
for night birds to begin a journey.

The scene metamorphoses.
Wrapped in a cocoon, I'm
lying in a hospital ward with a bevy
of nurses cradling babies in their arms,
as if they'd charm them out of Eden.
It doesn't matter. The road back is blocked
by white-frocked seraphim brandishing
hypodermic needles. The babies are being processed
like slabs of meat for the world's consumption.

They do this with the kindly air
of ministrants for the dispossessed. Soon
the children will be suckled at the breast
of lesser angels, on the first leg

of their fruitless journey. It's the last
succor they'll get before plummeting to earth,
where there'll be no survivors.

I'm feeling sorry for them
as I pull myself
out of the sweating wreckage
of night's suffocating sleep,
bracing for catastrophe.

Published in Stray Branch Spring 2010

God

(the sonnet)

“What have you done to affirm Him?” she asked.
“Absolutely nothing,” I said. “He’s great!
Too great to be arrested and unmasked
by pulpit prelates who pontificate
on unsolved mysteries. I like my God
untamed. A voice crying in the desert,
a whirlwind over plains where none have trod.
Fear keeps us guessing, leery and alert.
I don’t want my Lord domesticated,
as though a hired servant at man’s beck
and call, or a politician feted
for favors. Chained around a maiden’s neck?
I’d rather have him wandering the street,
a burning bush in every face we meet.”

Published in: Time of Singing (winter 2010-2011)
and Penwood Review

Pacem

Why is it death always gets a bum rap?
The best of us, who neither fear nor sweat
beneath life's taxing trials, have taken naps
without the slightest feelings of regret.
Yet, as we slept, our bodies could have slipped
past recall, for all it would have mattered.
Living's an aesthetic habit. We're gripped
by lush, sprawling canvases of splattered
paint, as if addicted to moody blues.
Such noxious fumes would make the fittest faint,
if daily doses hadn't made us used
to dying. Fleshed-out pleasures and complaints
that tincture life with happiness and hell,
would disappear if we could break their spell.

Published in Penwood Review

Gethsemane

I walk along congested city streets,
crushed beneath the heavy cross of memory.
Contempt is etched on every face I meet
along the twisted path to Calvary.
My former robust self is pale and drawn
as guilt and fear weigh heavy on my heart.
Old friends who swore fidelity are gone,
and I drift through the crowd as though apart
from everything I formerly held dear.
Laurels gleaned at Galilee didn't last,
and wary women hold their children near
to save them from contagions of my past.

Distressed, I stop inside some eating place
to get myself a sandwich and a drink.
The man behind the counter gives a sneer,
as if to mock the agony I feel
at being stripped and scourged with heartless zeal,
that stamps me with the stigma of disgrace.
Determined to continue till I sink,
my grief becomes a crown to the ordeal,

and glistens on my brow with beads of sweat,
as I tread toward the fate I must embrace.

On my way out, still visibly upset,
I glimpse a passing smile on the cashier,
whose fingers rise up from her lips to grace
the crucifix that dangles from her ear,
as if she'd kiss the anguish from my face
before I fall before your harsh decree,
God. My God! Why hast Thou forsaken me?

Published in Penwood Review Fall 2009

Birth Watch

"I'm sorry," Dr. Jones told the new mom
lying on the hospital bed in tears.
He held her hand in an effort to calm
her. "Your child has only 86 years
left to live." "Oh, God. Please don't tell me that,"
she shrieked helplessly. "I had ambition
for him. It just isn't fair!" Diplomat
that he was, the doctor pledged remission
of the disease would guarantee the child
a good life until the terminal stage
set in. His optimistic slant beguiled
her into seeing ravage as the wage
most people pay when exiting the womb,
like flowers on the earth for one brief bloom.

Previously Published in Language and Culture

Circe Victorious

(on seducing Odysseus)

To offset my diminished agency
which I see mirrored in my hapless men,
who've been transformed to pigs inside your pen,
I should be foaming at your harsh decree
and seek, with Hermes' aid, my liberty.
But, less a wolf you've tamed than cackling hen,
I shamelessly indulge my passive yen
and flap my wings before your sorcery
in affirmation of your potent charms.
When my brood spots the man of many wiles,
whose mission was to bring them safely home,
capitulating to your forceful arms
no less than to your patronizing smiles,
it's clear their cocky rooster's lost his comb.

Previously Published in Pearl 2010

Tristan's Lament

As love smolders, wafting the tune along
the stopped-up chambers of my aching heart,
it segues to the same old plaintive song,

adding measure to litanies of wrong.
Winds blow through open wounds from Cupid's dart
as love smolders, wafting the tune along.

Although harmony calms the whistling throng
of past discord whose overtones still smart,
it segues to the same old plaintive song

which once again proclaims I don't belong
beside the breast whose throbbing made it start.
As love smolders, wafting the tune along

the modulated grief that keeps me strong
enough to carry on Life's forlorn art,
it segues to the same old plaintive song.

And refrains echo that I'm doomed to long
forever, knowing that - till death's shrill part -
as love smolders, wafting the tune along,
it segues to the same old plaintive song.

Previously Published in Fullosia Press 5/31/09

Royal Mystery

Should I have traced that trail of black and red
that slinked behind a serpent aisle of books
as I left the library? Was it dread,
or did desire sow those pallid looks
that blossomed in her colors? Black - the dress
she wore on our first night out together.
Red - that furnace of undulant tresses
that warms her face like tropical weather.
But was it really her I thought I'd seen -
my dream Aurora slinking out of sight?
Or did she bear the mantle of my queen
without the regal head that lends it might?
I'd best prostrate myself with chastened doubt
before a more alarming truth comes out.

Published in Lyrical Passion Poetry E-Zine 2015

For Amy Winehouse

You worship at the altar of your muse
whose art is more important than your life.
But think of what the goddess stands to lose
if you snuff out your smoky voice with rife
discordance. How poetic that your art,
when you lack harmony and feel bereft,
should feed upon infusions from the dart
of Cupid, till you're smarting from the cleft
that's instrumental to the hits you've scored.
And though we all enjoy your sacrifice
to music, know the Muse is in accord
that you play more and pay a lesser price.
A tune in sync with life can still take flight,
and they most serve the Muse who sit and write.

Published in Current Acounts/Spring, Summer '09

A Clone of My Own

Last night I dreamed I engineered my clone -
a replica to comfort me in age.
My protégé in feature, skin and bone,
I coached him well, preparing to re-stage
dramatic scenes that I myself had tried.
But those premieres fell through the boards of life.
And now I had a chance to be my guide.
His opting to get married caused me strife
enough to wonder if I should provide
the apple of my eye a paring knife.
Not caring now if facts and art complied,
I penciled out the part of my son's wife.
She promptly moved 2000 miles away
with seven kids who thought their grand-dad strange
for expurgating their prize winning play.
I realized then my son could never change
his theater piece to imitate my own,
as I woke up to finish it alone.

Previously Published online in: Autumn Leaves, 2009

Plumbing Her Depths

What's indicated by that feral yawn
assailing men from women thy would wed?
Perhaps it's the symbolic way they spawn
in vitro or some way of giving head.
Why would a woman open up her mouth
with each encounter with the virile sex
except to breed or otherwise go south
behind contrived appearances to vex
us. Strange dynamics underline our drives.
The things we crave we oftentimes abjure.
Thus, wildcats often serve as gentle wives.
For some gals use resentment as a lure
to bait and reel in men they can't forgive
themselves for loving till they learn to live

as confidantes instead of sovereign queens.
For why else would they sit like they're on thrones
and thunder exhalations as the means
of lording over subjects who are prone?
Perhaps they take their stratagems from fish
who wait with gullets open in the sea
to treacherously make a tasty dish

of cods who dart into their cavity.
What matter that the latter spread their fins
from a genetic bent, to search for food,
conduct a school, or take aquatic spins?
Presumptive groupers prove their fortitude.
For while some fish use flashy lures to bait
a mate, they're also served who sit and wait.

Published in Aries: Journal of Creative Expression, v.34 '09

Fall from Grace

How like an Eden are the sprays
of youth. A stem becomes a rose
bud that's collected in bouquets.
Each seed disseminated grows
into a verdant memory,
perennial as May romance.
One revels in fecundity
beneath a canopied expanse
of trees where every sprouting branch
bears fruit and never seems to fade.
But Autumn deems that arbors blanch
which once gave seething passions shade.
And we whom scythes of winter trim
are left with just a phantom limb.

Published in Aries: A Journal of Creative Expression
24th volume/2009

Sound Advice

It's said that we should turn the other cheek.
But bullies prove that no one should entice
us to bear grievances and not to speak.

For they're just civil liberties we seek
when we start fulminating for our slice
of pie. Then we should turn the other cheek

but likewise put on hold the goals we seek
when social honors prove to us it's nice
to bear adversity and not to speak.

But though it's law that make most men act meek
and good folk recognize our sacrifice,
they soon forget we turn the other cheek.

In time we're stigmatized for being weak.
For when we're made not once or twice but thrice,
and yet again to suffer and not speak,

what's tragic turns to opera comique.
Or cynics see a mark of our vice
and scorn such turning of the other cheek.

Thus, their contempt's soon added to the bleak
existence that we've purchased for the price
of choosing to bear grief and not to speak.

When in the end we curse life with a shriek -
estranging men and ceding Paradise -
we rue our choice to turn the other cheek
amidst adversity and not to speak.

Previously Published in Hazmat Journal

Casting Call

Perhaps Life serves as tryout for a play
in another world. Bombastic bosses,
who scribble hackneyed bit parts to portray
employees, conclude their run with losses.
Practiced workmen are perfect for the role
of filling up a larger stage with skill.
Cold criminals, whose forte's grand guignol,
dress up as the heavies. Directors drill
extras, then draw from thespians their best
performances before they muff their lines.
For age is every artist's final test
until they honor contracts Heaven signs.
Those who, dying young, break spectators' hearts
already have received important parts.

Previously Published in Nomad's Choir 2010

Brazen Tactics

She strips me bare with her corrosive stare
from where I sit inside the subway car.
Do I look like a pick-up in a bar?
I feel my senses somewhat worse for wear
as soon as she pulls back her flanking hair
from cheekbones as if it's a silk peignoir.
And though her fancy cannot take me far,
her militant maneuvers seem to dare
me to collaborate in her campaign
to make aggressive inroads to my sex.
Indeed it seems strategically insane
to let her compromising glances vex
my pride. But even as I stand to gain,
I feel the thrust of powers she'd annex.

Published in Mad Poet's Review, December '10

Afterlife

On exiting the station of the cross
town subway, he trudges home with the news.
He nailed that big promotion from the boss,
and tells his mother while the coffee brews.
The matriarch had told her son: "It's time
to leave." Dying to this world to improve
the next is best, they find, as church bells chime.
What's more, he's at that stage where girlfriends groove
to beats of Nature's burgeoning romance.
Indeed. Better to marry than to burn
both ends of a candle. For some, the dance
is over. Neither will the dancer turn
again, despite the skilled embalmer's hand
that pairs with him as in a saraband.

Friends collect his books like alms; purge the shelves
with liquid soap ablutions that atone
for sins of omission. His sister delves
into the CD collection. The phone
has been disconnected. For only prayer
now helps him, where he lies immaculate
before he settles in the plot he'll share
with hermit worms. His ex, initiate

of renovated tenements, will learn
appearances matter. Before the shock
of recognition sets in, small lamps burn
to warm grave souls like votive candles. Stock
condolences and tombstone eulogies
dispense with incense, ghostly memories.

Yes. I believe in the resurrection
of the dead. The landlord sweeps away dirt
from the apartment; a genuflection
before dark alcoves. For this sole convert
who lived there last left toasted offerings.
A mohair carpet's flogged till purified.
The profligate son, at Mom's behest, brings
the surety like palm at Eastertide,
then celebrates his having borne again
a pilgrim's cross. He'd completed penance
for those spare lodgings, and intones "amen"
at the heaven housing their past tenants.
Phone mail left by a girlfriend baptizes
his enterprise, as martyred flesh rises.

PREVIOUSLY PUBLISHED in CHAFFIN JOURNAL December 2009

Piano Works

The girl does well without a man around.
There's just the guy who sits beside the score
she has before her, pages tightly bound.
Thus, she can pound the keys until they roar
beneath deft fingers hammering out sound
that fills the concert hall. Ardent eyes soar
past measures that she chews up like a hound
munches meaty bones her master left for
food and pleasure. Like a burial mound
submerged in weeds, their markings furnish lore
for her narration. Hands ply sacred ground;
sprawling notes - plundered for their secret store
of treasure. Kindled by the hoard she's found,
the audience, applauding, shouts for more.

Previously published in Nomad's Choir
October 2011

First Love

It's funny I should think of you
in the dread of winter
under the frozen mistletoe
before your fresh greening
when the lights of Christmas
merriment are all aglow
and the hearts are warming
and the children still are screaming
while they're awaiting Santa Claus
and the radiator in my empty room
is steaming with heat
that scarcely warms my frozen
heart - a part of it still
with you, always with you
and with the children
gaily screaming with a joy
I hardly think I'll know again
until my last greening
in the heart's winter
when the lights are low
and my few remaining friends
believe they're grieving
with despondent protestations
of a love I'll never know again.

Published in Abramelin
winter 2009. vol.IV

To Marie at 60

Of pilfering birthdays that burden your years
with burgeoning branches and new-fangled leaf
whose worming detachments will turn profiteers,
the 60th one is a swift-footed thief.
He filches the food you find hard to digest,
spends most of the savings you have in the bank,
then creeps through a body that gives you no rest
through tossing and turnings that make you a crank
to husband and neighbors. They can't comprehend
why such a sane person at 60 years old
and golden with wisdom, should so condescend
to clipping her wings and to be pigeon-holed
by banking on children and immature friends
whose stock is too new to afford dividends.

Published in Abramelin, winter 2009

Cuckoo Clock

If life begins its run at one o'clock
and youth gets settled in a quarter after,
adulthood takes in stride its bold tick-tock
a happy half-turn from birth's gurgling laughter.
Nor need we care or otherwise take stock
of any here or there, or hereinafter,
or fear the cuckoo down the line will shock
us with its coming hour's burgling laughter.
But when the small hand noses toward the two,
we cease to weave the yarn that time has spun
and starkly mark the ticking left to do
before the ticker tells us that it's done.
And we can hear the chirping cuckoo mock
us when we end our course around the clock.

PREVIOUSLY PUBLISHED ONLINE
FULLOSIA PRESS 2009

Approaching Port

This schooner's getting tedious to steer.
But even though my briny hands still clutch
the tiller firmly, making it appear
I'm in control, it took no sailor's touch
to navigate across the narrow shoal.
What option here to choose another course
or ply deep waters with some earnest goal
in mind? I move as though propelled by force
before a summons I can plainly hear
near shores emerging ominously stark.
I recognize with unaccustomed fear,
as my ship lists, that soon I'll disembark
in cold, uncharted regions, so bereft,
not even murmurs of the sea are left.

Published by Fulosia Press, online

Harbor Lights

Why should the stalwart captain, in the noon
of his sea-harnessing stride, relinquish
command of his enterprising schooner?
As it cruises smooth waters like a fish
from the quay's crepuscular light to some
resplendent port of call, he scuttles in
the hull of night for sleep's stern relief from
a calm, steadfast voyage. Yet, while sirens
sing sweet songs beyond Life's billowing storm,
in the tempest of my winded passage
on a wayward course, I cling like flotsam
to the wreckage of a rudderless rig
going nowhere. And in the tidal foam,
play dumb to voices that summon me home.

PREVIOUSLY PUBLISHED 2009 in WRITE ON

Whitewash

I need a paint job.
So much has accrued over the years –
through use and abuse; thumbprints,
grease, childish doodling –
a lot I never put there.
I don't have the money
for a professional overhaul,
or the balls to argue with landlord –
not to speak of the hopelessness
of seeing it through.

We poor people –
we take the roller and some latex
and paint it all – clean as a whistle –
cheaper than wallpaper; faster
than scraping off the old stuff

and more permanent than absolution.
I call it the steamrolling aesthetic.
No time needed to put pictures up,
or drill holes in the wall –
put a hole in the heart instead –
even the red gets whitewashed
after it dries.

Frank De Canio
fdecanio@hotmail.com
201-867-5346

See that white light tunneling effect
while the paint is still wet!
No fuss no mess
no asking friends to come over
and do the dirty work for you –
no messy clothes – at least
not something you'll have to wear again.
Ditto cleaning up afterwards.
Leave it for your relatives
(it's the least they can do)
after all they helped us get here
in the first place.

I tell you
it's not gonna last forever.
So why make the effort?
So someone can move into a spiffy apartment
after we're gone?
Let them do the work for a change,
or buy themselves a new house -
if they can afford one.

Published in Blue Collar Review
winter 2009-10

Democracy's Stern Mistress

"I'm not free," she told him, brushing aside
brash importuning, like loose strands of hair.
"Neither will they win me with misty-eyed
murmurings of need, or wrath's steely glare.
I'm not easily intimidated,
and whining doesn't mean you care. I heed
only suitors who have demonstrated
wholehearted commitment in word and deed.
Nor am I seduced by the sly, shark-skin
smoothness of moneyed men in business suits,
or roughnecks who hide behind masculine
posturing. Let them bed with prostitutes
and sleep in borrowed dreams of ecstasy
until their time is through. But not with me!"

Published in Deronda Review as:
Democracy, Stern Mistress

Reading Room Zippers

(for nuisances at public libraries)

A zipper here! A zipper there!
Convinced I can't take anymore,
I run tense fingers through my hair

suggesting that she's so unfair
for grating on my mental door
by zipping here and zipping there

assorted luggage, as it were.
She still repeats her harsh encore
as I run fingers through my hair

before her bag is worse for wear
and snagging fingers start to sore
by zipping here and zipping there

metallic teeth that scrape and tear
with rasping strains I can't ignore.
As I run fingers through my hair,

I start to moan a fervent prayer
that some steel-snipping omnivore
gnaws zipper here and zipper there,
then bores through roots beneath her hair.

Published in The Poet's Art, March 2011

Seasoned Musings

In the Spring all I thought about
was sowing seeds in distant lands.
I feasted on the fruitful yield of summer
waiting for the gathering of Fall's harvest.
Now my labor's almost done,
and with the first frost of winter
when fields are covered with snow
my thoughts turn homeward.

Published by LONG STORY SHORT, 2010

Beguiling Amy
(for Amy Winehouse)

You versify your demons with a wealth
of melody desalinating brine.
Aside from Sirens undermining health,
they intersperse with your iambic line
subversive substances that they supply.
Though lyricists write only what they need,
they just as often seed ideas they try.
Indeed, addictive verses merely feed
the appetite they're anxious to assuage.
And every stanza serves as stepping stone
that lures you to the adulating stage
with more addictive verses that you hone,
until the verse and the addiction merge
with the toxicity you need to purge.

Published online in: Commonsense 2

Tuning Out

Just as an artificial limb
can function for the missing part,
so cell phone chats with her or him
can compensate the faint of heart.
What is that cell phone at her ear
if not a prophylactic arm
that aurally impounds her fear
or serves as fetishistic charm.
The nursery she's since split from
now functions electronically,
just like Rapunzel or Tom Thumb,
with ring tones that soothe sonically.
And after hearing her beau peep
with sign-off chimes she falls asleep.

Published in The Lyric, Spring/2010

A Neighbor's Death

They fall down like toy soldiers, one by one,
before the entrance to the battered door
that traps in heat and keeps away the hoar
frost of impending grief. Youth's taped rerun
of early bliss is worn. Spring's schoolmarm sun
now sports the wan demeanor of a store
clerk. Life grants me sufficient light to pore
through sales receipts before the workday's done
and the store shuts down. Former bustling streets
are empty and their neon signs torn down
along with delis selling ice and sweets.
Grown kids have moved their own kids out of town.
I'm at the crossroads where the graveyard meets
the grandson in his graduation gown.

PREVIOUSLY PUBLISHED (in a slightly different version) online March 2010 in Wild Violet and both online and in the 2010 issue of THE LISTENING EYE

Concords

She storms Town Hall's stage, determined fighter,
sporting formal dress. A toothy giant
Baldwin grand stands keyed-up to ignite her
thrust. She attacks his body. Defiant
with fierce forays of floor-shaking fortes,
she crows her show of strength. Legerdemain
fingers stress criss-crossed wrists as she essays
pianissimo passages that strain
her battery of skills. These tasks spring traps
to challenge her defense force till it cracks.
But swift sforzandos show how fast she taps
into her arms, till hammered pedals tax
sapped resources. Despite the closing chord
she hunches by the ivory for sore
resistance from the pummeled sounding board.
Unnerved by battles with this rattling score
she stiffens, poised to muffle overtones
that resonate from her prolonged assaults.
They slowly fade away with dying groans
beneath her respiration's starts and halts.
She slackens following this pregnant pause,
then smiles triumphantly to loud applause.

Published in "ILLOGICAL MUSE"
SUMMER 2010

Midlife

The ripest apple on the tree -
that gives the rest a deathly pall -
while tasting best, ironically
becomes the first of all to fall.
How bittersweet that piece of fruit
that beams like an unblemished gem,
which, while it claims a common root
with others, has a weaker stem.
Indeed, it's easier to pluck
than those whose skins are tan or green -
though one might be disposed to suck,
not eat, the pulp that's in-between
its skin and core. Thus, weep and wail
for fruit that hang on such a tail.

Published online in Foliate Oak March 2010

Flower Power

Pity those who can't enjoy a flower.
They only see the insidious worm
underneath the fragrance of the bower.
Wary, they feel the cold, corrupting term
enkindling life, without its warming fire.
Succor those who can't distinguish the rose
from the prickly thickets of its briar;
who see its splendor only as a pose.
And there are those who can't endure an hour
of raw Nature without the troubling thought
that what engenders Spring's fecund shower
floods earth with the tumult its wonders wrought;
that the pigeon, hawk and roosting tower
are shaped by the same creative power.

Pity those who only see the flower,
or savor just the sweetness of its fruit.
They don't hear the buzzing in the bower,
or sense the sleepless plower at the root
of God's fertile field. Life's budding power
rules his realm, donning varied foliage

like a wardrobe that helps marauders scour
the land. Markings camouflaged, they forage
for dinner. Some plot in a quiet hour,
spinning silk entrapments for their guileless
guests. Others prowl plains where quarry cower,
eluding stern predation with finesse
to vanquish the rest. Weaklings scan a sky
filled with vultures, and settle down to die.

But those who see the hoe near the flower
know what stratagems nature needs to grow.
They're aware that buried in the bower
are compost heaps which eloquently show
that under perfumed posies lies power
decomposed. For blossoming plants become
fodder for cows, whose dung helps the plower
sow fertile fields, where thriving worlds succumb.
Flowers are flirtations that keep life's dour
mistress dumb in her lascivious swoon,
while she's being ravished in its tower.
Despairing that at last she's come to ruin,
she wallows in its underside to scour
for God's sympathy: its wildest flower.

Published in: Samsara #16 Spring, 2010

Tart

Let others seeks out common fare
to satisfy an appetite
averse to meats (well-done or rare),
rich brews and turkey breast not white
enough. Bores crave vin ordinaire.
Dullards hide behind candlelight
dinners and fancy suits they wear
at posh banquet halls and "invite
only" functions. Bland eaters tear
at tender lambs or something slight.
But foods, like tunes, that are foursquare,
have little power to excite.
It's mutton then, whose claws are bare
and paw at me when they don't bite.

Published in Timber Creek Review, winter 2018

Bristling Lament

Who will love you when I am gone
when all the curtains have been drawn
and love remains a mystery?
When your frenetic ecstasy
lies settled on a wrinkled brow,
now, who will harmonize your vow,
when yet unwritten songs are sung,
and rusty churchyard bells have rung
to toll the fading reverie
that festers in your memory,
and drowns the din that echoes near
to sound the death knell in your ear
when death is left to dwell upon,
who will love you when I am gone?

Published in Long Story Short, June 2010

Parting

Because we did not kiss goodbye,
the tears that should have fostered bliss
now stain my cheeks.
The breast that should have cradled sleep
now bears in folded arms my grief.
And love, which might have had a start,
lies buried in my distant heart,
while I lament, as one apart
from love.

Published in Long Story Short, July 2010

Photographic Remembrances

We who are doomed to die,
will not yet perish,
nor fade amidst the fixed impressions
of this pristine eye.
But tucked away behind the gloss,
in this plush array and afterpiece
of images, we may still arrest elusive bliss,
and salvage mortal visages.
For baptized in a wash,
translucent sheets of cellulose
become a mirrored soul.
In this emulsion's coat and brushed-up artifice,
we may still forestall the passing imperfections
that soon beset us all, who are doomed to die.

Published in Long Story Short, September 2010

Elizabeth, New Jersey

A winter's morning flurry fell
like makeup on this ancient belle.
But she's not haughty or distraught
at what these frosty lashes wrought.
For she now dons a vestal glow
as if it were a bride's trousseau.
And revelers in masquerade
of winter garments, serenade
with ruby faces, bright and gay,
delighting in her special day.
Still, this loquacious socialite,
parades in silence through the night,
beside an elongated train
of softly swishing cellophane.

Published in Long Story Short
Dec 2010

Flirting with the Muse

No matter how you skirt around the thing,
desire's what the chatting's all about.
In lieu of taking her out on a fling
you start a conversation, draw it out,
do anything to keep her next to you;
if just because she's commandeered your mind.
And fantasies which you want to work through,
become the very elements that bind
you to an enterprise you know is vain.
But still you keep discussing with the girl
polite irrelevancies that sustain
the throbbing pulse that sets your heart awhirl.
And when the conversation's finally complete
you're left depleted by your vain conceit.

PUBLISHED IN THINK JOURNAL
JUNE 2010

Near Calvary

I won't remain in shadows of love's loss,
wear sorrow like some penitential mask
nor bear old courtship's relics like a cross
to weigh me down on earth until I ask
the groaning ground to say what I did wrong.
I made a vow when my first heartbreak passed,
to neither feel remiss nor strung along
the primrose path, should love's last trumpet blast.
And so I've sown with care my words and deeds
anticipating this bleak judgment day,
when passion's fruit lies withered with the weeds
that fresh enchantment cleared to give it sway.
Thus, I accept loss as your just decree,
God. My God! Why hast Thou forsaken me?

Published in Soul Fountain, Spring 2010

The Trembling Leaf

Trees shed their leaves to survive the winter.
Does it matter that this or that one grieves,
while many scramble to the topmost eaves
of shuttered houses like winging, splintered
reeds, to whistle in the breeze their story?
A host are swept, at close of season, sere;
others squashed beneath God's greening glory
before the full disclosure of their year.
The rest are rustled by the Fall's first gust
of wind, then blown across barren hinter-
lands, there to curdle on some frozen crust
of earth. That these die like drab refugees
in outposts, isn't the concern of trees
who shed their leaves to survive the winter.

Published in Soul Fountain, Spring 2010

Love's Lottery

Though it be granted all the numbers match
on that spun cylinder whose arm we hold,
the lover who's presumptively a catch
is one whose jangling jackpot bells have tolled
already. Subsequently, we excite
ourselves with fantasies of moneyed pots
that render such investments a delight
that reinforces putting coins in slots.
But that's no indication that we'll win.
Still worse, instead of numbers duds are drawn
with worries that entail another spin
of teasing bandits riddling us with scorn.
So is it really worth a taxing cost
to win the jackpot given what we've lost?

AKA Casino Player.
PUBLISHED in SUNKEN LINES

Boarding Bus Passengers

They rush the aisle as if I don't exist.
I'm more the hassled captive forced to march
ahead of shoves whose gist's an iron fist
than someone who wears shirts my cleaners starch.
Forget it if I pause before a seat,
deciding if it's one that I prefer
to something else. I feel their marching feet
behind my own, employing force majeure
to make it easy for me to decide.
And even as I make a sharp right turn
to slide inside a seat, they storm my hide.
For my maneuverings are no concern
of them who, in the solipsistic fog
they're living in, are tails that wag my dog.

Published in The Taylor Trust/Feb 2010

Vacation Blues

I've started on a working vacation.
There's much to do, a lot is on my mind.
So there isn't time for relaxation.
I've got to find a way to stop the grind.

There's much to do, a lot is on my mind.
I ought to find a worthwhile vocation.
I've got to find a way to stop the grind.
I'm starting with self-examination.

I ought to find a worthwhile vocation.
I've got to stop not being productive.
I'm starting with self-examination,
as the budding spring becomes seductive.

I've got to stop not being productive.
And I'm trying to get off the treadmill,
as the budding spring becomes seductive
and I begin to lose my vaunted will.

So I'm trying to get off the treadmill,
and begin exercising more freedom.
But I begin to lose my vaunted will.
The more I think, the weaker I become.

Though starting to exercise more freedom,
I sink in a groundswell of abstraction.
The more I think, the weaker I become;
the more intent, the greater my distraction.

I sink in a groundswell of abstraction,
darting frenetically from thought to thought.
The more I think the greater my distraction
from fantasies that leave me overwrought.

Darting frenetically from thought to thought,
I ponder if I'll see that girl again
with fantasies that leave me overwrought,
as I start to think of her more often.

I ponder if I'll see that girl again,
imagining her naked and supine.
As I start to think of her more often,
I'm coming closer to the finish line,

imagining her naked and supine.
I've started on a working vacation.
I'm coming closer to the finish line,
so there isn't time for relaxation.

Published in Grand Little Things 10/16/20

Bearing Loss

What kindling love is this that sanctifies the earth
with memories proliferating like the grave
turning of a second birth? What enterprising arms
disseminate their charms like seeds on fallow fields
to function as a lavish yield for autumn's harvest?

Suspended on such tensile roots, they bring forth fruits
which thrive on sappy juices of their germinating tree -
if just to nurture offshoots for posterity.
But what use cultivating heartbreak's fertile soil,
that promises abundance from such husbandry?

Tears scarcely save the desiccated oak. Nor does grief
breathe life into a reverie. Then pity us who savor solace
from eulogies, assuring us that death is just a passing.
For with this ever-passing hour, when time
sits still and time is never ending,
then this and every passing is an everlasting death.

Previously Published online in Wild Violet, 10/11/20

Kant Be Any Other Way

The actions that our people entertain
should function well as universal law,
at least as far as Kant's philosophy ordained.
So, let the proud electorate guffaw,
while those who served their interests are defiled
by people who would scarcely last a week
without protections that they've hence reviled
in order to secure the ends they seek.
Oh, they will face the justice that prevails,
despite the approbation of the mob
who seem intoxicated by the tales
of what a failsafe, comprehensive job
they're doing to the hapless victimized.
But rogues who give societal support
to them in such a way that minimize
their crimes - as though legitimized by court
decree - hurt more than any brief assault
where juries castigate the one at fault,

and vindicate the victim's injury.
If not, our social contract's in arrears.
Do they think that our Bill of Rights is free
who go about adjudicating peers?
So, lest they get deprived of what they deem
is just for those who've served democracy,
I hope the fellow denizens of fiends who seem
to entertain ad hoc autocracy
bestow on them a sample of the same
beneficence they smugly delegate
to others, wanting any dose of shame.
Leave rank emotions free to legislate
the justice folks deem fit for this man's grief,
that woman's pride, and any hotshot's pique,
and render it the governing motif
of people's justice, howsoever bleak
the consequences for finagling folk.
We'll see then how they'll bear beneath its yolk.

Published in Dissident Voice October 4, 2020

Bureaucracies

are functionally fascist in disguise.
No armed battalions flashing swastikas
to make sure citizens don't vocalize
their grievances to tacit commissars;
they let them rattle to their heart's content,
assuming they can find the comments page.
And later on, their grievance can be sent
so they can garner as their proper wage
that "someone will get back to you" who won't!
A representative democracy
cannot be blamed if electorates don't
have fortitude to brook hypocrisy.
And be resigned that patience is the word
when customer objections aren't heard

by corporate heads. For they are scarcely tea
that we can dump in Boston's harbor when
they tax our patience and autonomy.
Besides, their robots aren't businessmen.
And what use is America's free press
if it can't promulgate it's owners views
without according readers a redress?
Accordingly, it gives us cable news,

like CNN, to rally listeners
like demagogues of yore. But they're no more
accessible than air conditioners
in deserts, or a school of albacore.
in swimming pools. Thus, those who'd hook a catch,
will reel in empty lines from their dispatch.

Published in Dissident Voice October 4, 2020

Old Strychnine in New Bottles

How readily a social smear or slight
against a person, notwithstanding law,
becomes a celebrated plebiscite
that makes imprudent citizens guffaw.
No longer out of fashion ethnic slurs
to undermine their laissez-faire conceit.
No brown shirt bullies flashing swastikas
to scare off immigrants they're poised to treat
by way of grassroots generosity;
just obviating contracts that they've signed
ensuring we get reciprocity,
once they've amassed the clout to change their mind.
And even as their victims stand appalled,
warped minions seem subversively enthralled.

Published in Dissident Voice 4/12/20

Hard Times

He used Ramona like a rug
to wipe the dust off from the feet
when courting women for a hug
he made the liaisons complete.
he'd flirt with every girl he'd meet.
For he was young and she was old
enough to suffer his conceit.
Now his betrothed's as young and bold
as when he dallied in his prime,
and just as arrogant and cold
in love as he was in his time.
And painful antics he beholds
in her that he can judge a crime,
she's sadly fashioned from his mold.

Previously Published, slightly varied, in vol. 38 No.'s 1 &2 of the California Quarterly, 2012

Heart Blossoms

It's always Spring in the past. The first buds
of love, friendship, or insurgent passion
take root before we witness fertile floods,
or fathom seeds were planted. The ration
seems a windfall of delight. We're enthralled
by the lush green of our growing season.
Yet, how fast freshness dissipates from scrawled
colors on Life's canvas! For drab reason
screens out enchantment. Cloying abundance
replaces the thrill of the first lily
that burgeons. Chaperoned by its fragrance,
April fades to November whose chilly
climate assails us while our minds are May.
And in our heart's agenda, frost holds sway.

Published in Avocet's Fall Printed issue
2020

Sucker

Before the trematode co-opts the bird
to mediate its predatory ends,
it's discharged on the mudflat in a turd
to be engorged. Therein the scrounger rends
the reproductive tissue of a snail.
Just so, before conceit subsumes my word
and drops off its expository tail,
it infiltrates desire's tissue, spurred
to metric verse by its subversive quest.
And once inside a metaphoric cyst
it puts my pen to paper without rest.
There, beckoned, my poetic formalist
dissolves the images around the thought
till future parasitic poems are wrought.

So why then scribble verse if closures sought
serve fishy notions burrowed in a worm
that renders me less predator than caught
by verbal cysts? Their insides make me squirm.
For I'm assigned the status of a snail
whose procreative apparatus hosts
expanding daydreams. Then they drop the tail
within a seminal conceit that boasts

poetic permutations in my brain.
And still they're picked up by my gleaning pen
if only to alleviate the pain
that surfaces to start the work again.
For thereby worming fancy's free to roam
and germinate another sponging poem.

The cure then is refuse to feed on fish
from fantasies that harbor a conceit.
This way the latter doesn't find a niche
by walking through the door on metric feet.
Nor should the poet cast his craftsman's rod
in murky lakes. For formal verse can't bite
if there's no lure. Intense impressions prod
the songster to assuage his appetite
by swooping down on budding metaphor,
disseminating ripples through the skin.
These soon become a poem's thematic core.
But such a journey never could begin
without an idle study of the sea
of images that seed each simile.

For hunger motivates the bardic bird
to search for nurture in the psychic deep
his skills metabolize with thought and word,

informed by an imaginative leap.
And with his heart's ambitions compromised
he's prone to ponder from his poet's perch,
insinuating fantasies, disguised
as metaphors, that leave him in the lurch.
But mavens seek their food supply in heights
appropriate to noble birds of prey,
while wings unfold in literary flights,
designing arabesques above the bay.
Nor are they lured by wheedling slime to eat
desire's worm, entrenched in its conceit.

Published in Consequence 2020

A Piece of Mother Teresa

(and Emma Lazarus)

I get a kick out of the way the smug
reporters of the border crisis at
cable news use the occasion to mug
before the cameras with a welcome mat
of sympathetic sermons for the plight
of immigrants. What use the photo ops
that put them in a laudatory light!
In truth, the misery will never stop
as long as they're averse to volunteer
their services to feed and care for those
they love to talk about with cavalier
regard. For it's a picture-perfect pose
whose gloss photogenically counterfeits
the cost-intensive labor needed. It's

on par with someone in a car who tells
a passerby to help a blind man cross
the street while his complacent ego swells
with self-importance at another's cost.
Instead of cursing the oppressive dark,
they'd do much more as avatars of light
and jumpstart what alleviates the stark
conditions that inform the migrants' plight.

But rather than assisting those exposed
as needing help, they show a cavalier
concern for the logistics thus imposed
on burned-out border guards. Thus, let them hear
the Saint advising those whose virtues foam
with smugness: "Charity begins at home"

and not in understaffed internment camps.
So, let us all begin to play a part
in making sure the migrants see our lamp's
imprisoned lightning. This way they can start
to consummate their yearning to breathe free,
instead of hearing pols and Cable news
pontificate with rank hypocrisy.
As such, each state should start collecting dues
from us for decent home facilities.
The lucky masses get East River views,
the rest will get no less civility
from mothers of exiles, glad to infuse
the difficulties refugees endure,
with domiciles they're able to procure

for them. Though there'll be hardships as to trials
of integration, from their beacon hands
glow world-wide welcomes and a thousand smiles.
For each and every mother understands
the difficulties settling here entails.

It’s when communal chic begins to shove
on them encumbrances that countervail
exigencies pertaining to self-love
that problems will ensue. The smug romance
of deference to others might give way
to scarcely granting even peers a glance.
But though ‘yours truly’ strikes them with dismay
when with my own concerns I start to yelp,
I’m sure there’ll be somebody who can help

those “huddled masses yearning to breathe free.”
It’s when do-gooders have to pay you mind
that they then cease to be at liberty,
and leave their charitable mood behind
them. Not a nod do I receive from those
when I ask them to help me find a street,
beyond a sneer and a dismissive pose.
I should have done the same when asked to meet
with the selective service for the draft.
And, when our liberties are trampled on,
how liberally they look smug and laugh
when stringent terms for civic claims are drawn.
Thus, pray these champions of human rights
will not be in control of oversights.

Published in Another Chicago Magazine
2020

The Cavalier of the Rose
Prelude

Sooner or later. "Heut oder Morgen."
After a tryst of trumpeting thrusts, their
lust subsides like the symphonic fanfare
approximating it. The Marschallin
broods on life's transience, to the protests
of her beau, and then leaves to greet some guests.
She wryly suggests her earnest lover,
Octavion, as the cavalier who
bears to the betrothed Sophie, a silver
rose (from Baron Ochs, her parvenu
of a coarse cousin). Refusing to wed
the buffoon, "die Fraulein, die Fraulein, kurz
und gut, die Fraulein" falls in love instead
with her rose-bearer. The boy, later masked as
the shy chambermaid, Mariandel, has
the bald baron chasing her skirts, then flirts
with the libertine in a gender-bending
rendezvous that ends with his disgrace.
The Marschallin reappears just in time
to render the ridiculous sublime.
She dismisses her cousin, gives Sophie

to her Rosenkavalier, quietly
muses as she watches the rapt pair extend
undying love, and then resigns her place.
The lovers embrace blissfully. As if
lured by the luster of silvery calls,
the page retrieves a dropped handkerchief
that glimmers like grace, as the curtain falls.

Act I

I couldn't leave with her and that was that.
And all because of the corduroy hat
Dad gave me for Christmas. I never knew
what mischief losing just one cap could do,
until I saw Der Rosenkavalier
at the Met. My date didn't have an ear
for music and left before the third act.
How's a modern cavalier to react?
I returned to my seat preparing for
its singing ménage of women to soar
above infatuations of a world
as radiant as satin on unfurled
banners. Nestled in thoughts of clustering
bursts of harmony, I start mustering
the courage to talk to a girl sitting
in the sole seat remaining in my row.

Act II

"I'm waiting for the third act," she tells me,
playing Octavian to my Sophie.
"The most beautiful music in the world,"
she goes on, with her program notes unfurled.
She "sang with the chorus in Elektra
at Spoleto." Will I play Baron Ochs,
annoying Sophie with his barren jokes
(though mine left because she didn't feel well)?

Act III

Now I fantasize she's Mariandel,
Strauss's counterfeiting, coy kitsch-kitten
weeping in a run-down inn who's smitten
by this nostalgic sentiment like I am.
My now beleaguered heart is on the lam.
And when shimmering voices start to blend
with harmonies suspending measured time,
I felt a rupture only they could mend.

At this point, my stand-in Mariandel
starts growing almost as emotional
as Strauss's ersatz sentimentalist

who cries in coyness, rather than be kissed
by her duped suitor. But with mine it was
music not wine that gave to her the buzz
as she sat enraptured by this long-spun
lyricism. The wistful lovers sing
a last duet, then leave the stage, wherein
the page retrieves, as though with a closing
benediction, a hankie. This token
exhilarates as much as it consoles,
beneath the velvet curtain's falling folds,
where it flickers like moonlight's silver glare.

Are operatic patrons unaware
of the almost ecstatic pleasure of
a dominant-tonic cadence? It's love
in sweet repose. She called it a basic
3-5-8 with the practiced flair of quick-
witted club fighters who put in digits
hand combinations they might soon forget
when plying their trade. I use this sportive
metaphor as someone left contortive
from this tonal slugfest. So Strauss comes through
with a smashing, good old-fashioned one-two
punch. A winning finish to the opera,
it crowns the whole like a gold tiara.

It sweetens with sumptuous effusions,
like syrup at the bottom of a dish
of ice-cream, or wine after meat or fish.
And may those untutored audiences
who covet curtains more than cadences,
find all their efforts come to naught because
their concentration's broken by applause!

But wait some! I haven't even come yet
to the conclusion of this piece. Bravos
dispel the mists of lingering regret

as my Mariandel blows through her nose.
When she gets up to leave I try to stall
her with conversation. "I could hear you
whimpering," I muttered, gathering all
my belongings to let the girl go through,
so I could follow her down the plush aisle.

Suddenly I was looking for my hat.
On top of that my lady's wistful smile
had all the passion of a caveat.
Though frankly vain as I'm completely frank,
I looked at her face and filled in the blank.
Clearer than any silver rose could be,
Mariandel was abandoning me!

So through the course of one exhausting act,
I lose a love I never had in fact,
and I'm morosely pining after her
departure, like an ardent amateur
who suffered the millinery mishap
of looking for a sentimental cap.

Likewise, Octavion rushed out the door
of the Marschallin's boudoir. "Ich hab' ihn
fortgehn lassen und ihm nicht einmal gekusst,"
I brooded in the style of the sad-eyed,
Act I Marschallin, who let her anguished
lover leave without kissing him goodbye.
Unlike her, I could only reminisce,
"I have let her go, and without a kiss."

That's because she called her servants to run
after him. I had only a fervent
longing, as my handsome Octavion
left to kindle yearnings of emergent
Sophies in the wide-eyed world. Now I bend
a knee, not with the grace of a princess
resigned to her age, "in Gottes Nahmen,"
but as somebody trying to assess
just how I'd been demoted to a page
looking for my hat on an empty stage.

In the post-tonal mist this was certain,
filtered through an operatic format:
the tempi stopped with the falling curtain,
and minus hat, the melody fell flat.

PUBLISHED in:
PENNSYLVANIA ENGLISH 2018

Language Session

"Your German ist sehr gut," she says. Indeed
sehr gut enough for her to till the soil
she needs in preparation for the seed
she'll plant within me. Thus, she can embroil
me in semantics of her native tongue.
Linguistically at home, she's in control
of any future flowering that's sprung
out of its duly cultivated scroll.
And every word's a kernel in the ground
that grows in her accommodating ear
into a rich, reverberating sound.
It blossoms in mutations that I hear
her speak through sweetly redolent two lips,
suggestive of inseminating scripts.

Published in Horizons magazine, 2020

Marion, Pert Librarian

This straitlaced girl who'd disappeared
behind his solipsistic self
has just as passionately reared
from where he placed her on the shelf
of his concern to gather dust.
But now her text is loud and clear
with boldfaced lines to be discussed
from dog-eared pages that endear
her to him. How could he ignore
the solid binding of the book
he'll so assiduously pore
through, once the cover starts to look
enthralling? He would check her out
if that's what dating was about.

Published in Horizons magazine, 2020

Forest Murmurs

Some nature lovers see her tree
as wads of green from which to plunk
down berries from the treasury
of vaulting arms that crown its trunk.
They criticize its spendthrift leaves
as borrowing off sun and earth,
and branches on which each bud cleaves
as banks that fund their season's worth.
But such withdrawals don't belie
the wealth of maple, oak and beech
which, though their assets liquefy
can still mint leafage, nut and peach.
Such coinage is the tender fruit
of pure gold standards at their root.

Published in Woods Reader, Summer 2020

Scholastic Scrimmage

Her fluency's alive and well.
And not just on the podium
when she, while fielding questions, fell
afoul of backfield odium
from hecklers taking her to school.
But rushing one as he recapped
his triumph with conceited cool,
her metaphoric tackle zapped
him harder than the verbal bricks
that fell on her like an assault.
It hit him like some forward chick's
improper pass. For by default,
her spirited, linguistic sack
became an aphrodisiac.

published by Stepping Stones
Magazine Mar Apr/May 2015

Love Ties

Forget that talismanic gunny sack of oils. Face-pasted dolls dripping honey merely made you squander hard-earned money. Even that twisted arm behind my back could hardly pick up Aphrodite's slack, tickling less the pubic than the funny bone. Though trussing up my hands would stun me, in spite of this incendiary tack, you left me flaccid, off the beaten track, if only to avoid a felony rap. But watching you, all worked up, runny nose, disheveled hair smelling of lilac as it dispensed its aphrodisiac, roiled my blood. Eros rose as - your sunny disposition darkening - you spun me all about. Such miffed scrambling for the knack of disentangling that quadruple knot with which you'd gingerly secured my wrists, worked magic to assist love's steaming pot to boil. You champed at the cord, pounded fists, as your frenetic body stewed to hot, then wet. Though no man worth his salt enlists prolonged restrictions sitting in one spot, you - baffled, huffing mad - puffed catalysts that tripped me to discharge my pleasure shot much quicker than the rope's abrasive twists

Published online in 'Fleas on the Dog' September 2020

Salaciously Served

Though smitten senseless by the handsome thief
of hearts who brashly swaggered in her store,
she was accomplished at preparing beef
her gourmet peers and family adore.
As such, she clasped the fellow in her arms
and pressed him to her appetizing ear,
then seasoned him with hot and spicy charms
like thyme, until she felt his passion rear.
With aromatic preparations done,
she took the silken ribbon from her hair
and, just as if he were filet mignon,
entwined his hands with gastronomic care
which later, like porchetta, she then tied
in nuptial knots with culinary pride.

Published online in 'Fleas on the Dog'
September 2020

Wheedling Wedlock

is sort of like the lovelorn out on bail.
He stumbles on his girlfriend's house to rob
her of her valuables, until she flails
to hinder her armed, if ardent, heartthrob.
She manages to confiscate his gun,
but not before he cocks it in her face,
believing she'd be stunned and overrun.
Instead, with frantic thrust, her arms embrace
him in a stranglehold that makes him rear
in desperation, writhing to escape.
With no recourse then biting on her ear,
he breathlessly concedes to her the scrape,
if only so he get sufficient rest.
Of course, the case contested in the court
of public opinion, he hence confessed
to charges that require child support.
And with the evidence inside of her,
the court remands him as her prisoner.

Published online in 'Fleas on the Dog'
September 2020

Nurturing Her Animus

Exasperated with the gender role
assigned to her, she first stopped using rouge,
then makeup altogether. Mind control
sufficed as a becoming subterfuge,
before she took karate and Tai Chi.
But still she needed thumbs up from her peers,
besides subverting femininity
by putting triple piercings in her ears.
Enjoining older men to take her seat
on bus and train accorded social clout
to her. And though policing on the beat
afforded her pro forma ways to flout
the stigma she felt compromised her sex,
just running down a suspect purged the hex.

Published online in 'Fleas on the Dog'
September 2020

A Scrumptious Hero

What matter if it's raisin, rye or wheat
bread sandwiching the food stuff that's inside?
It's meat, plus lettuce, cheese and all you eat
with it that makes you feel so satisfied.
Such appetizing victuals can slake
your hunger. Nor should spice in mayonnaise,
and red-hot peppers force you to forsake
them for less pungent flavors that won't braise
the sensibilities. For they're subsumed
within the context of a proper lunch
that doesn't leave one's healthy diet doomed.
But listen up, before your features scrunch!
Those condiments affording you a thrill
as seasoning, uncoupled make you ill.

**Published online in 'Fleas on the Dog'
September 2020**

Munch Hour

Where's that sultry French girl I saw in the heat
of a Summer afternoon selling fruit on Park Avenue South
in the Flat Iron District of Manhattan? "The Tide is High"
was blazing on the radio like waves buffeting the sweaty
shores of my body. Did the dust settle on her pretty cropped
head like that of Jean Seberg's in Joan of Arc? Or have tresses
of time embalmed it in a coiffure of sackcloth and ashes?
Nothing remains except the sultry air of her. Ah! The permeable
suture of youth, where women enter stitched into our mindsets
at their behest and there's no gainsaying it, before the armature
is settled on our bodies like an embalmer's primer. I remember
her boyfriend appearing as if from back stage of a play
unfolding on this patron of her parts. How I envied him in his
youthful exuberance, embracing and missing her. Has the sun
set on his enterprising affections? Or have they sublet some
tawdry apartment on the lower eastside where he's fodder for
her plebian tastes? Oh, those dog days of summer. How they
cling to me like a wet blanket on a hot beach reaching out to
tides of passion that ride me like a surfboard on their surge.

Published online in 'Fleas on the Dog'
September 2020

Constitutional Cancer

Americans treat free speech like a crime
and kidnapping or murder like free speech!
A fool who says the wrong thing's rendered slime,
while those committing murder's out of reach
of judgement that's beyond a court of law.
Free speech is subject to the lynching mob
while rapists seem to have a passing flaw.
Though glib remarks can render one a slob,
rape's treated like an inconvenience.
It leaves the violated girl intact
enough to grant the suspect lenience
by smug interpretations of the act.
A felon's still a suspect should he rob
somebody, meriting a costly trial.
But those who aren't PC lose their job,
while self-styled liberals sit back and smile.
And those who piously promote the flap
perhaps would not survive a wiretap.

Published 7/12/20 in Dissident Voice

Corona's Apocalypse

I don't believe a missile-launched attack
could wreak such havoc on those living it
Although our buildings still remain intact
there aren't many people giving it
a second thought, for all the friends they've lost;
familiar faces who'd been working there
who now must suffer the financial cost
of businesses whose coffers may be bare.
The smoldering that follows bombed out ruins
is mirrored in the thoughts of those who brood.
I ponder thus, the seething social wounds
inflicted on those wanting fortitude
to put the fractured pieces of their lives
together in the body that survives.

Published online in Poetry Kit:
"In the Plague Year" April 2002

A Senior Bussing with a Threesome

An episode from Charlie's Angels could
have functioned just as well. The blonde rose from
her seat near a brunette to play the good
Samaritan while urging me to come
sit down, as if by ordinance, and bide
her charge. Was I suspect for ceding ground
to some conspiring bloke preoccupied
with stealing leg room? Blondie would impound
his pilfered space, and then insinuate
herself beside his seat with book and specs.
Although I made attempts to mitigate
my designated captor's random checks
on me, she finally seemed prepossessed
by what she had been reading since I sat
beside her at her colleague's stern behest.
This notwithstanding, she'd at last combat
my quest with nods to an arresting friend
who'd overseen the drama that ensued.
The latter laughed that it approached its end
with just the duo's dose of fortitude.
Considering the three gals were allied,
resignedly I sat back for the ride.

**Previously published in Old Red Kimono,
May 2020, less 4 lines subsequently added**

Elegy for George Floyd

It's strange that a man should be arrested and then killed merely on suspicion that he's using a $20 counterfeit bill. Forget that apparently a black man's life isn't worth more than $20.00 in the eyes of America! The world is filled with counterfeits that serve as currency toward self-serving ends. Counterfeit democracies that give minorities freedom checks that bounce. Eastern Colleges that banked on black labor to enhance its coffers and those of its student body. Southern states who used counterfeit currency in the form of slaves to serve the welfare of plantation owners; or the cheap labor amassed through the African workforce in the South, even after the Emancipation Proclamation; counterfeit education in minority enclaves and the rest of the disenfranchised concentrated in underserved cities so the rest of us can cash in on racial inequities; the blank check accorded our black fighting men who risked their lives so we could live freely. The counterfeit gold medal that the great Muhammad Ali got from the Olympics that couldn't barter a seat in an all-white restaurant. The counterfeit court trials allotted white serial killers accorded a jury of their peers that merit them a lifetime of prison food, while black men get a summary sentence of death handed down by policemen for selling cigarettes on the street. The counterfeit sympathy of otherwise clueless people like me and many in my generation who bewailed the violence going on in the South in the 50's and marched only to the newspaper stand to read about it. The world is filled with counterfeit. What it needs is empathy and men of character with real currency who can finance change with political acumen.

Previously published in Jerry Jazz Musician June 2020

Diablo!

he yelled at me in the fast-moving car.
And though not physically accosted by
the sniper, vocally he'd petrify
me with his brash invective. It would jar
my senses, just as if it left a scar
inside of me so raw I'd soon as die.
Perhaps his anonymity was why
it rattled me who fostered the bizarre
conceit he was a plant. How mobilize
defensively and let the tension out
for what was after all a sanitized
offensive by a surreptitious lout?
Had he *done* something, I could galvanize
against the tacit threat and move to rout

the miscreant. Besides, he screeched in front
of my apartment, on the quiet street
where I reside. I felt it was a stunt
to show me I should beat a fast retreat,
in lieu of any quest to stand my ground
amid adrift, inflammatory words
res publica had helped to spread around.
Such excrement is strictly for the birds.

For there are scarcely seeds in crap like that
to feed my democratic appetite
for civil rights without a caveat -
whatever scavengers are in mid-flight.
I trust the country that I'm living in,
however its electorate might grin
approvingly. "Diablo," I could hear
him yell again, confused as what to do.
Intimidated, I could see him veer
his car around the corner, anxious to
engage my spleen. Instead I let him hit
me with bewilderment, then speed away
with cunning, having managed to acquit
himself of any input in the fray.
My body smoldered like a battlefield,
with him and me combatants in my breast.
There, neither of us seemed disposed to yield
positions that the other one possessed.
And so, the conflict waged alarmingly.
For I was target of my armory.

Hence, battle weary, I could hear grenades
exploding within distance of my head.
As I approached the city's barricades,
I crawled to safety, wishing I were dead.

And so, I'd done the dirty work for him,
while managing to hide my injuries,
except the self-inflicted loss of vim
and other corporal contingencies.
Forget the sense of being stalked like prey
in social spheres where guns are frowned upon.
I look upon my future with dismay
while, flaunting cockiness, he carries on.
I feel like I'd been booted in the ass,
and only wish his destiny's as crass.

Published in Words and Whispers
September 2020

Homage to Those Who Serve

(in a viral age)

Forget the knight in armor at a list
who advertises daunting jousting skill.
I yield devotion to the scientist
in labs, and health providers with the will
to take up arms against Corona's scourge.
No mere medieval damsels in distress,
our nurses storm the battlements to purge
the pathogen with cavalier noblesse
oblige. Their foe deploys our friendly arms
as turncoat soldiers serve as breeding ground
to pass on its incendiary harms
pandemically. Nor can its source be found.
As such our health providers chaperone
potential victims into quarantine -
removed from front lines of the battle zone,
in lieu of an emergency vaccine.
And still our white-masked warriors advance,
as fearlessly as cavaliers of yore,
without the latter's rapier and lance.
Their weapons are a single-minded core
of industry, endurance, cotton scrubs,
proficiency and antiseptic rubs.

Published in The Voices Project 6/23/20

Viral Trials

(during the time of Corona)

Freud wrote, "The unconscious doesn't know death,
but as the loss of love." That rings so true.
For it's a passionately labored breath
that respirates among our forlorn crew.
I rue the close-knit people whom I've lost
to this eviscerating quarantine
we're in. We'll pay a devastating cost
emotionally, pending a vaccine
that lets the blood flow back into a world
on life support. No heartbeat stirs this street
that looks like an internment shroud unfurled
across a corpus wanting body heat.
My mind's been transferred to intensive care
for those bereaved, since severed arteries
to downtown haunts are aching for repair.
Strong bonds are ruptured by this heart disease.
And even as societies convulse,
I'm at a loss to feel the slightest pulse.

Published in Dissident Voice 5/17/20

Life Support in a Viral Age

It isn't easy to live anymore.
This cancer's grown so that it's hard to walk
unwisely. Mom and Pop's grocery store
serves as limit of my travels. I talk
to walls because my peers are ill at ease.
I'm quartered now, restricted to a chair,
since made aware that crucial arteries
have been occluded or in disrepair.
I scarcely see life in the district where
I live, and hear still less its throbbing beat,
who once heard children laughing without care
in games they played. My heart's a lonely street
where I mark time. And daylight's hazed with dread,
while I keep watch at pastimes that are dead.

Published online in Dissident Voice 4/19/20

Amorous Tick

It's not that I'm alone
that makes me sick with grief,
but that you sap my bone
and flesh without relief.
How well I felt before
you burrowed in my breast,
encouraging rapport
with what would soon divest
me of autonomy.
Indeed, you're in my hair
with rank economy
of means. For you're not where
you physically should be,
but thrive in memory.

Published in lpe-zine 2020

To His Beloved

That men have died before their time,
I will not to the distance tell;
before the springtide leaves its rhyme,
and summer spins its midday spell.

Until the labored day is done,
and night betrays a winter chill,
when darkness shades the setting sun,
and loneliness oppresses still,

I will not stir this settled mind
with sorrows that within me dwell,
or dare confess to humankind,
the love for whom I cannot quell.

Forestalling hopes of happiness,
until the tolling of the bell,
I'll end my days in emptiness,
and bid you of my life, farewell.

Oh death, that sounds the fatal knell,
and sears the grieving heart with pain,
if fear will give me faith to tell,
can dying love be born again.

Published in lpe zine 2020

Ardent Foreclosure

Although I brandished her a harmless gift,
it only took her seconds to disarm
me. She gave fugitive feelings short shrift
through agile demonstrations of her charm.
And even though I bargained that she'd spare
my sensibilities, she drew me near
so I could feel, impressed behind her hair,
the hardware of her cockleshell of ear.
Her firm embrace constrained my face beside
hers with maneuvers that would scarcely spare
me. Since I couldn't run, and still less hide,
I sighed, relieved that my designs were good,
despite the heat still hidden where I stood.

Published in Pulsar Poetry Webzine
June 2020

Delicatessen Gal

With matronly efficiency
she teases pieces of roast
from the meat slicer
into the damp rose
of her opened palm.
Slim, dexterous fingers toss
soft slivers of cheese
on sodden slabs. Scattered parts
of my white-breasted hero
are stretched-out on the marble
counter. Naked to the warm
insouciance of her touch, the bread's
diapered with assorted cold-cuts,
then handily dressed with tufts
of lettuce, like bibs on a driveling child.

Published in Fleas on the Dog
September 2020

Kant Be Otherwise

Don't just suggest it's universal law
by way of telling others how to act,
while giving citizens a deal that's raw.
Through modeling create a moral fact
which like a planted seed sprouts in the hearts
of men who'd overrun domestic plants
despite good husbandry the law imparts.
For in the end they're autocratic rants
that water any seedlings that we've sown,
until they're toxic as the hyacinth
whose flowers turn to poison once they're grown.
Indeed, such actions sprout a labyrinth
of foliage from which there's no escape,
but to assume a more complicit shape.

Published in Conceit Magazine, April June 2018
The Ultimate Writer's Quarterly
and Dissident Voice March 2020

"You Need to Calm Down"
(intones the pop star)

Just as a quarry's brash response
brings to the fore, one laid to waste,
a stance conveying nonchalance
implies its source has been outfaced.
They're adversaries Taylor Swift
can handle with good-naturedly
aplomb. She doesn't let them rift
her measured sensibility.
Nor does she blithely shake them off
with just a sisterly rebuke.
For less Patrón than Molotov
cocktail she just as well would duke
it out when trolls step on her gown,
were she not bent on calming down.

Published in New Verse News, 2019

Medusa

He's mesmerized by snaky rows
astride her head. And piqued by her
provocatively deadpan pose,
he fantasizes force majeure
behind her sobering allure.
Because, by his own balance sheet,
vexation's an imprimatur
of strength he scarcely could compete
with, daring her exacts a wage.
Like Perseus, he's more to lose
than she has, should he thus engage
her in a brawl where egos bruise.
And since a shameless drubbing hurts,
he stiffens at the risk he skirts.

Previously Published in Star*Line 2020

Fancy's Harvest

How luscious was this island tryst
which blossomed such a little while
that every sepal shall be missed
as I pluck petals from your smile.
Oh, false conceit of this romance
that keeps its produce out of reach!
For if there were the circumstance
of garnered bliss, what bitter breach
would wend into my fertile dreams?
And though it's closeness that I seek
it's distance that preserves what seems
to be my heart's florescent peak.
Then let me weep for fruits I'll keep
forever ripe but never reap.

Published in Poets' Espresso, 2020/v.13 issue

For Evelyne

I sent legions of desire to conquer
you. Battalions of affection to bring
Venus to her knees, and force surrender.
I might have shot darts with Cupid's bowstring
and watch them be deflected off breastplates
of steel, as try to storm your citadel
of alabaster skin and delicate
bone, flanked by pride's stonewalling sentinels.
The siege failed when embattled regiments
of love's campaign, wasted by your winter,
hastily retreated to repentant
murmurings at the ramparts of your ear.
Vanquished by arms that promised my release,
I yielded passion for deserts of peace.

Published in Poets' Espresso, v.13/issue 8

Aural Sex

Your honor, I demand my date be charged
with using learnedness to cast a spell
on me. I roused his ego, hence enlarged
by Shostakovich, Mozart and Ravel,
and other conquests that he made in art.
But I don't put on costly jewelry,
and get made up to entertain how smart
guys are when banking on tomfoolery.
Your honor, this I barely could endure.
I bought myself a chic Versace dress,
a perky permanent, and manicure
that would have made a tone deaf guy assess
me as the kind of girl inclined to love,
and all I got, instead of turtledove

were Bach cantatas ringing from above
the couch whereon I lay. He talked of Freud,
Nijinsky, Ailey and Baryshnikov,
along with Baudelaire and Carlisle Floyd.
The only sheets he rumpled on my bed
were those he put there from the music score
of La Boheme; and the only head
I got from him was nodding in rapport

with arias Rudolpho sang. He sowed
no seed, but tickets to a concert in the Spring
contained the sole affection that he showed.
Nor did he try to crown his offering
with bubbling champagne glasses we could clink
while heeding overtures by Humperdinck
instead of those he should have given me.
Thus, all in all, he was a dreadful date,
committed less to love than chastity,
and sacrificing prurient for prate.
But why did I engage at such expense
a fellow who seemed more enthused about
the Tristan chord that left him in suspense
than leaving me without the slightest doubt
that he was interested? Since he was not,
I heard the chorus in Messiah ring
out hallelujahs, while my Lancelot
did not touch any keys to make me sing
with similar enthusiasm. Hence,
my date was less elixir than expense.

Published in The Listening Eye 2019

A Fool Ponders Rules

"You know what you can do with rules,"
he said. "Give them to corporate heads
to ply the organizing tools
they need as their conglomerate spreads.
They'll gobble up the poor in need
of meager wages at the cost
of laborers who fed that greed
before they found their jobs were lost.
Bequeath then to the privileged class
who seem to think that laissez faire
affords them license to act crass,
until they purge the guilt they bear
on those first scapegoats who agree
to give them moral solvency.

Bestow them on the Catholic Church
who need them to keep heathens out;
to bigots; members of John Birch
Societies who aim to rout
socialists; to those who need laws
in order to protect themselves,
but eke out an exemption clause
to put them right back on the shelves

once they've sufficient force to wield.
Impose them on advancing flanks
of demagogues to make them yield
from flogging us once we break ranks
and they can fend off felony
charges, but don't pin them on me."

Published in Dissident Voice, 2/2/20

Graveyard Reverie

Nebulous in moonlight, sleep's afterglow
suffuses her breast as she bunches hair
buffeted by wind. Amorous, she grows
heavy. Love's outgrowth is cribbed in her care.
Those doubtful that the dead can ever rise
should see the seeds her cradled consort's sown
branch up from causeways wherein he lies.
They'd trace this metamorphosis of bone
and sinew along tributary arms.
She'll gather from this liaison with earth
ripe fruits that serve as fertilizing charms
before she brings to term his second birth.
And thus she quickens detumescent men
until her throbbing lover comes again.

Published in Samsara, Issue #22, 2020

Poignant Parings

Freud thought the unconscious doesn't know death
excepting loss of love. In that case,
I know it when I think of my strained breath
while fixing on your slowly fading face
amidst the peers and friends to follow suit.
It dawns on me when I know my address
will soon be fallow strangers will take root
in as their plans begin to effloresce.
It looms when restaurants where our hands entwined
have since emerged as nondescript hotels
facilitating foreign ties that bind.
It pricks when my new-kindled passion swells
with budding fervor that will spawn no shoot.
It dawns as sadly I recall Times Square
emerged from seedy squalor to a fruit
as succulent as any tree can bear.
For harvests gathered can taste bittersweet
beside the teeming produce heirs will eat.

Published in Samsara Issue #22, 2020

Lest We Forget

The present plight of immigrants
is sad indeed. But paring of
our moral stance shows congruence
with other forfeitures of love.
"Have we lost our humanity?"
The Governor John Kasich asked,
assured in his urbanity.
Did he forget slaveholders basked
while separating families,
as servants labored in the field,
and masters muttered homilies
about God's blessing on their yield?
Such sweat and toil without respite
our government won't still make right.

Recall the bloody massacre
of Indians at Wounded Knee,
importing slaves from Africa,
for lynching mobs in Tennessee.
The slaughter reappears today
with sanitized veneer as drugs
to keep downtrodden folks at bay
or jail those selling them as thugs.

And don't forget our Japanese
internment camps before we wince
at coolness to atrocities
against the Jews. A long time since
humanity has lost its clout.
Surprising John just found this out.

Published in Dissident Voice, 10/13/19

Instrumental Asylum

I know a Hank where the whiled time goes
as fast as a CEO's income grows.
Though nursing fixed views in his head, he'll schmooze
with more civility than cable news,
without assuming hoity-toity airs.
He says whatever points of view he cares
to. In the sheltered building where he lives,
he's snug as corporate executives;
but his lobby's more keen for an ID
than special interests. Clearly, he can see
the many homeless living on the streets,
but leaves it to policemen on their beats
to do the work that he's disposed to shirk.
At least he doesn't give a righteous smirk

if it's not done. He cares, but isn't swayed
to do much more than protest in parades.
Nor are there cockerels and clucking hens
pontificating in his cloistered pen.
For he's sequestered from the smug decrees
put out by CNN. At perfect ease,
we chat. There are no wires in his ears
to obfuscate the mandates that he hears

inside his head to give more than a yen
to help the needful, weary veteran.
He doesn't keep repeating gibes deemed cheap,
to serve as mantras for a good night's sleep.
I would have shared with him another cup
of tea, but visiting hours were up.

Published in Dissident Voice, 8/4/19

Yet Again

They weren't swastikas that swept through streets
in Germany preceding World War 2,
but tactics voiding patriots' receipts
and swapping them with payments that were due.
And that, in time, would bring into relief
the wretchedness of those deemed in arrears.
The charge outstanding would inform their grief
by stigmatizing them to paid up peers.
There, citizens, traduced by heads of state,
who held groups patriotically in debt,
were more than eager to initiate
proceedings that would be their epithet.
For wormy imprecations loom like bait
to sate the tastes of those who vegetate

beneath the thrall of fascist militants.
But in a country like America,
where democratic laws keep vigilance
to guard against a Nazi replica,
there're sycophants who would traduce the state.
For threats that wouldn't resonate beyond
those saying them, das folk reiterate
until more feckless followers respond

in kind. They're thus, the camps and dungeons laid
on grounds good people built as guarantor,
until the latter find they've been betrayed
and creditors start knocking on their door.
Thus, every menace given currency,
are breaches on our homeland's warranty.

Published in Dissident Voice, 8/18/19

Art

is the life gourmet's chief comestible;
filleted experience seasoned in spice.
It isn't some dry, indigestible
roughage doctors prescribe to force a nice
bowel movement while on the fast track to
success. It's neither a grocery list
that goes into the making of a stew,
nor a quick snack that's wiser to resist
before partaking of the heavy meal
prepared by corporate executives.
No. It's the staff and protein of life; real
fare that nourishes and helps people live
as though at lavish banquets fit for kings;
idling near bowers where the skylark sings.

Published in Art Times, 1/28/18

The Closing Fugue of Mozart's Jupiter Symphony

Canons unfold like limpid layers of fat
straining the bodice of this straight-laced
goddess as she bears the symphonic fruit
of her miraculous conception. The brood's dispensed
with fluid counterpoint from her embryonic theme -
first inverted, then eased outward
with deft, compositional forceps.
Melodic snippets trip on heels of kin.
Interweaving lines knit a warm,
incubating blanket of sound. I swoon from bliss -
as though the proud father of these sextuplets.
And well I know, they'd choke in polyphonic muscle
before completing life's cycle
were it not for art's dear sustenance.

Published online in Eye on Life, November 2011
and later In the Eclectic Muse Christmas 2011

Our Ninth Hour

We too are Jesus forced to bear the cross
of law and suffer man's iniquities.
We too deny our providential source
of power to redress inequities
when mobs with club cards crown us king of fools.
We wear a coronet of PC thorns
and suffer vinegary ridicule
at Golgothas complete with social scorn.
And still we're slated to be crucified
by arrogant, self-righteous Pharisees
who, not content to see our hopes have died
of ever rising from our Calvaries,
shout merciless forewarnings of our doom
to keep us in a metaphoric tomb.

Published in Ancient Paths 9/8/18

Lost Harvest

No matter what good shepherds say,
the meek shall inherit the dearth.
No restitutive second birth
to resurrect his wilted spray
or chance to reap some other day
the fullest measure of his worth.
A seasoned grief won't crown with mirth
the summer, once it fades away.
No wreath of ivy leaves adorn
or justify the destitute.
The object of another's scorn
for letting blight destroy his fruit,
or waiting meekly to be born
again, his fig tree spawns no shoot.

Published in The Magnolia Review 2019

Lucky Loser

I didn't think the volley to and fro
was more than just a passing pickup game.
And yet, with every service, stroke or throw
your deft returns were fanning passion's flame.
And so I kept in play the tennis ball
that you forehanded with apparent glee,
while I kept waiting for the judges' call
to stop exchanges with a penalty.
Instead the play continued through a set
whose match point volleys caused my head to spin
awaiting for the referee to let
me serve again with shots that help one win.
But when you flouted my lob just above
the net, and left, I knew it wasn't love.

Published in The Magnolia Review July 2019

The Princess of Labor Lost

(after Shakespeare's Love's Labors Lost)

Like soldiers poised to wage a war,
she maps positions of her foe.
She asks her cohorts what they know
of the belligerents who swore
off love. She mocks the canon's roar
that bellows from their pompous show
of abstinence with digs that sow
the seeds that grow into rapport.
For well she knows man's scathing wit
will wither even with increase
of powers that engender it.
And he will never get release
from servitude till he submit
to disconcerting terms of peace.

Published in The Magnolia Review, July 2019

What the Cell!

The walking cell phone user's smirk
is telling me to get on queue.
I have to focus on the work
required not to bump into
this prima donna while she squints.
The way she starts approaching me,
I have to learn again to mince
my footsteps patiently should she
decide to stop short in her tracks.
Forget that I may miss the train
while she takes time off to relax
and digitally entertain
herself at my commute's expense.
Her texting keeps me in suspense.

Previously Published in Amulet May/June 2019

Champagne

You palmed my offering, then held
it fast against your dungarees.
With sensual finesse you shelled
the foiled, intoxicating tease.
Slipped loose, its bubbles seemed to rise
s though poised to intimidate
you to suspend your enterprise,
and passively capitulate
to its still stoppered eminence.
But you constrained it in a grip
that flaunted the hard evidence
of your undaunted gamesmanship.
Then with a few judicious jerks
you popped it and discharged the works.

Published in Amulet, May/June 2019

Amorous Karma

A fan of Indian philosophy,
I touched on Yoga with the frisky girl.
But then as though she feared apostasy,
she asked me not to play pedantic churl
and slight the mental practice she observed.
She said this with such affable control
that I became a little bit unnerved.
As such, she doffed her sari for the role
of bold protectress of her heritage.
She prompted me in turn to acquiesce
my virile role and tender patronage
at her behest. How quickly she'd redress
my apathy in amorous affairs,
till she, as suitor, trumped my prissy airs.

**Published in India-USA Punjabi
English Magazine May '19**

Correspondences

How beautiful those summer leaves
were, blossoming along with your
infectious tugging on my sleeves
while talking. All this was before
I pared your flower from the branch
of self-regard that nurtured it.
Then both of you began to blanch
before my seasoned counterfeit.
Now autumn leaves are falling down,
befuddled by a gusty wind.
It's scathing as my forlorn frown
that's vainly trying to rescind
the wages of my cavalier
response, as more leaves start to sere.

Published in Caveat Lector 2019

Meshugana Dance

What stylized truancy is this?
A prototype of living dead
performers moving all amiss,
while, with their oscillating heads,
they move apace as in a trance.
I feel a little powerless -
considering their wayward dance -
to do much more than acquiesce
to what looms as subversive grooves.
For what's the use of my cache
of seasoned thoughts when they're removes
from reasoning. And thus, at bay
from doing much more than a child,
I cede myself to it, beguiled.

Published in Art Times 6/21/19

Orally Corralled

“Hahah, really? I don’t think so,”
was her insouciant response
to my suggestion that she stow
a smart phone with her when she wants
it for exams. No thinking twice
when dealing with my flip remark
about her honor - although spiced
with humor. Neither was a stark
demeanor shown to cover up
inadequacies in her breast.
For old west cowboys mouthing “yup!”
while routing rustlers don’t suggest
proficiency with more aplomb
than she did rendering me dumb.

Published in Poet’s Espresso
May 2019

Amiss Missionary

"You're mocking me," she sneered when I asked her
if I should cancel any pending dates
beyond the one creating such a stir
her fundamentalist group advocates.
No pass for riding on the wave of scorn,
and her own abdication to her Lord.
It seems the only spirit that was born
again in her was when I'd struck a chord
with the resolve she'd given up for dead.
Forget Apocalyptic promises
of some impending judgement day, the dread
of her induced this doubting Thomas's
belief that doomsday would indeed arrive
if my respect for her did not revive.

Published in Poets Espresso 2019

Blue Collar Beef

To no avail, I tilled the soil that served
the interests of agrarians. Their seeds
would foster lots they scarcely had deserved
and left my own plot festering with weeds.
The social contract that my parents signed
before the fine print was explained to them,
was dubious. For some kids were designed
to serve electorates who'd, down the line, condemn
them on the very ground that they themselves
enjoyed. Nor can we bank on norms we've got.
For what use are the law books on our shelves
if pols decree things that subvert the lot.
It seems this country hasn't any rules
except the ones they lay on docile mules.

My labors helped to foster privileged ends,
while streetwise tactics stopped me in my tracks.
My job was serving fellow citizens,
while grantees siphoned off what I'd been taxed.
It's clear that I should help my fellow man,
through payouts that the government expends
at my expense. But what if what I can
do on my own entails no dividends,

because self-righteous demagogues constrain
my rights by banking on the fruits of theirs
unlawfully, And still I entertain
concerns regarding humanist affairs,
and helping people threatened or in need,
of any nation, color, faith or creed.

But though it's nice to help an immigrant
to get around, it isn't if I can't
surmount a language hurdle that's relaxed
for him, while my linguistic skills have lapsed.
Bus drivers may not speak my native tongue,
yet I would nonetheless with glee have flung
my grievance out, if buses that I'd hop
on won't insist I do it at the stop!
For I don't care whatever numbers come
here, if the tally isn't zero sum.
Why fuss that border crossings have increased,
were citizens in turn not so policed
when visiting a corporate building in
the city they were born and living in.
For isn't it just rank hypocrisy
to lay the cost of generosity
on some, while the elite have entry rules
concerning those inside their vestibules?
And now they sit in judgement of the rule

of law, while taking underlings to school
regarding these same laws. But, by the way,
do not those laws supposedly convey
the people's will, not gainsaid by decrees?
Yet demagogues defy them with esprit.
So tell me then the rules I should abide
by, short of being taken for a ride.

Published in Blue Collar Review of 6/15/19

The Mote's in Their Eye

(with this one at CNN)

Did I hear what I thought I did?
It seems this knowing African-
American had blown her lid.
For she mentioned on CNN
that it, 'of course would be a white
guy - influenced by Trump's regard
toward women' - to believe it's right
to grope one. Wasn't Roseanne barred
for such stuff? Someone must have heard,
since tape and transcript both fell short
of capturing the quip referred
to, lest it end up in the court
of broadcast opinion. But some
are crumbled while others play dumb.

For Cuomo didn't clean his ear,
or Ruhle have bated breath expelled.
Nor would we get a haughty leer
from Lemon had its import jelled.
No witch-hunt here. This gal's okay
with me, thus shooting from the hip.
If we are going to make hay

of all that's said - a verbal slip,
or not – so little would get done
beyond promoting cable news.
But what's amusing is that none
of the news police who peruse
the most unfocused, rambling speech,
found this remark within their reach.

Previously Published in Conceit Magazine June 2019
Erica Hill substituting for Brooke Baldwin
conversing with Leah Wright Rigueur,
(the accent's on the first syllables of her last name)

Nettling Her Mettle

How self-effacing, gentle and demure
a woman is when dealing with the men
she's raised. But when someone acts like a boor
or is amiss, she's visceral again.
For when it comes to motherly concern
Clark Kent, who dons the cloak of Superman,
could scarcely muster means to overturn
conventional assumptions as she can.
And then her politesse is put on hold,
beside the prowess she's with pride professed
beyond the context of the social mold.
accorded her - which we're averse to test.
Indeed, instinctively we're not as bold
and tend to do just what we're told.

Published in Amulet, July /August 2019

Yeezy Does It

We don't allow the government to send
psychotics to institutions to shield us
from whatever violence they portend.
Yet, there's Kanye thrown under the bus,
by the smug demigods of CNN.
This dude, who'd fly over the cuckoo nest,
might fare better with a flock of mother hens
than with corporate shirts determined to go West
with their diagnostic tools. He won't fit
into the strait jackets of straight-laced minds
who want him acting likewise to acquit
himself by spinning mental wheels that grind
into a halt, just short of independence.
It was a really cogent speech he made.
But Mother monikers just don't make sense
like squeezing Lemon, grinning, throwing shade
at him to a parade of sycophants
determined to consider them as rants.

Previously Published in Amulet, July, August 2019

Magic Lamp

I'm Scheherazade. Telling my inner sultan tall tales, I survive another day. At night I start another poem to pique his interest. He follows the exotic lines of my cunning concoctions to arousal. Bewitched as he is by my iambics, he spares me. Indeed. The fantastic stories I spin beg closure. For well I know the fate of my previous lives. Death awaits me should I cease enchantment during this forced marriage. And I'm scared, lest unceremoniously, nuptial tensions be brought to a head.

Previously Published in Fleas on the Dog September 2020

Dubious Bargain

McDonald's sells 4 chicken McNuggets for $1.59 and six for $3.59. This means you're paying $2.00 for an additional 2 McNuggets, 50 cents more than you paid for the first 4! I told this to my fiancée, remembering she costs me more than my 2 previous girlfriends put together.

Previously published in The Poet's Art April 2013

Miss Appraisal

Every man's a fugitive from justice as far as women are concerned. He saw the girl reflected on the window of the subway car where he sat suspiciously engaged by her resemblance to a singer he was fond of. Propped against the exit door beside him she didn't leave at the next stop but occupied the seat opposite him when one of his familiars left. Put off by his expropriating looks, she sat resolved to confiscate his stolen goods. Furtive glances ensued. Stared into submission, he was arrested by her tough demeanor. After he was placed in custody, she frisked him for any contraband involving wife, children, present liaisons or seminal associations. Pursuant to being ID'd on the way to the next station he was booked at the restaurant where he was charged with a 3 course meal. In the interrogation room he confessed to Miss demeanors that shadowed him all the daze of his life. Handcuffed to her waist, he was later fingerprinted by her neck and shoulders. Preliminary tests on the hickies he left behind - coming out positive for his being a good kisser - he was remanded into custody where he's serving a wife sentence with little possibility of parole, unless under strict supervision that he pay child support.

Published in Fleas on the Dog
September 2020

Black Ladies Sing the Blues

(after a huge payout for sexual harassment by Roger Ailes)

We also have an axe to grind my friend,
and brooked harassment of a much worse kind
than some guy complimenting our rear end:
rear-ended by some jobs we'd been resigned
to. Notwithstanding bosses asking sex
from us, they did cut hours when the flu
entailed we take some days off. That would vex
us to no end. And though respect was due
us black girls for the OT we put in
to make sure that important jobs were done -
without a buck for working ourselves thin -
why pay for work done underneath the gun?
We're speaking metaphorically, of course!
But what *ails* most regarding the award
our peer received from such a wealthy source,
is not that we'd be treated like a bawd
from someone who appears to be a slob,
but that, back then, we'd never get the job.

Previously Pub in NEBO Spring, 2019 V.37#2

Transformative Encounter

(with a six-year-old)

I might as well have been her other child,
as far as importuning her to "Look!
Look!" at the sneering face her juvenile
daughter was making at me as I took
my leave. I felt more like a sibling bent
on ratting out a rival to secure
his parent's love than stranger poised to vent
an interest in her child's verbose allure.
For she had demonstrated a panache
at recollecting being in a huff
with boys at school where she averred: "Don't touch
me!" in a breathless manner that would snuff
out flambeaux. Thus, she certainly seemed rough
enough to neutralize an urchin's guff.

Alarmed, her mother quizzically peered down
to see her toddler roll judgmental cheeks
at me with an authoritative frown
left over from describing those past piques.
She seemed to be eliciting the peer
in me to scramble to her mother's side
as I might not do as a cavalier

endeavoring to win her as my bride.
Indeed, she claimed she once had dreamt of me,
as noble prince, though we had never met.
before. This made her mother beam with glee
considering her clever child's vignette
was countermanding logic. Such falsehoods
didn't stop her selling me a bill of goods.

Perhaps she wanted the devoted Dad
she fantasized from my paternal bent,
and marked me as her mother's Galahad.
Whatever was the girl's precise intent,
be it to wheedle my paternity,
or marriage to her mom, was not clear yet.
In any case, her mother's bel esprit
while humoring her child, made me regret
my pending separation from the pair.
But most of all, the mother's heartening bliss
at cherishing the toddler in her care
informed the child in me what I would miss.
And, mesmerized by her maternal charms,
my fancy took to cradling in her arms.

Published in Pennine Ink Issue#40, May 2019

Copperhead

Desire's bad penny returns again and again
through layers of fancy even as we dig
up academic nuggets. Preoccupied
with the labor it takes to excavate ideas
we're somewhat surprised to see it lying there.
The find was an unexpected turn
from the last time the penny was struck.
At last, we stoop to pick it up.

Previously Published by Krax #51

Love With Lemony Twist

It isn't that your balled up fist
subverts my sensibilities
to revel in the pugilist
you imitate with perfect ease.
More hedonist than masochist,
I'd just as fondly shoot the breeze
or let myself be sweetly kissed
as be thus pummeled to my knees
by some virago acting dissed
to tease out passive fantasies.
But though I understand a tryst
would tender me more pleasantries,
precluding this I must enlist
your penchant to do as you please.

Published in Chantarelle's Notebook, February 2019

Comedy of Errors

Your honor, my pedestrian date began taking her prose off even before we dated, insinuating she'd like to pay a visit to Shakespeare in the Park. She had already investigated his loft at the Open Air Theater in London's Regent Park. She hankered to see some drama there and, in lieu of that, we flirted with one at Clapham Common. My suggesting to her doing, "As You Like It" wasn't rebuffed. Nor would I try to beset her with an intimidating Lear. It also didn't hurt her sensibilities for me to spike her thinking with "A Midsummer Night's Dream" at Richmond Park. But she was wide awake when she lay on the grass with me. Yes, there was indeed a beam of pleasure in her eyes - for Shakespeare's sake, not mine. But I swear your honor, The Tempest wasn't in my breast, but a downpour that came after the Twelfth Night with her. And, notwithstanding "The Taming of the Shrew" in Victoria Park, "A Winter's Tale" was the only one I'd get, when we went together to Hampstead Heath. It's true, she seemed to yield to my come hither look when I attempted to take her to my treasured "Hamlet". Unfortunately, close to our departure, while understandably drunk on pentameter, the girl said no. Of course I was disappointed. But when a girl says no, your honor, she means no. And so, I let her go, holding a copy of Love's Labour's Lost, which I'd given her a week before. And that was the extent of it. So it's all Much Ado About Nothing.

The Magnolia Review Volume 5, Issue 1 January 2019

Joplin Mania

Great Scott! I feel uplifted by your rags.
Forget the ones concealed in garbage bags,
discretely tied so they seem nice and neat.
I love those tossed out of a measured beat.
And I'm amazed you'd flippantly throw out
melodic jewels, whose preciousness I tout
has all the clout that fills a Mozart strain
with logic it seems only gods ordain.
What tuneful threads you weave through hand me downs,
whose cleft notes march to syncopated sounds;
fleet fugitives from their 2/4 time.
Were ever rag infusions more sublime?
For woven thus into a formal coat
they give their trappings even greater note.

Published in Jerry Jazz Musician, February 2019

Drummer Girl

Let Pollyannas play the flute
or dote upon guitars they strum;
I toot at gals who prosecute
their argument upon a drum.
They aren't as irresolute
as cellists who, legato, plumb
the depths that leave us destitute;
or oboists who render numb
those senses heightened in pursuit
of resolutions yet to come.
But what bliss when a gal en route
to final chord delirium,
gives valedictory salute
by pounding mallets on her drum.

Published 2019 in Nomad's Choir

Her Bleeding Heart

She cares about the universe,
and every passing soul she meets.
She rummages inside her purse
to give the homeless on the streets
a token of her deep concern
for all the grievances they bear.
She's game for any friendly turn
accorded those without a prayer.
Her rage against injustice mounts
when itemizing all the wrongs
we do in life, but doesn't count
the tribulations that belong
to my estate. She makes me add
another dollar to the tip
I give the waitress, and seems glad
to entertain such fellowship.
She dotes on all humanity,
but doesn't care a whit for me.

Published in Penwood Review, Fall 2018

Toxic Airs

The real bane of a poison plant
is not the swelling on your skin.
It's more than warnings that you can't
be natural and that you've been
seduced, deluded by the green
appearance of a shrub or fern.
Such noxious plants assume a mien
of eco-friendliness to burn
the hand that reaches out in trust.
But coups depend on camouflage.
As such, we subsequently must -
at risk of desert vistas - dodge
each branching salutary leaf
in fear that it will bring us grief.

Published in Floyd County Moonshine
Fall 2018

Crippling Lien

In lawful states a threat's despised
when even issued face to face,
because its violence is disguised
as something that will soon take place.
There's not much you can do about
assaults that haven't happened yet,
except to shrink in fear or shout
in vain at what you're deemed to get.
And, since we're bound by rules of law,
this isn't any honest fight.
One's goose is cooked, but comes out raw
enough to make it hard to bite.
And, if the threat gets social thrust,
then one's the butt of every man
who thinks the bully tactic's just.
You're doomed to muster what you can
from those who think it's not a crime
to stomach living on a dime.

Published in Miller's Pond

Auguries of Winter

How beautiful those summer leaves
were, blossoming along with your
infectious tugging on my sleeves
while talking. All this was before
I pared your flower from the branch
of selfless love that nurtured it.
Then both of you began to blanch
before my seasoned counterfeit.
Now autumn leaves are falling down,
befuddled by a gusty wind.
It's scathing as my forlorn frown
that's vainly trying to rescind
the wages of my cavalier
regard, as more leaves start to sere.

Published in Poet's Espresso Review
V.13, Issue #4

Ashes

"Can I have the funny pages, old man?"
the fellow sitting opposite me asked.
One year ago I boasted youth's élan
with Kate. Now dumped, summarily unmasked,
I'm Cinderella, midnight at the ball.
The sweet effusion from her bee-stung lips,
now emanate from his as bitter gall.
How readily love's disaffection strips
the youthful carriage I was wont to bear!
My husky horseman's voice now squeaks like mice,
and my springtime demeanor's worse for wear
where summer showers have congealed to ice.
The magic moments of affection's spell
are over, and my slipper's tight as hell.

Published in Poet's Espresso Review
v. 13, Issue 4

Interrogation Womb

No waterboarding tactics so compel
a prisoner to waver and confess
as her salacious probes did in the cell
constricting him with amorous duress.
Notwithstanding sweet words in her ear,
which he pronounced like mantras in the hope
the chains of his constraint would disappear,
her supple limbs would scarcely give him scope,
until he ceded what she wanted most.
And that was written in the DNA
she garnered from him after her riposte
insisted she held unremitting sway.
Thus, yielding up this data for surcease
of torture, he was granted his release.

Published in Westview #33, issue 2

Shades

I'm thinking there are grimmer fates than death,
as loves, like specters, pass by in review.
The basking in a sweetheart's laughing breath
before embracing in a parting rendezvous.
Such memories are pictures on an urn
that fissure into pieces over time
till fixed by sentimentalists who yearn,
beyond the destined passing of their prime
for there to be some permanence above.
Some say that death's a briefly blown out flame
on everlasting candles lit with love.
This image casts a shadow just the same.
For if mortality's a passing breath
each passing is an everlasting death.

Published in Nomad's Choir
Summer 2018, v.26, Issue#3

Sheep in Wolf's Clothing

"In that case you'll be coming in my car,"
she said, when I told her I'd take her out.
My effort to woo her didn't get far,
before she had turned the tables to rout
my sensibilities. Watching her drive
with fierce determination and control,
I winced, and wondered if I would survive
the enterprise in such a passive role.
For although she was pretty and petite,
I was in no position to do much
but play the captive to her indiscreet
mishandling of me like I were a clutch.
But just when I felt I was in the lurch,
while nervously cavorting with her hair,
the speedster parked her car beside a church.
And I who thought I didn't have a prayer
to ward off her lascivious advance,
would pray in lieu of subsequent romance.

Published in Blue Unicorn as of 2/6/18

Cancer Diagnosis

But why do you look so upset and pale
because I have a tumor in my chest?
Is it not part of Nature's firm behest?
I'm sure the beam that's riven by the nail,
if it had feelings, would protest and wail
at being thus, metallically oppressed
by the invasive spike. It'd be distressed
because it couldn't see the larger scale
of being part and parcel of the house
that's being built. Indeed, there'd be no new
construction if the studs and double plates
on which the walls attached began to grouse
at necessary changes they await.
Then why lament old structures I outgrew?

Published in The Lyric

Shirking Work or Perk?

What openings do I create
who leave my office door ajar?
For rather than depart, I wait
on those whose scruples have no bar
to trespass on my poor estate,
nor rankling fears that they might mar
the expectations of my date.
Perhaps they think I'm some bazaar
for entertaining sloths who, late
to work, are first with au revoir
and no compunction to negate
my plans, however small they are.
And though I know firms terminate
employees who will not go far,
I just might be a profligate
whose office functions as boudoir.

Published in Blue Collar Review 2018

A Mother Surrogate Dresses Me Down

The Lord giveth but mommy takes away.
At least that's the impression that I got
when after amorously holding sway
with Cathy busing me back home. I thought
we could be a ménage a trois. For she,
with flair, engaged the other passengers -
including still another bon ami
she knew. But an arresting lass sent her
disclaimer by displaying her regard
for just that gentleman the driver knew.
Indeed her exit, kissing him, weighed hard
on me. I felt she wanted to outdo
my dash, conveying scowling glances pat
enough to tell me I was not all that.

**Published in Amulet/Conceit Magazine,
July/August 2018**

Passion Prone

The body whets the appetite it feeds.
Without it farmers wouldn't till the soil
into the furrows where they plant the seeds
which grow the wheat that compensates his toil.
Desire shapes the object that it needs.
But who'd choose to be fried inside its oil
to satisfy the hunger that it breeds,
if just to stoke the flames that will embroil
him further in the appetite he heeds?
A fencer needs a swordsman as a foil,
as rosaries require strings for beads,
or lotuses the crops that they despoil.
But he is wisest who with cunning cedes
attachments and forsakes this mortal coil.

**Published in Amulet/Conceit Magazine,
July/August 2018**

Percolator

I stand and watch her fix with care
my coffee at a chic café
while she chats like a bored au pair
about the problems of the day
with some guy working in her crew.
Forget that I can barely wait
to drink the aromatic brew.
She starts to huff, gesticulate
and cough without a second thought
that she has made, with this bequest,
the salutary draft she wrought
alluring as a mother's breast.
And thus, intent to drink it up,
I salivate before the cup.

Published in Amulet of Conceit
July/August '18

The Bitter Fruit of Crass Pursuit

As though she were the limit of my world,
and I was just a child in custody,
I tried enquiring what dispute unfurled
beyond the front desk where, insistent, he
was saying something touching on my plight.
"Oh, he's just babbling," my attendant said,
as she made sure the knot she tied was tight
that she would use to take me to the bed
I made myself. For she had placed her trust
in me which I imprudently betrayed
with some offhand remark. It seemed unjust,
in lieu of the investments that she made
in me while she embarked on her career.
My world thus shrank to her unheeding ear

and I was pared down to a naughty child.
she'd neither patience nor the will to heed.
Nor was it easy to be reconciled
where kindling seed turned into rankling weed
that strangled love. And, since I fell from grace,
I was a pariah whose every word
to curry favor forced me to lose face
before dismissive glances I incurred.

The former, pampered boyfriend in her arms
became a frenemy she'd since surmise
was scarcely worth her being put in harm's
way. Thus, she assumed the matron's guise.
And tired of me getting in her hair,
she relegated me to foster care.

Published in Nomad's Choir, Fall 2019

Abortive Siege

Could I, who planned to storm your citadel
and consummate my expedition's quest,
be so deficient in matériel
that I felt less oppressor than oppressed?
And later when I murmured terms of peace
before the flanking sentries of your face,
your militant maneuvers wouldn't cease
to hound my weary legions back to base.
Thus I surrendered, startled by your glare
of triumph at seducing me to breach
a stony fortress whose chargés d'affaires
would mock the furthest limits of my reach.
For there, although mere outpost of your heart,
my armored Mars was pierced by Cupid's dart.

Previously Published in Illya's Honey 2017

In Hades

Returning to the restaurant where you worked,
I saw a graveyard with the walking dead.
And since I felt your absence where they lurked,
those bloodless bodies filled my heart with dread.
I might have crossed the fabled River Styx
to find souls who were refugees from life.
But I, sojourner, didn't want to mix
with them, while searching for my would-be wife.
Odysseus, with reason to enquire
the way to get home to Penelope
could not have greater cause than my desire
to find what happened to my bon ami.
But none could give me answers I could use,
and so I'm stuck with shadows of my muse.

Previously Published in Chiron Review, October 2017

Subversive Cells

I wonder what she stores inside her phone?
She holds it like an unpinned hand grenade
before a fortress that will soon be blown
away. Sometimes it seems she's on parade
to scare potential adversaries who
must surely think the woman's poised to raid
their heartland. But as soon as she's in view
of my advancing, militant brigade
of spying eyes, she brusquely turns away.
There must be something that she can't abide.
For shameful thoughts of an impending fray
already start to bristle deep inside
my loins. I stare, immobilized by fear,
as she sprints off with cell phone to her ear.

Previously Published in The Poet's Art
Issue #61

Training Weal

She stripped me bear with her corrosive stare
from where I sat inside the subway car,
as though I were a pick-up in a bar.
I felt my senses somewhat worse for wear
as soon as flanking tresses of her hair
unveiled her cheekbones like a slipped peignoir.
And, though her fancy couldn't take me far,
her militant maneuvers seemed to dare
me to collaborate in her campaign
to make aggressive inroads to my sex.
Indeed it seemed strategically insane
to let her compromising glances vex
my sensibilities who stood to gain.
And so I let the vixen flex her pecs.

**Published in Muses Run
on the Sunway Tracks 2018**

To the Woman who Scowled at Him

Sorry I walked into the ladies' room
when you were just about to get undressed;
or at the very least disposed to groom
yourself so you could look your very best.
But I thought I was on the downtown train
whose final destination's Bowling Green.
So I'm a little shocked at the disdain.
implied by your eviscerating mien.
I know some women like to be alone
and don't like anxious men to glance at them.
But I have I have crucial duties of my own
which sadly grow out of our common stem.
And since your ego needs protected space,
I promise you that Bellevue's just the place.

**Published in Muses Run
on the Subway Tracks 2018**

To the Woman who Scowled at Him

(a metaphorical variant of the preceding theme)

Sorry that I rampaged through your perfumed
garden, where singing thrushes have their nest
among the golden marigolds that bloomed
while you were lying supine and at rest.
But I thought I was on the downtown train
whose only flowering was Bowling Green.
So I begin to wither from the bane
that's part and parcel of your wintry mien.
I know some farmers like to sow alone
and don't like predators to stare at them.
But I must plant for harvests of my own,
which sadly grow out of our common stem.
And though your fallow wants protected space,
I promise you the subway's not the place.

**Published in Muses Run
on the Subway Tracks '18**

Rush Hour

A cop won't place a perp under arrest
with more implacable authority
than she whose collar managed to divest
me of my quest to travel rapidly.
A police officer walking his beat
scarcely gets a fleeing felon to freeze
like she who asked me if McDougal Street
was coming up. For I was poised to squeeze
my way out, after having reached my stop.
And I was not in any mood to heed
the summons of an ersatz traffic cop.
That said, to be obliging, I would plead
no alibi during her stop and frisk
operation to satisfy her shy,
if importuning glances with their brisk
pat down. And so not to play the fall guy
to a quota system seeking a bust
for her conceit, I curbed my wanderlust.

**Published in Muses Run
on the Subway Tracks 2018**

Gender Bender

Appearing to recount the day
her husband came home drunk again -
with antics leading to a fray -
she crowed more like a cock than hen.
"I beat him up", I heard her tell
her girlfriend on the subway train.
I sensed the vaunting woman swell
with pride that she could entertain
such conquest of the guy she wed.
Perhaps, committed to disguise
her prowess, she'd discreetly led
him down the altar to surmise
he was in charge before she stormed
his citadel. This clueless catch
of hers apparently had warmed
to alcohol; a better match
for this meek, lily-livered man
whose wife now blustered, "Yes, I can!"

Published in Muses Run
on the Subway Tracks 2018

Aphrodite's Hound

Love's fugitive, I'm turning myself in
for peace of mind - if not for room and board.
I cede my arms to stay the downward spin
a felon feels beside his stolen hoard.
Though on the run, I scramble to the place
which I escaped from with her love in tow.
Returned to its proprietor I'll face
arraignment by her side, relieved to know
the sentence for my passion-driven crime.
Constrained within the prison of desire,
it's simple justice that I serve my time
inside the jurisdiction laws require.
And since my stringent warden holds its key,
I'm praying her good turn will set me free.

Published in Illya's Honey October 2017

Dreamscape #2

Out of the shadows of sleep, only one image remains from a procession of others that loomed pregnant with foreboding. I wanted to escape the shutter of the camera a devout Christian girl I knew held before me, poised to have me fixed in celluloid. As she snapped my picture I winced at its grave finality. I didn't like the way I looked and asked her for another to weather the tribulations of time. She complied. I wasn't satisfied with that one either, as I anxiously maneuvered to squirm out of the metaphoric box that opened up before me in the presence of my enemies. Surely this would shadow me all the days of my strife. She smiled dismissively, as if to say, I could do no better. Rising and oblivious to, my protestations, she moved on with my future impaled in the palm of her hand.

Published in Cura April 2018

Dreams

When stress becomes a bit too hard to bear,
and feckless friends have left me in the lurch,
resentment so entangles roots of care
that in despair I put on hold the search
for happiness. My tears bestrew the earth,
scorched with the heat of a pitiless sun
that promises no fig leaf of rebirth
from salutary rains till day is done.
So I wait on the night's benevolence.
And just when Nature's fecund realm seems dead,
love's stubborn flower rises up and rends
its leaden shroud. Rearing its prickly head
like a cactus, it caps shimmering strands
with lush mirages on my desert sands.

Published in Cura April 9th 2018

Terminal

It's nice this queen can keep her clothing clean.
So what if she gets food crumbs on the floor,
and some on me? Her manner is pristine.
She eats away, then brushes with still more
authority. It seems she cannot stand
the thought that flakes might soil her regal suit.
Just so, she puts to use her royal hand,
as though the locus of a guy's commute
from work to home were one huge garbage pail
that's put there to contain subversive crumbs.
She wipes her hands. And then, to crown her trail
of eminence, she scoffs like we were bums
intently eyeing her beside the seat
where she's enthroned, imperially neat.

Published in The Writer's Block, May 2018

Subversive Muse

Long after I put metric cuffs
on her so I could pat her down
for bawdy verse, the suspect bluffs
me and takes license with a frown.
She says the metaphor's too tight.
I loosen it and give her scope
to make her verses watertight.
Of course she uses every trope
to skirt around the charge,
until she slips away from me
and back into the verse at large.
She wraps it in a simile.
which, notwithstanding her command
of style, reveals its contraband.

Published in The Writer's Block, May 2018

Brahms' Trio for Horn, Violin and Piano

(with female ensemble)

When my proscriptive parents go away
for the evening, I turn my inner child
over to the performing arts speedway.
There my young imagination runs wild
in the backseat of a fast track Baldwin,
empowered by some highly strung au pairs.
They keep their harnessed stripling in a spin
percussively with wind and high-strung airs.
The threesome flirt in concert from the stage.
A brassy gal soon blows the bubbly horn
that cedes its mouthpiece so it can engage
her like a nipple to a newly born
babe. While the fiddler plucks her eyelash strings
and bows pubescent dreams, I ride with glee
the throbbing cadences another wrings
from baby grand's white-diapered ebony.
How tirelessly their ivories appease
me with salubrious sonorities.

I quicken as she, pulsing pianist,
ensnares me past the bugler's swaddling song,
on galloping triplets. Dreamily kissed
from where I swoon, those hands can do no wrong
flaunting skilled command. I reel in tandem
around the bend of her near dizzying
athletics to the precarious brim
of counterpoint. Still she romps, busying
herself with polyphonic repartees
to the brash, insouciant attitudes
of her two consorts. Triplets each one plays
are hushed by cooed, legato interludes,
until I'm palpitating for release
and molto presto swinging, homeward bound.
The pianist embarks on a caprice
whose figurations skittishly resound
to soothe, and yet preclude my being bored –
until she bangs the last, consoling chord.

Published in The Writer's Block, May 2018

Messing with Her Animus

He swooned in her interrogation room, where he endured her third degree's incriminating stares. He quickened upon hearing what appeared to be exculpatory words in his defense. But that was not a part of her judicial standards. "He's babbling," she replied when he enquired what her colleague said. He kept on thrashing just to get beneath her grip on his arrested sensibilities. For he'd betrayed her filial belief in him and thus enkindled what would be her faux crusader's harsh parental bent. Nor would she let him focus on whatever narrative the aforementioned father surrogate accorded him to soothe his open wounds. For this would just preempt her dishing out the just desserts she had in store for him. They'd subsequently end in the surcease of their rapport along with the relationship. Thus, like a mother with a colic child soliciting enticing tresses of her coiffured nature for support, she turned his headstrong effort upside down and pinned on him the diapered narrative that suited her involuntary rage and put self-serving arguments to rest.

**Published in The Ultimate Writer Quarterly,
April, May, June '18**

On the Mend

She'd glibly show she had a tough-street streak
in her to counter the sarcastic jabs
he'd thrown her way. For he'd expressed the pique
he felt inside recovery from labs
whose meds implied post-surgical concern.
As such, she parried his linguistic fray
with "fuckin comes with cardio." A stern
rebuttal phrased in gritty terms to flay
his senses. Neither did she compromise
her perky mien, but brought it in relief
beside the more antagonistic guise
that would have brought him haplessly to grief.
Thus, having been confronted by her tough
cop manner first, her sweet demeanor looked
auspicious if he didn't give her guff.
but played the prudent felon being booked.
Nor did he feign indifference at the smile
she flashed at him who quickened at her guile.

Published in the Ultimate Writer Quarterly,
April May, June 2018

On Being Questioned By a 3-Year-Old

No foreign agent locked inside
a dank interrogation room
could feel a sense of pending doom
linguistically as I did. Tried
by her interminable tide
of questions, I would just assume
her words - who knows from where and whom -
were appropriately replied
to from the quarters where I lay,
recovering from surgery.
This daughter of the guy who shared
my space would function as a ray
of light to make sure perjury
was not part of what I declared

to her. But since she hadn't squared
with my idea of questioning,
instead of her deemed unprepared
for my linguistic reckoning,
she limited my practiced tongue
to phrases in her lexicon.
As such, communication hung
on words she had been working on.

Though some of it was poppycock
that brought into relief her charm,
it made of me a laughingstock
who'd schooled on some pre-lingual farm.
But such disarming third degree
accorded me what liberty
her language left me privy to.
Her mother tried to intervene.
"Simone, he can't understand you.
Leave him alone!" And still she'd wean
me from linguistic skills I'd known
across the years to those she made
from random pieces she had sewn
together. They were words assayed
from parents and her older peers.
I'd be the tutor she could learn
from if it weren't that her years
had managed thus to overturn
the system I was taught at school
to one where I'd play Fortune's fool.

**Published in The Ultimate Writer Quarterly,
April, May, June '18**

A Knight's Tale

He might prefer the sweet allure
of graceful lass with pretty dress,
demure coiffure and manicure.
But he'll as readily regress
to times when gender didn't tax
the scarce resources of a man
to compensate for what she lacks.
Indeed. A jousting gal who can
acquit herself - with arms as buff
as any stalwart knight's - might do
as well as femmes who strut their stuff,
in getting men to rendezvous
with them. For blows her skill affords
might serve to sharpen blunted swords.

And although festering rewards
may not bestow upon a knight
the bliss that mistresses give lords,
it gives him fancy-free delight.
He courts a stalwart woman thus
in lists that scarcely would avail
him an advance before she'd fuss -
did she not ardently assail

the thrust of his swashbuckling quest
with pluck that penetrates his shield.
And though this triumph's second best
to that which makes the woman yield,
it gives his spiritless pursuit
a salutary substitute.

And what economy of means
he uses to secure love's grail!
No damsel in distressing scenes,
that he will later on bewail,
will spoil his fantasied romance.
Instead her dauntless derring-do
suffices as a mounted stance
to this schlemiel whom she'll pursue
with passionately prodding spurs.
She's scarcely armored on the horse
whose course of action will be hers
to choose through gallantry or force.
Yet he'll sagaciously disguise
the import of her enterprise.

**Published in The Ultimate Writer Quarterly,
April, May, June '18**

Doggone

Though dogmatism isn't meet,
of course all canines should be leashed,
or owners otherwise beseeched
to let us safely walk the street
without the fear their pets might eat
us, flesh and bone, before we've reached
the portals they've so safely breeched.
Why must the innocent entreat
dog fanciers for civil rights?
Scared prisoners, we dare not run,
lest some irate "police dog" bites
us on the ankle, face or bun,
should we thus pique the appetites
of beasts whose trust we haven't won.

Published in The Taylor Trust v.4, Feb 2010

On the Fast Lane

My wife goes back for a brie, olives and anchovies. There's a new refrigerator to match the dining room set; maybe even two, before the move to the large apartment down the street. There's a house in the suburbs, not far from the grand opening of the new supermarket before the kids return shouldering their own and holding, with the daily news, a series subscription to the opera. "Grimes" ends with a slow curtain on a sun that hovers on the horizon. I, too, sailed on ships that docked at a few foreign ports, unloading weary passengers. But I'm close to home now. The cashier tallies produce which I purchase with a credit card. A few items have to be taken out of my shopping cart, though no child's sitting there, and I'm left with two bags of milk, veggies and cold cuts that I'll schlep back to an empty flat.

Published in Down in the Dirt, April 2010

Beware

Pity the furious Ajax. He'd slay
those Greeks who mocked his plight by killing sheep -
which his nemesis, skilled in cunning ways,
would fleece for pillows and a good night's sleep.
Consider the impetuous King Lear,
puffed with rage in his self-destructive pride.
The prized Cordelia he once held dear
is dammed because she lacked the craft to hide
behind a fixed veneer of honeyed words.
Brave Moor, lord of fleets in far-off lands, lies
vanquished at the feet of half a man, spurred
by jealousy. Love's flaming candle dies!
So guard against despondent moods. Be glad!
Whom the gods would destroy they first make mad.

PUBLISHED IN ARDENT! online, fall/winter 2010

For Sondra Ball

(in memoriam)

The animistic universe withdrew
while you lay in your salutary lodge
awaiting Nature's shaman to renew
your sprit with a seasonal corsage
of teeming trees and iridescent plains.
But from the rippling river that you've crossed
your scintillating spirit still remains
amidst a flux where nothing's ever lost.
Between the water's horizontal weft
and vertical warp of a mountain range,
you'll sleep beneath the blanket nature left
embroidered with the verdant season's change.
Does death much differ from a mystic dance
or posthumous repose from sacred trance?

And if the winds of Wakan-Tanka talk
throughout creation of the mysteries
of bison, snake and swooping hawk,
your graceful voice will resonate through trees.
Is there less animation in the breath
informing pregnant words that poets write
than skin of bear or deer surviving death

in rites that spur the sharpened arrow's flight?
Now freshly vested in your native suit
of rolling hills and verdant fields
the fertile seed of your rebirth takes root
while mourners celebrate the fruit it yields.
For every feathered soul of Nature's heard
as it wings skyward with the singing bird.

Published online in Autumn Leaves, 2010

Sea Drift

Possessions are flotsam in the sea
of memory. Excessive ballast can sink
a ship. The gale's too rough to cast anchor,
and it's late. Amidst storm waves, I abandon
my vessel and swim to nearby islands.
Efflorescent shores suggest safe harbor.
There, I'll practice novel skills, adapt old
habits to fresh environs. But drift wood
plays havoc with the coastline.
Remembrance is a hazard for old navigators
who, like me, ply new routes. Castoffs
from the past cling to my knees; tarnished
prospects that remind me of distances
traveled, and far-off harbors long since closed.
Tides recede, as I listen to the foghorn
bellowing in the encroaching darkness.

previously published in Yasou Engine

Mater Dolorosa

If there's a Heaven somewhere, it's on earth
beside a Mother. She nurtures her child
while stationed at the cross of giving birth.
How well she cleanses diapers he's defiled
while father rests besides the world he's made.
There's seven days of formulae to buy
and floods of tears through which she'll bravely wade
though few the witnesses to sanctify
such deeds. Her hand on baby's fevered head
works miracles that bless his troubled sleep.
Like Lazarus she rises from the dead
of night to guard this lambkin counting sheep.
She beams like he's the godsend son who'll be
commended to her after Calvary.

Published in Aries Vol. 25, December 2013

A Neighbor's Death

They fall down like toy soldiers, one by one,
before the entrance to the battered door
that traps in heat and keeps away the hoar
frost of impending grief. Youth's taped rerun
of early bliss is worn. Spring's schoolmarm sun
now sports the wan demeanor of a store
clerk. Life grants me sufficient light to pore
through sales receipts before the workday's done
and the store shuts down. Former bustling streets
are empty and their neon signs torn down
along with delis selling ice and sweets.
Grown kids have moved their own kids out of town.
I'm at the crossroads where the graveyard meets
the grandson in his graduation gown.

Published (in a slightly different version) online March 2010 in Wild Violet and both online and in the 2010 issue of The Listening Eye

For Van

(In Memoriam)

Come to think of it, I'd see you mostly
behind the lobby's black oval booth
in your dark velvet security jacket.
We shot the breeze for seven years
worth of working days. Brief encounters that time
stitched into quilts of friendship across
the bare bones of daily routine,
like some cozy blanket in a cold-water flat.
And in the often long-spun exchanges,
that ranged from your mother's home
in North Carolina, to the combat zones
of Vietnam, with interests, jokes and talks of
baseball games tossed in-between, it never seemed
like I was being warmed against the coming chill
of winter. For I'd weave the loosened yarn
into yards of habit, and let the lot hang up -
shirt, coat and hat - inside my closet rack
that you could pick up for our future chats.
And so it was, until one day, you put them on,
wandered off and did not come back.

Published in Poets Espresso 2010

On Her Toes

She suavely struts her stuff at the ballet.
With jazzy stride or classic relevé,
she uses pointe as Cupid might his darts
if just to warm the cockles of our hearts.
But notwithstanding swans and Juliets,
I'm more enamored of her pirouettes.
And if she doesn't entertain concern
for meek aesthetes who merely watch and yearn
as she performs soutenus and fouettes,
her nimble movement fetchingly purveys
seductive thoughts of maenads who control,
with haughty port de bras that bares their soul,
audacious choreographies men make
to see how much those supple torsos take.

Published in The Lyric, Spring 2010

Revised Review

How strange that someone I ignore
because of her prosaic look
begins to read, the more I pore
inside her, like a darn good book.
Despite her page's dowdy mien
that contravenes aesthetic norms,
she grows poetic in-between
the lines as irony informs
those sentences I read as prose.
But when her fancy fashions tropes
she dons a literary pose
that almost rivals Poe's and Pope's.
And mannerisms I deplore
develop like a metaphor.

Published online in Stepping Stones
August 2010

Patricia Manterola Touts "The Rhythm"

Honey-tongued Delilah! Who do you think
you're kidding, descanting with charisma
your injunction to dance? A melisma
from woodwinds, modulating on the brink
of song, hardly gives resistance a chance.
Spiced with Mideast, reed-chromaticism
you're concocting more of paroxysms
with your sound stew than dance's whirling trance.
Nor do you give your guy the A-OK
to speak while you get down and acquiesce
to him beside his "boom boom boom." You sway
to the beat, so close to flesh, his lips press
against yours. And all you're able to bray
midst murmurs are "yi yi yi-s" of distress.

Are these the moves your guy enjoys so much
they'll keep him grooving through the night? Indeed
its rhythm's so relentless he won't breathe,
still less resist the ardor of your touch.
So why can't he just heed his addled brain
and, with those trembling lips you find so sweet,
start osculating to the crazy beat?
Indeed. He's wanting options to constrain

his movements. For his hands are in the air
and "bumping's something that I can't control."
You say he likes it. But you hardly care
that he's still moaning. Sultry arches roll
astride him, as your mindless "yeah yeah yeah"
envelops both his body and his soul.

Published in Quest Fall 2010

Love Games

Averse to trading liberty for love,
he gave her piquant charge a stern rebuff
while she responded with an ardent shove
that gently urged him not to give her guff.
But sensing it'd be harder to control
a mollycoddle with sufficient force
than using sweet inducements to cajole
belligerents, she tried the wiser course.
"Come on. I brought you this," she coyly cooed.
The "this" was just a little piece of cake
which, like a sop from cops with attitude
inside interrogation rooms, helped make
him blissfully submit to her behest
as though divorced from his subversive quest.

Published in Quest Fall 2010

Winehouse Odyssey

(for Amy)

Honeyed Ulysses, bound to music's mast
of staffs and clefs! What Sirens engineer
those strident sounds which, were you not held fast,
you'd scarcely have the fortitude to hear?
And we're dumb sailors on your dauntless cruise!
Our ears are plugged with processed record wax
which filters out narcotics from the blues
and adds as ballast, trumpet, harp and sax.
We countenance the narratives you tell
despite the torments that you suffer through.
But take care! Harpies lie behind the spell
whose music fascinates your faithful crew.
And strains production values sanitize
remain inflamed beneath their deft disguise.

Published in: Pennine Platform 2009

Going Home

Your car's constructed for the engine,
not the engine for the car. Of course,
it needs solid bodywork, a good set
of tires, and a driver with some sense
of direction. Upholstered seats make
the journey comfortable, if not less
monotonous, as you putter (which will
sometimes be the case) along the backroads
of your destination. You may even want
to fuss over its simonized sheen or spiffy
interior, as though they were parts of yourself.
But the car's purpose is functional.

And if there's room for more than a passenger
or two, so much the better. Just don't forget
where you're going - what with the diverse
attractions along the way to stop and marvel at.
Not to mention the music coming from the radio.
And what gorgeous music! Full-throated
songs that burnish jaded landscapes
with green velvet mountains, lakes of emerald
and flowers jeweled with glistening dewdrops.

But the windshield's frosted over. And that
squashed armadillo at the side of the road
jolts you from otherworldly musings.
If it doesn't, the truck collision should,
a little further down, around the bend.
You'll find there's not much left to see
beyond the smoldering wreckage.

And the next time your car stalls, or you
get lost in the boondocks and have to walk
the rest of the way, remember this: Long
after your clunker's stripped beyond
recognition and is recycled from the junk-heap,
its essence stays the same through countless
permutations, though nothing else remains.

Published in Down in the Dirt March 2011

Strindberg in Paris

He saunters in his black-hooded cloak,
scanning the distant blue line
of the harbor, which he can see
across dust-covered walls of
a lunatic asylum. He boards in a nearby hotel.
Later, he's forced to duck behind the hedges,

having injected morphine into the twig of a leaf
to test the drug's effect on plant life.
He's chased back to his hotel, chastened.
Chapped hands caked in sulphuric dust,
he tries to transform base matter into gold.
As his love grows cold by the blue flame
of the crucible, he dons his penitent's cloak.

Published in Down in the Dirt, Dec 2010

Television

Odd. A sitcom in Chicago
picks up the slack of my business trip,
takes on the contours of desire,
feeds on the meal I'm eating,
digests it in commercial breaks,
repackages its contents. Whimsy absorbs
the tartness of the bass I drink
while flirting with fancy
after a hard day's work,
pollinates the rose of its conceit
with kinetic fauna,
breaks into the compact of my dreams,
couples itself with soulful yearning,
breeds a contagion of images
which, stealing its fragrance, parades
in masquerades. Nor can I shake the shades
of daydreams from its aftertaste.
Fiction steals my affection
with graphic measures, sets up house
in prime-time recesses of my heart.
And love, since blind, takes the imposter
for the fling, sweetly consummated
in celluloid, as it beams flitting images
on the screen of memory.

Published Down in the Dirt/Dec 2010

Reverie

The lines are drawn. Too many words
the page swears at night
for such a piddling wage.
But you're in the right turn of phrase
for my subordinate clause
to pique your interest
if think banks fail
with ideas that brainstorm
the teller takes all. The writer
transcribed glasses filled with
20-20 proof against deep sea wishing,
where he scribbled at the margin
of a world, recovered in the ocean blue
of melancholy thoughts of you,
as in the beginning, God-willing.

Published in Down in the Dirt, December 2010

Valedictory

I don't know what lies beyond the classrooms
of this pedagogic world we live in.
Does death preserve degrees beneath our tombs
on brittle bones instead of onionskin,
when we've completed half the arduous
curriculum at Nature's Academe?
Will grand commencement of Life's final course
confer on all of us succes d'estime
despite poor grades? I guess just having been
matriculated in a mother's womb
constitutes a valid education,
perfected when the body's been consumed.
We'll grow into our wisdom lying down,
distinguished in our mortuary gown.

Published in Language and Culture, 2010

Against the Ropes

Rewriting's like a rubber match
with adversaries hard to beat.
You corner with iambic feet
retreating meanings hard to catch
while transformations help you snatch
from feeble phrases pros delete
a more appropriate conceit.
Sometimes it means you have to scratch
out "tell" with "images" that "show".
At other times you're forced to clinch
with content you'd as soon let go
of while you scrutinize and flinch.
And still you're going toe to toe
with text you'd forfeit in a pinch.

Published in WESTWARD QUARTERLY
winter 2011

Passover Thoughts

I know there's nowhere to go
in my flight out of Egypt,
nor any law of Moses that can
lead me to the Promised Land.
But that the road to Canaan
cuts across the Moab
of my desert thoughts
with the staff of understanding,
and the haggadah of my heart.

In this season of growth
and renewal, I sweep, searching
for at least ten pieces of hamez; feather
my dusty room, search in dark
corners with a cleansing light
that purges pride and clears
the way to righteousness.

Yet every year I get lost
amidst crowded wheat fields
and, with fast-fermenting thoughts,
wander along loaded caravans
of second-hand goods, gathering loaves
of leavened bread that others left
behind in their exodus
from tribulation.

Along the way, I get the urge
to bundle into sheaves
the whole lot of my long-grained
baggage, and burn the least trace
of hamez from my cluttered mind.
All that I'm dependent on,
that keeps my flesh in bondage
and the heart confined, I'd scatter
to the wind, roam across desert sands
with nothing, but mazzah dipped
in haroset, and the afikoman
in my hand.

Published in Poetry Now Jan/Feb 2011

Same Old Song
(of recriminations)

You drive me mad, command
my attention, then use dulcet tones
that slowly turn staccato.
Like a crafty composer you play
endless variations on that jarring tune.
Here the theme's so hackneyed
it's ignored. There it breaches my reverie
while dressed in whipping winds.
And even as I lean in my seat
to bolt from the discord
it vanishes in a host of glissandos
that strain the ear to search
for its abrasive ghost. Is it lost,
primed for harmonic resolution?
Not to worry. Beneath subdued
cadences, the braying brass
begins da capo with a donkey's laugh.

Published in Poetry Now, Jan/Feb 2011

Christmas Eve

All spruced up in frosted furs,
and muffs of evergreen.
Preening herself in the gusting wind,
her bristling pines, glistening
with powder puffs of winter's affection,
she bends in salutation to the warming sun
of the coming solstice.

Stirred by the sudden quickening
of her brown-breasted lover,
throbbing near her tufts of hair,
she thought it was love
to be thus uprooted
by the cutting tumescence
of the forester's edge. She found instead,
the groundswell of her wounded passion
on the mound of earth where she spread
her branches to the blade's advances,
before she fell.

Huddling in the cold night air
among her sisters, she stands,
as though abandoned, against the drab

buildings of the city streets,
where smartly tailored gentlemen
pound the pavement with their bustling feet,
like clients in a red-light district
braving sleet.

In the provocative glare of the electric night,
they flash their wares like brazen harlots, aglow
among the flickering rows of psychedelic lights,
in the multi-colored brightness and slick, ever
greening district of Christmas cheer.

It's not long before the kindling spirit
of the holly season drowns out reason
with its siren's song. A lusty John appears,
blushing amidst the naked trees,
flustered with passion.

He cradles in his probing arms
the full extension of their charms,
and chooses one among the throng
to bundle up and carry home,
like a fallen woman, newly born
among the demimonde.

The amorous man caresses with his hand
the swooning concubine, swaddled in his room,
like a doll from a foreign land;
golden globules dangling in her hair,
a shawl of silver garlands
sprawled across her shoulders,
and strings of colored pearls,
swirling amidst the contours
of her tinseled dress, like an arabesque
of dancing stars. A coiffured crest
of clustered leaves adorns her bowing head
crowned as with a diadem.

There's more of merry than of Magdalene
kept within this woman pregnant
with redeeming hopes of dreamers yet unborn,
she bears within the woodland inn
of her pine-scented womb
the perfumed trappings of beribboned boxes,
blazoned with hosannas for anxious children,
who await the promised coming
of her godsend groom.

**Published in Eclectic Muse,
Christmas 2010**

Taylor's Swift Ascent

(Kanye West Disses Taylor Swift)

She's also served who stands and waits
while holding VMA awards
as some usurper arrogates
attention that the prize affords.
But although this West wind was swift,
and tailored, thus, to aggrandize
its source, who dissonantly riffed
on concords craftsmen harmonize
with, rather than eclipse the star,
he made her radiance more bright.
For just as climbers show they're far
more seasoned, measured by the height
they've weathered at the mountain's peak,
so Taylor's silence seemed to speak.

"It's like stepping on a kitten,"
a stricken songstress would attest
to, apropos of Kanye's quest
that Fortune be rewritten.
to make it seem she'd bitten
this frozen singer chosen 'Best
New Video', this music fest.

And the rest of us were smitten
by stylish Taylor, center stage
with flattering fragility,
preempted of her proper wage.
A deer in headlights all could see,
it prompted us to thus assuage
her, nodding, "You Belong with Me!"

Published in Eclectic Muse, Christmas, 2010

Naming of Hops

(July 30, 2009)

Today there will be naming of hops.
Today they'll have a beer outside
the oval office of the White House.
Likewise our planet rotates with an oval orbit
around the sun of no determinate God,
whose purity and innocence informs
the white bars on the American flag.

Today President Obama, Professor Gates
and Officer Crowley will have a beer
without discriminatory roots.
Vice-President Biden will grab a Buckler
and ward off journalistic gibes.

The President will have a Bud Lite.
Just so, cherry blossoms bud lightly near
the President's office, and all around
the grounds of the White House.
And today there will be naming of hops.

The professor wanted a Red Stripe.
Indeed red stripes emblazon the American flag

with the hardiness and valor of patriots
who fought to make this country free,
with brotherhood from sea to shining sea.
But, fermenting, with true revolutionary fervor,
he settled on a Boston-based Samuel Adams.

So today there will be naming of hops.
And four men will bond with beer outside the oval office.
The officer in blue will have a Blue Moon.
Indeed blue is the color of justice, perseverance
and vigilance; and upon this cerulean hue,
the stars representing our states are fixed,
as in the celestial spheres. It's the color
of sad, chromatic notes, flat as the moon
rising over the jazzy circuits that light
the music scenes of America like dancing stars.
For today there will be naming of hops,
fermented in a brew of friendship and hope.

Published online in Eye on Poetry 2010

Life Boat

The captives in a labor camp
with hopeful prospect of relief
will huddle close against the damp
in hopes of tempering their grief.
Yet people who are on a boat
that has no chance of being moored
before it casts its crew afloat
until they're terminally shored,
make no attempt to bridge divides.
They scarcely dare attenuate
the terror of engulfing tides.
You'd think their need to navigate
against the coming of the storm
would make their common watch a norm.

Published in Eye on Life
online mag, pub Dec 2010

Poignant Post

I'd rather be on Cornwall's shore
despairing for Isolde's ship
than monitoring e-mail for
Isolde's electronic blip
on my computer's message box!
Incoming mail adorns my site
like sailboats seen beside the docks
that mock my landlocked heart's delight.
For I see flagging on my screen
bright signals that my love arrived
with white displayed on its marine
horizon. Sadly, what's inscribed
in black is not my heartthrob's name,
but fans desire's unquenched flame.

Published online in: Eye on Life, December 2010

Warmings

Foraging Autumn leaves
for remembered sweetmeats
of Time's teething brain,
I kindle still-dawning butts,
like sprigs of fiery rose
out of the day's ashen.

Salted by lusty stains
of longing, I don the top-hat
of heart-harded meat, masticating
with stir-crazed forceps
the escalating stairs
of long-winded desire.

I sing ringing accolades of spring
in love's seasoned athletes
aching to be reborn and touch down
on hustling, mainstreaming streets,
line-backed with sun-turbaned chicks
in halter tops, and biker babes
in swaddling arms doling out
amorous soup kitchens to souped-up
cyclists pitching small-talk

in well-stacked aisles near shopping sensors
of the sun's intense summons
to youth's translucence.

Oh! The shrieking soprano of mad Lucias
piercing pants-blue navies
of the sky with top-mast decibels
above the crazy cruisings
of hazy afternoons, bugged
with ear-tapping memories
and high C seethings
of the operatic night!

My bird-wing brain begins
to blossom into dog walking bard
whose long-leashed compass
hounds the tall storied
shaggy word into bachwurst
of barking meters which I savor
like mustard seed for my daily bread.

Published in Down in the Dirt

King Lear

Two daughters scheme within my breast.
Time hobbles me with needling age.
And my physician would divest
me of the trappings of a sage,
when I decry her rank abuse.
Just when I give up fatty food,
she offers me a lame excuse
to snatch lean morsels with a rude
injunction to reduce my weight.
Time castigates my limb and bone
while she, who's licensed by the state,
provides a wheelchair for a throne.
And when I let that daughter nurse
me, Cronus purchases a hearse.

Published in Abbey June 2011

Fix-It Gal

It's just as if she wants to show us how
it's done. Like mothers stir the frying pan,
while men sit squabbling, she confirms she can.
Intense beneath the furrows of her brow
she bankrolls bankrupt senses like the Dow
informs the pockets of the businessman.
She's neither candidate nor also-ran
but funds her politic exchanges now,
though shyness and societal constraint
impose a limitation on her means.
Not only does she serve without complaint,
she maximizes pleasure from routines
that turn her budding martyr into saint
dispensing blessings from where she convenes.

Published in Magnolia Quarterly
Winter 2010

Postmortem

Death's a gourmet chef
gutting mangled carcasses
hanging from blood-basted butcher shops
of morticians. Cleansed
of impurities, our meat and bones
are ground with blends of fame or notoriety.
Predigested by posthumous worms
turning in the compost of posterity,
only the worst leave an aftertaste
not sweetened by the seasoning
of time. Death turns entrails
of remembrance into a dish
carved for connoisseurs.
Mashed memories
are sopped in the piquant sauce
of sadness and remorse.
Thus, spiced with the condiment
of tearful thoughts,
we're cordially served at Life's banquet.
A good glass of wine
makes it easier for friends
to stomach us.

PUBLISHED IN BLACK BOOK PRESS 9/08

Home Wrecking Actress

(nude in a staged play)

How dare she flash love's currency at me
and bare her private assets on the stage!
Her moving in without a finder's fee
deprives my agency its proper wage.
She even starts reneging on the rent
which, after all, she's honor bound to pay.
Though she co-opted me without consent
I'm not averse to meeting her halfway.
But she's distinctly not disposed to share.
Thus, I'm pent-up where penury resides
while she sits smiling in my easy chair.
And I'm compelled to comb the classifieds
for women looking for a single male
or else to buy a house that's up for sale.

Published in The Poet's Pen, March 2011

Good Copy

Never regret what brings us grief.
The bitter loss of faithless friends,
exposing fraud and cut-purse, lends
to mourning, tokens of relief
that coins more prized are spared the thief.
The threadbare manuscript that rends,
when thumbed, defies the hand that mends
it to belie Time's scathing brief
upon each desiccated sheaf
whereon our fruitless story ends.
Life's sermonizing author pens
corruption as its leitmotif.
Romantics let poor writing blot
awareness that their structure's weak
and doesn't justify the plot
it's built on. Pruning's the critique
revealing underlying rot
that fuels the havoc age will wreak.

Published in Soul Fountain, 2011

Forging Majesty

This drama queen is every inch a prince,
portraying Harry in the Shakespeare play.
I bow before her talent to evince
an aptitude for holding courtly sway.
And though she seems reluctant to outflank
me, I'm determined to impose on her
the agency incumbent on a rank
that resonates with force majeure.
Some deem me abject subject to her rule,
a foppish member of her entourage,
a Falstaff risking censure, or a fool.
But I cede sovereignty, and sabotage
scant privileges attendant on my own,
if just to glean a post-performance nod
before this prince is seated on her throne.
For thus seduced to wield a royal rod
as acting lord before her prostrate liege,
she might dispense the fruits of her prestige.

Published (slightly differently) in:
River Oak Review 2011

As You Like It

She starred as Ganymede the night before,
transgendering her Rosalind of yore.
A masquerade that Shakespeare would adore.
And now as I walk past the acting corps,
she and her Aliena start to roar
with laughter, maybe thinking I want more
of her clad in the doublet she once wore.
Do they presume I'm boldly in rapport
with Rosalind's agenda and foreswore
my own in order thereby to explore
the tender distaff side of either-or?
Do I hope Ganymede intends to score
with some guy fixed on women who abhor
the salutation, Miss, but not Signor?
I hurry home and bolt the bedroom door.

Published in River Oak Review, Spring 2013

Mother Dear

I deeply dread the woman you've become:
that crooked sorceress who took away
your magic strength and made my senses numb
with aches and pains that hold you in their sway;
who blanched your hair and parched your aged skin,
then mocked my grief, and made you deaf and dumb
to childlike groans that used to make you grin
with tender solace at your doting son.

She sits disheveled in your rocking chair,
whose wizened shape usurps your pride of place.
She stares at me, but doesn't seem to care
that both of us have fallen out of grace.
What witching potion simmers in her brew,
consumes your love, and breaks my heart in two?

Published in Italian Americana
winter 2013

Dead Weight

No matter how much the mortician tried
to coffin McLaughlin in the oblong
box, he wasn't able to stuff inside
sixty years of indolent pride, headstrong
eating habits, and the 400 pounds
comprising his puffed-up hide. Pallbearers
paled at having to haul appalling mounds
of coarse corpulence on their frail shoulders.
So they held him in the air, as they praised
the monumental place he filled in life,
the comprehensive largeness of his ways,
and the grievous burden borne by his wife.
Then they laid him down with groans of regret
for what was left behind, and made them sweat.

Published in Italiana Americana 2012

Guiding Tower

A moon beam in the thick of night
could not exude a warmer glow
than you, whom I'd presumed took flight
like sunlight when it sinks below
the skyline. Skewed rays from a cloud
could not make hazy hues so bright
as when you burst forth from a crowd.
I savored the bereaved's delight
at finding what was reckoned lost,
and reveled in that sweet respite
of sailors being tempest-tossed
before the beacon looms in sight.
And thus amidst Poseidon's roar
I trailed your beaming eyes to shore.

Published in Iodine Poetry Journal
Fall winter 2011

My Stars

"You notice? All of them are girls," she said,
when I reeled off names of performers
who I like. As though she grabbed
the driver's seat beside a fellow
liable to wed a woman having agency
she shifted into high gear. Aware
her car's petroleum had lead
in it to power ardor in my breast,
the rubber on its wheels began to burn
in tandem with her purpose to exploit
meek leanings in my amatory quest.
And this put import in her sudden turn.

Previous Publisher uncertain

Elegy for My Mother

I waited out the days allotted you,
like a cad in a one-sided romance;
postponing dinner date and rendezvous,
while you sat out my philandering dance.
But charming as an old-world gentleman,
disease's courtship swept you off your feet,
then sent you cards and flowers till you ran
away with him. Wrapped in your winding sheet,
it might have been the silk, cathedral train
of a bridal dress. Transfigured by light,
your pale cheeks glowed, as though they'd still maintain
a maiden blush, until that solemn night,
when prepossessing as a newly wed,
death sealed your lips and carried you to bed.

Published in The Lyric, Spring 2011

Age

How practiced the part and how well-rehearsed
its stages. What seems strange and difficult
at first becomes easy when one's immersed
in the plot. It's the ironic result
of having rejected the script ten times
during the rushed decade of the forties.
Reducing stage business to pantomime,
I reconnoitered the set with sorties
into one belabored activity
or another, till I became attuned
to ruin. Being cast, the proclivity's
been honed. Now I just need to be festooned
with wrinkles, use a walking stick, and groan
from spastic pain to make the part my own.

Published in "Still Crazy" Spring 2011

Conceptual Surgery

This vain conceit metastasized too far.
But how remove a tumor from the brain
and not destroy the portion that we are?
Yet neither can we brook it till insane.
I thus employed a delicate technique
to keep alive in vibrant metaphors
what's workable and purge the parts that pique
my senses with insinuating spores.
As such, I'm forced to tread the passageways
that rend my mind in order to excise
the dread disease. For in its crucial phase
I doubt if expurgation or disguise
dispenses the salubrious effects
of cleaning up the body of the text.

Published in The Haiku Quarterly
#39 & 40 September 2011

Starting Over

I'd gone beyond a woman's tutelage,
I thought, before I called to activate
my mobile phone and shrank to pupilage.
Indeed, I let her savvy captivate
my sensibilities. With sweet finesse
she walked me to the cradle of the phone
to reconnect its power source, depress
the menu key and let her chaperone
me through connections to the world outside.
As such, dependent on her expertise,
I followed her instructions, fortified
by how resourcefully she seemed to seize
control. Assured my phone was programmed right,
she waxed indulgent, wishing me goodnight.

Published in Foliate Oak December 2011

Bemused

Just like a child who wants to play outside
implores her mother with a voice that's sweet,
my muse - when she wants feelings versified -
- promotes her cause with an iambic beat.
And if that doesn't open any doors
to my suspicious sensibilities,
she dresses her conceit in metaphors
that punctuate her sentences like pleas.
She knows I'm troubled when her clothes get soiled,
so roughs it up in corduroy and jeans.
And still she ends up getting me embroiled
in arguments. For reason intervenes,
complaining that she's making too much noise
amidst the play of words that she enjoys.

Published in Foliate Oak, December 2011

By Ophelia's Grave

What's he whose brief bears such an emphasis
as though he were an advocate in court
and not indeed preemptive nemesis!
You used subversive tactics to abort
the buds that blossomed in her virgin field.
For both of us had sown that kindling seed
which you preferred to harvest as your yield.
Then you took umbrage at corrupting weed.
As if such growth does not proliferate
from turf untutored gardeners produce!
And thus you banished me from your estate
who used the steadfast, salutary spruce
I was until your blight destroyed its root.
By grafting your resentment on a shoot,

you sapped the tree and made it destitute.
My efflorescent leaves began to blanch,
till, growing heavy with embittered fruit,
I went from blooming bough to withered branch.
Then you gave friends a rap sheet, marked with gall,
of parlous imperfections that I bore
to cause my perfumed greenery to pall.
And I who'd grown - atrophied by the hoar -

conservatively skeletal and lean,
droop, all but pruned, to perish in my rot,
while mocked by fruit you liberally glean.
It makes me laugh to see you in my spot
dispensing boysenberry, pear and plum
to her, with love that can't make up my sum.

Published in Ardent July 1, 2012

Spring Fever

They told me to wait till springtide
before moving beyond the mountain crossing,
with its crevices and steep incline.
I told them Spring was the problem
in the first place. Those smooth, sharkskin
afternoons littering calm, tepid waters
with cast-off carcasses of fresh beginnings.
I've done enough fishing for a dozen lives,
without having to plunge in murky depths
again; dragging up seared, auburn leaves
that autumn left behind. I'd rather end
this long journey in the clear glaze
of winter, while there's time to trek across
cracked ice. I'll arrive before the warming thaw
entices me with fragrant clusters
of brightly colored blossoms, and birds and bees
seduce me with their bawdy show.

Published online in Eye on Life, November 2011

Page Turner

In contrast to the pianist
she's sitting perfectly erect.
Her eyes are focused on the notes
like she's a marksman poised to shoot
the music printed on the sheet.
And when the work concludes, she smiles,
as if she not just played each bar
but then and there congealed the whole
from fragments forged inside a brain
that now is tempered with relief.
When the pianist leaves amidst
applause, she rises from her seat,
a tree emerging from the floor.
She exits, straight-laced, from the stage,
an apparition dressed in black.
The puppeteers of Bunraku
could hardly be more circumspect.
When the pianist reappears
to play the concert's final piece,
she trails him with a leisured pace,
as if a bashful confidant
or prissy at a high school dance.

Then, latterly, she takes her seat,
resuming focus on the score,
as if the music on the sheet
flowed from her meditative stare.

I'd think it's she who pulls the strings
of the pianist who seems poised
to fade into the ivory,
did not the posture of this girl
inform him with its gravity.
For, armored in her two-piece suit,
she leads him in this nimble dance
of fingers on cascading keys.
A pause to thrust subversive strands
of jet-black hair behind her ear
gives substance to insurgent terms
imposed by her protracted stare.
She scans the notes to the last bars
of the piece, hands still on her lap,
as she smiles in approbation,
then disappears amidst applause
for the performer still on stage.

Published online in Eye on Life Magazine, Nov 2011

Air Conditioner

Heat-snuffing dragon
of hot-house nights.
How soundly the midnight hum
of your metal machinery
dumbs down the evergreen Eden
of my flowering past

when cubes of ice
conspired against the fire
of the melting sun,
and popsicles made it nice
to smelt in the withering heat
while humid flights of fancy
overdosed on the hormonal rush
of summer's first coming.

Excuse me if I now sit out
those white-noise surges
of relief with watt-not urges
riding astride the sea breeze
of memories. They squeeze friezes
through my window
of stalking grass
harnessed by a blitz
of sassy mosquitoes
bombarded by pesticides
that filled the air
like perfume in the hair
of languid afternoons.
I've done 7th inning stretches
with a wooden Breyer's ice-cream spoon
that school-kids used to beat the heat,
before the advent
of your indiscreet electric storm.

Published online November 2011 in EYE ON LIFE

For Katie Spotz

(who sailed the Atlantic, solo)

Since she disarmed the jousting waves
while thus crusading coast to coast,
the catapulting dolphin raves
about her chivalric riposte.
She plied an ocean for the hoard.
Though not in armor on a steed
with sword, she dubbed the boat she oared,
Liv. Neither would she taint her deed
with aid to brave the rising tide
of roaring dragons she subdued.
But pliant mettle forged with pride
accompanied her buoyant mood
as, disembarking from her boat,
she kept our sinking hearts afloat.

Published in The Storyteller, Pub. Spring, 2011

Schmoozing the News

Of all broadcasters, stout or trim,
who give this tv viewer grief,
I cringe at those who groan with "hmm"

when reportage on items grim
suggests that mawkish leitmotif.
Of all broadcasters, stout or trim,

the ones who are a paradigm
of buttressing an anchor's brief,
are those who smugly murmur, "hmm".

For, mulling news, they start to brim
with obbligato disbelief.
I cringe at anchors, stout or trim,

who, thinking news needs vocal vim,
attempt to bring it in relief
by suspirating with a "hmm"

or some such wordless homonym
that gives news flashes needless beef.
And though some news is rather trim,

must anchors go out on a limb
or moan, as with a handkerchief,
by punctuating it with "hmm?"

They think my light of reason's dim,
or else imagine some naïf
who, unconcerned by news that's trim,
requires an emotive "hmm".

Published in Fullosia Press/winter 2011/2012

Beyond Good and Evil

Morality has little use
protecting us from headstrong folk.
They seem addicted to abuse
of scapegoats primed to bear the yoke
put on them by these haughty fools.
The latter think it's native might
and not the equitable rules
of law that let them dictate right
and wrong against those same decrees.
If that's their wont, then make laws void
that guarantee their liberties
at the expense of those enjoyed
by us. If not, chuck righteous creeds
for those our constitution heeds.

Published in Fullosia Press, winter 2011/2012

A Strong Constitution

The law and civil rights are all I need.
And although there's a God men court with awe
to foster their endeavor to succeed,

I just want what the Bill of Rights decreed.
A winner of fate's fickle-fingered draw,
the law and civil rights are all I need

to start an enterprising life. Godspeed!
Ah, yes! In every system there's a flaw
subverting one's endeavor to succeed.

There's slanders, threats, ill-will, vindictive deed
and sometimes even right cross to the jaw.
But law and civil rights are all I need

to justify myself. Though men impede
my liberty, then heartlessly guffaw
at my derailed endeavor to succeed,

I grieve not when I scorn to take the lead
advancing selfsame ends with tooth and claw.
For law and civil rights are all men need

to shrewdly mobilize a ruthless breed
to set afire law's adaptive straw
we trusted them with so they could succeed.

And hell ensues when people won't pay heed
to rules that temper minds innately raw
enough to scorn the civil rights men need.

The latter, thus betrayed, must meekly plead
for rights respecting which they staunchly saw
the ones who now emerge as foes succeed.

Indeed. They exercise destructive greed
who use law as a craven means to gnaw
away the civil rights that all men need
to foster their endeavor to succeed.

**Published im Fullosia Press
Winter/2011/2012**

Odysseus Confronts Good and Evil

Twin sirens of life's ambiguous deep!
How tantalizing is your wheedling song.
Springboard of action, and cradle of sleep,
buttressed with harmonies of right and wrong.
Sentiments that power our sails on wings
of rippling currents, tempting them to port.
Though mesmerized by lusts illusion brings,
I steel my crew against your chant's report.
For well I remember Circe's warning,
and see for myself, shipwrecked near the shore,
hordes of cocksure sailors, now past mourning,
whose placid waters raged to tempest's roar.
I prefer more sober notes of reason
to guide me on a safe and steady course;
where justice is never out of season
and failed seduction doesn't foster force.
And so with laws I'm bound to my ship's mast
until your charmed, compelling song has passed.

Published in Fullosia press, winter 2011/2012

Defending the Duel

It's not a brutal enterprise.
The duelist doesn't get a rise
from mortifying other men
with slanderously poisoned pen
and threats on advantageous terms.
And seeing how a fellow squirms
is not the purpose of the duel.
It doesn't wish to make a fool
of someone challenged on the field
of honor. Better that they yield
to reason settling their dispute.
But if one party doesn't mute
his accusations he must stand
on equal terms or cede his hand.

So what if duels give you dismay!
Would you prefer a bloody fray
where someone spurred by bulk and might,
deciding that he's in the right,
impugns your manhood and your pride?
With duels, your rights are not belied.
Nor are you wracked by shame and fear.
And if the challenged won't appear

to back up his vindictive claims,
the challenger can't stoke the flames
beyond his having rendered right
the wrongs he suffered out of spite.
In any case, the referee
wants fairness mixed with amity.

Published in Fullosia Press, winter 2011/2012

Gossamer Girl

Could artifice work such a toxic kiss
despite its guile? Demure, yet filled with grace,
she glares at me as if she might dismiss
me out of hand, and put me in my place.
She doesn't play like novices who scowl
to snuff out flames of passion that they stoke.
But like some hungry spider on the prowl,
she's poised to pounce on quarry with one stroke,
as soon as they're entangled in her web.
Indeed. When I approach this stern cashier,
her sweet hello accelerates the ebb
and flow of my heart's racing blood. And fear
in my glazed eyes assures her she holds sway
as her smile spins the silk that dooms her prey.

Published in Adept Press/Small Brushes

Politic Ponderings

What message are we giving citizens?
Our dogs are safe from troubling pranks of Vicks,
and Plaxico will never threaten clubbers with a gun
he carries for his own defensive use!
But don't try saddling killers with a charge
that never sticks or get restraining orders
if it's wife abuse. For guns are not allowed
for citizens who try to shield themselves.
They're only used by felons violating civil rights
of those who heed the law books on the shelves
officials use to keep the rest in check.
How economical becomes this scheme.
The laws are broad enough to keep the rich secure,
and make the rest of us unsure of talking
out of turn or even walking streets at night.
And don't reach out to the long arm of the law.
For that's been set for minimum mobility
by those who move on the fast lane.
And there are stronger arms in store.

Published in Jerry Jazz Musician

Grooving to Shakira's Ciega, Sordomudo

I ride beside her while she sings her song!
The more I hear her moan she's gone to waste
because of love, the more I prance along-
side sixteenth notes of her adroitly paced
racnchera. And - yippee ay aye away! -
she canters down its mariachi course
as runs - staccato! rapido! - convey
her, crestfallen vaquera, on the horse sing
she trots across the forlorn parts of town.
Aggrieved, she harmonizes "yi yi yi"
whose winded consolation is the crown
that rises from her agitated sigh.
Concluding mexicano hounds of brass
salute her cancion with braying sass.

Published in Jerry Jazz Musician/Jan 2012

Sharp Accords

She storms Town Hall's stage, determined fighter,
sporting formal dress. A toothy giant
Baldwin grand stands keyed-up to ignite her
thrust. She attacks his body. Defiant,
with fierce forays of floor-shaking fortes,
she crows her show of strength. Legerdemain
fingers stress criss-crossed wrists as she essays
pianissimo passages that strain
her battery of skills. These tasks spring traps
to challenge her defense force till it cracks.
But swift sforzandos show how fast she taps
into her arms, till hammered pedals tax
sapped resources for her cadenza's pitched
assault on major key positions that bewitched

her captive audience. And what display
of firearms begins her forte siege
toward a triumphant finish of the fray!
Downplaying any subsequent prestige
or plaudits following the final chord,
she hunches by the ivory for sore
resistance from the pummeled sounding board.
For primed by battles with this rattling score

she's well-equipped to muffle overtones
that resonate from her prolonged assaults.
They slowly fade away with dying groans
beneath her respiration's starts and halts.
She slackens following this pregnant pause,
then smiles triumphantly to loud applause.

Published online, with 22 lines, as "Concords" in Illogical Muse, Summer 2010

Talking Tchaikovsky's Violin Concerto

Her tonal discourse has some strings attached
to buttress her expository flow.
And fortes of the orchestra are matched
by strong sforzandos with her horsehair bow.
Though hushed by clamorous fortissimos,
once disputatious passages subside,
acute reflexes deftly interpose
her repartee. Its sentimental slide
draws pathos from the argument addressed.
As such, the listener gets her side of
the score, beyond the music accents stressed
inside the staff or bowing marks above.
And just before the final chord is heard,
this fiddler interjects her edgewise word.

Published in Jerry Jazz Musician January 2012

In the Pink

The Mobile girl connects with me.
Delectable in cupcake dress
transmitting domesticity,
she percolates with politesse.
Her swanlike, elongated arms
are moored demurely at her side,
with standing at attention palms
whose slides alluringly provide
direction to her product pitch.
They skirt just past her garment's waist,
as though reluctant to unstitch
its seams with seeming brazenfaced
routines. But signal vibes that she
transmits are mobile to a T.

Published online in Eye on Life
November 2011

Postscript

So that poet's perplexed about the turn
in a Petrarchan sonnet? When this field
of words I'm cultivating bears a yield
editors cut; when wary readers spurn
my scribbled produce even as I burn
the midnight oil; when I can neither wield
my pen as sword, nor dress my wounds till healed
by inky salve on quill, then I adjourn
my fruitless enterprise and cease to write
beyond the octave. To the end I sigh
from writer's block that gives my critics might
beyond due currency. What's worse, I buy
their estimate with mix of scorn and spite
that stays my hand and lets my well run dry.

Published in WRITE ON! January 2012

Peregrinations

What's Life? It's just a moment's breach
with death; a sentinel in place to guard
the heartland which we left behind us
in our quest to help restore a troubled peace.
Life's a brief respite from bliss; a kindling light
that seeds the night with harried fields. These yield
the harvests that we reap till turning over in the heap
from which we stirred. Life's a bankrupt state
of past desires' vested interests; arousal's panoply
of hypnagogic images; a posthumous jostling
of death's headboard by collapsing stars;
a personified Pleiades who tuck us into cosmic pockets
when we're young and rocket us to Mars
when sleep's deep enough to reach the Morning star.
Life's a nova in the galaxy of death; a fracture
in the fortress of the universe, a dissonance in music
of the spheres; death's bad dream before awakening.

Published in Down in the Dirt, May 2012

Cellblock Row

This life's a lockup that we'd best avoid.
Genetic blueprints are the prison clothes
we wear. But native threads have since alloyed
themselves with alterations guards impose
like chains which add to sentences we serve.
Some break from the ordeal; some stay in shape.
Delusions that we're free afford us nerve
to entertain ideas for an escape
from what appears to be our destiny.
And books allow us prisoners to read
while we await release and liberty
to cash in vouchers from our chosen creed.
But all who burgle life must serve their time
till death affords atonement for their crime.

Published online February 2012 in:
Ascent Aspirations

Cashing in the Jackpot

We win the lottery when once we're born.
For no amount of youthful escapades,
where vim holds up mortality to scorn
and moxie proudly swaggers on parade,
can stay the hand of death's advancing scythe.
No mesmerized attachment to this life
can help make aging ballerinas lithe,
or put the cutting edge back in the knife
that's wielded past the season of its use.
But, notwithstanding palliative pills,
our bodies suffer limitless abuse
that undercuts the most resilient will's
endurance. Neither can we long withhold
the winning ticket that we've once been sold.

Published in Ascent Aspirations, February 2012

Unfinished Business

If Schubert could do it, I'll do one better. My symphony's
consummately incomplete from the beginning. The
signature
in my flat's the opening key. Nothing to speculate about, no
random notes in my music room to be orchestrated by tomb
raiders; no posthumous arrangement after my death. No
speculation as to why I stopped its inception when I did.
Just a long-drawn-out diminuendo that starts legato with
no strings attached. The quiet work radiates off the page
like a Cabernet's bouquet. It needs neither baton nor
metronome. It's keyed into seething sympathies. Like
loaves of leavened dough, it rises in silence. I give
posterity smoked piano on bar lines that aren't drawn.
The chord is my shepherd, I shall descant; retards on
my staff, they comfort me in the absence of my melodies.
Major sharps are flattened beyond repair. Tacit symbols
clash against the passing winds; drums roll into the distance.
There're processionals of pundits parsing empty staves in
A flat bridged with ties that boast a subdued resolution.
My taciturn score unfolds in schoolrooms, on turned-on
laptops, and at business meetings. Its music's piped into
children's nurseries as they sleep. It's heard in churches,

as Low Mass - between standby lines of the liturgy. It
modulates through rosaries of meditation in temples and
monasteries. It's performed by commuters who gaze
musingly through bus windows, tuned to horns like
patrons of the Philharmonic. My ambitious work's,
like Minerva, pulled fully formed out of my dread.
Its scales line my face. And designated rests leave
grave markings on tombstones trumpeting eloquence.

Published in The Puckerbrush Review 2012 spring/summer

Queen of Swords

What pluck informs the steel you wield?
Such thrusts betoken more than fencing skills.
Incisive strokes encourage men to yield.
But spunk subverts the firmness of their wills
as well. And even your clandestine strength,
released from trappings that you're made to wear -
embroidered skirts descending ankle-length -
remind us that you've potency to spare.
You hammer jaws of hapless miscreants
with cuffs that cause unkindest cuts of all.
For more than sword that fosters your advance,
or cape and mask that give a deathly pall
to foes, the latter sense you've tapped a source
that trumps accessories with native force.

Published in The Fifth Di.... Sept. 2012

Female Fan Lands Jim Morrisey

How cunningly she stalks her prey
while he struts by with vigilance.
No predator with an array
of claws or pincers could dispense
with wary quarry like she does.
For she not only bides her time
while raging hormones are abuzz
inside her, but will wisely prime
her tensile tendons to be sprung
so that he turns up where she lands.
And then with lightning speed her tongue
injects the captive in her hands
with serum. If he were a roe,
her booty would be good to go.

Published in the Eclectic Muse
Christmas 2011

Giggling Girl

What murky thoughts were harbored in her breast?
For just a humorous remark from me
about her firm's proposed hegemony
in the United States left her possessed
by brusque guffaws suggestive of a quest
to rule the world. Of course, transparency
of such intent made her seem more trustee
in charge of some guy's passionate arrest
before her stern behest to rule his heart
than claimant of impending city-states.
But neither would I loathe to serve my part
in some despotic realm that legislates
with such preemptive amatory art,
were I conveyed inside her city-gates.

Published in The Eclectic Muse
Christmas 2011

Devout Tillage

Whoever is afraid to bloom
because of Church theology,
should ponder what made Jesus fume
that time he importuned a tree
to tender him a humble fig.
Of course, the fig tree bore no fruit
upon its disobliging twig
to justify another shoot.
Since Jesus was a bit perplexed
to see its teleology
aborted, he succinctly hexed
it unto perpetuity.
For everything in life must bear
the fruit for which it's planted there.

So what if some bananas rot,
or there's a toxic tree among
the fruitful teeming of the lot?
And though some tulip picker's stung
by a productive honeybee,
the flower that it pollinates
can justify its felony.

And everything that's living grates
to some degree on people's nerves.
The thorns amidst the scented rose
is just what Mother Nature serves
up when her precious garden grows.
The only sin is want of strife
because there's no productive life.

Published in Ancient Paths 2012

Weather Report

The summer's hot, the winter roars
and in the spring there's too much rain.
This is a time to stay indoors.

September's oceanic shores
play havoc with the weather vane.
The summer's hot, the winter roars.

Today the temperature soars.
Despite the kindling on the plain,
this is the time to stay indoors.

Precipitation prickles pores
of those who cannot entertain
humidity, and winter roars

in ways the fisherman abhors
and horticulturists disdain.
This is a time to stay indoors.

Forget those freshly teeming moors!
Eighty in June is inhumane!
The summer's hot and winter roars

in ways the weatherman deplores.
And when the warnings seem inane
it's always time to stay indoors

as you investigate wherefores
with your intimidated brain.
For while prognostication roars,
it's always good to stay indoors.

Published in The Same, winter, Spring 2011

Diamond in the Rough

Assaying like a precious jewel
refracted features of your face,
I need no spectroscopic tool
to thus appraise it. Love's strong case
will make a conversation piece
of what remains in the exchange
of passion for my mind's caprice.
And though restricted to the range
my faceted recall affords
you, who are neither quartz nor glass,
your sparkle when I hold you towards
the light of memory can pass
examination from all sides.
Thereon my sharp-eyed fancy rides.

Published in The Same, winter/spring 2012

Shakespeare's A Midsummer Night's Dream

(in a New York City parking lot)

His play, performed beneath a sunset glow,
gives meaning to the nature of this dream.
There, spry but catty ladies steal the show
and frisky female fairies beam and gleam.
What fun to see these starlets play their part
where they exude a captivating charm,
until their real demeanors show what art
informs the sprites and lovers that disarm
our sensibilities to cede to night's
dissembling spirit. Thus, upon the stage
of life, attracted by cosmetic sleights
of hand, a dreamy jackass might engage
a drama queen until her breaking dawn
awakens him with a dismissive yawn.

**Published online in Ascent Aspirations
August 2012**

Commedia dell'Arte

My heart's set on that free-fall girl
who, scarcely injuring herself,
gets tossed like some rag doll awhirl,
as if she were a feisty elf.
Her mannerisms - crystallized
inside her Columbina dress -
have mischievously neutralized
with wry, kinetic perkiness
impassive aspects of her sex.
Her face blush mocks her pasty mien.
As such she's stamina to flex
the muscles of her in-between
identity and muster steel
enough for harlequins to reel.

Published in Nomad's Choir

Hedging Their Bets

I scarcely think that they believe in God
who venerate the heart above the soul,
who vehemently rage against the sod
or seek relief to make the body whole.
For otherwise they'd countenance disease
as though it were a prophylactic gift
that promised painful tensions quick surcease.
Would doctors leave the healing patient miffed
if they removed a tumor from his brain
so that he wakes up in a better state
despite the surgery's attendant pain?
Then why not let God's doctors operate,
unless they fear the body they've divined
cannot replace the one they'll leave behind.

Or maybe it's the home post-mortems get
that undermine their interest in a place
seraphic brokers advertise "to let"
in neighborhoods whose streets are paved with grace.
It might be that the price they have to pay
for otherworldly digs without a lift
exacts a cost they're anxious to defray.
But how could it be anything but thrift

if they acquired valued real estate
they've prayed for all their lives at such low cost?
Then why should they not purchase Heaven's gate
unless they fear that once that threshold's crossed
the most impressive palace that they find
would not replace the walk-up left behind.

Published in the Penwood Review 2011

Good Heavens

Religion's the bus stop where cars
illegally park when the space
is available. It's a face
whose grace replaces cosmic scars;
a stained glass window hiding stars.
It's an outsized, overnight case
for sleep-ins of the human race;
a podium for avatars;
a glib response to questions raised
that parents shudder to discuss;
memorials to having praised
the firmament with such a fuss;
a history that's paraphrased
to suit the time allotted us.

Published in Ancient Paths, 2012 #17

Ghost Whispering Madness

While Jennifer Love Hewitt seems so nice,
the sappy prittle-prattle of her ghosts
suggest affections short of Paradise.
Do we require sentimental hosts
to cross us over to the other side?
And would I want to disappear so fast
when lovable Love Hewitt is a guide
who'd make my crossing-over want to last?
But in-laws who you thought you left behind,
when you began your journey as a sprite,
would not elicit whispers should you find
them hovering post-mortem in the light.
Yet, what's the point of finding any dear
ones after you have crossed the great divide
when most of them were loath to have you near
them, taking you for dead before you died.
And what sort of a blessed soul would keep
in light so bright that it could scarcely sleep!

Published in Soul Fountain Spring 2012

Screw It!

I wish I could be an electric bulb.
Assuming that my mistress kept me cleaned,
I'd flash white teeth - quite the eclectic bulb -
in all her lamps, unless she intervened
and used me for the night-light on her porch.
Despite wear and advancing lumens' age
as she made use of me, I'd be her torch -
though I grew old, and she were at that stage
of beaming women who are prone to wed.
For filament - unlike arthritic joints,
decrepit bones, bad eyes and balding head -
while it's still glowing, never disappoints.
I'd be as bright lit as the newer light
bulbs. If she needed my own hundred watts,
my luminescence would be no less bright
than lights she purchased with last evening's pots.
So blissfully I'd help her get about
till, in a blaze of glory, I burn out.

Published in Third Wednesday 2012

Actress Punk'd by Male Peers

(to his male readers)

Forget presumptions of her sex
which in the context of the men
she dates preempt the need to flex
her muscle. In this mise en scène,
engendered by a playful sting,
she sits near a precocious lad
who fancies a romantic fling
while he sits waiting for his dad
to pick him up. The dad returns
and later vows to go to court,
pretending wicked word concerns.
What bliss to see her face contort
when she proceeds to make a fuss
demoted thus, to one of us.

Published 2012 in Third Wednesday

A Night's Romance

How aptly did her arms begin to tense
their muscles with the load she had to pull.
They showed incredible resilience
as she adroitly dragged a basketful
of clothes that hid her paramour inside.
And though it wasn't meant as an affront
to my integrity or sense of pride,
it wasn't part of my desire's wont
to watch the rosebuds in her supple arms
discreetly blossom from the tensile shoots
surrounding them like radiating charms.
Then I remembered how the bitter fruits
of shame that Lancelot inside a cart
abjectly bore were seasoned by his heart.

Published 2012 in Third Wednesday

Preemptive Critic

If you had said you didn't like my face,
at least you would have shown me one of yours,
and exorcised my demonized disgrace
by playing one of art's inquisitors.
I would have felt I was a Salem witch
condemned as sorceress by your high priest
who, being badgered by his inner bitch,
worked famine at life's literary feast.
But yours was an evasive, shifting charge,
ambiguous as those at witches' trials.
And I suspect the suspect's still at large -
not in my craft, but in mephitic wiles
of your own heart. Before you start to shelf
my poetry, physician, heal yourself!

Previously published in POETALK 2012

The Pussy Prince

A woman walking down a dusty road
discovers what looks like an antique lamp.
Her touch, as if it breaks some secret code,
lets loose a genie from its rusted cramp.
"Ah, that feels good," the sprite says with a grin.
"Because of this I'll grant you any wish."
"Yahoo!, she shouts. "Can you turn my Persian
cat into a horny prince who'll ravish
me in bed? My husband died and I've had
nothing since to satisfy my needs." "Done,"
chimes the genie. "Tonight a handsome lad
will come to you before the clock strikes one."
"Whoa," she clamors. "And I still have to do
my nails." After shower and powdered puff
on breasts, she dresses for the rendezvous
in some sexy negligee. Sure enough,
the young stud enters, skips the final stair
leading to the bedroom where his mistress
lies lasciviously. Stroking her hair,
he straddles her, pursuing happiness;
then murmurs, words and honeyed tongue admixed
inside her ear: "Too bad you had me fixed."

Previously Published in Nuthouse 2012

Hay Fever Blues

I met a former girlfriend in the park, last summer, who I hadn't seen in years. She smiled and said I looked great. I thanked her and said she seemed to have aged somewhat since I saw her last. As I fished for my cell phone to take her number down I heard what sounded like sniffling. I asked what the matter was. Blowing her nose she complained that she suffered from allergies and needed to leave. That's the darn thing about humid summers.

Published in The Poet's Art April 2013

Heaven as on Earth

Faith selects scriptural heads of state crowned with immaculate renown akin to in-car feted movie matrons waving right hands in beaming limousines streaming down streets populated by star-crossed disciples fazed by streaming cavalcades braying sovereignty on wheels squealing hosannas that trumpet the unseen thrust of their parishioners' reverential gaze.

Published in The Poet's Art 2013

Puccini's Madama Butterfly

Three years ago I left you, Cio-Cio San,
in front of the doors to the opera house.
I'd spurned your perfumed textures of chiffon
as you waited, like a dutiful spouse,
for me to backtrack from my loveless quest.
But I preferred the counterfeit bouquet
of pleasures where the sun sets in the west
of beauty. Dulcet harmonies that sway
like breezy cherry blossoms in the Spring
were too constrictive for my wayward heart.
I opted less for nightingales to sing
enchantment with their salutary art
than for the harsh tonalities and mind
benumbing movements of a disco grind.

And now I'm back, like Pinkerton returned,
though not with western wife. But yes! The child
that you gave birth to with suspensions churned
inside my breast sleeps sweetly domiciled
within the pages of my memory.
I hear kimonos rustling in my ear
beside your theater's tonal alchemy,
chrysanthemums and porcelain veneer.

And I can feel the dagger in the breast
you pierced yourself with as those crashing chords
brought down the curtain on our nuptial nest.
But agonized regrets, like sounding boards
rebounding with harmonic consequence,
gives reconciliation resonance.

Published in Lucid Rhythms
Issue #2, 2012

God Sends

So you're the "friend" addressing me -
not with the reverence I need,
but as the butt of OMG!
Forget the object of your creed
who used to be your BFF.
It seems the techno-gods that be
changed digital to devil's cleft
foot in *My* Space above. TC!
For in the text of Luke and Mark
that's written on *My* pad, you'll find
your post computer days are stark,
considering you've undermined
my sacred status with your cell
phone texts. You think it's NBD
preferring Fios, Sprint Nextel
and some PC instead of Me,
when you connect online? Well,
you can go to Dell! LOL!

Published in Lucid Rhythms 2012

Brahms in Arms

With crack brigades of fingers mobilized
at the composer's posthumous commands,
it's strange the keyboard isn't pulverized
by those sforzandos from her practiced hands.
She deftly executes staccato notes
besieging battered bar lines on the score,
then marshals energetic antidotes
to the composer's auditory war
of nerves, which she'll astutely prosecute.
Nor could he have conscripted better troops
than those skilled fingers armed by this recruit.
Behind their dexterous arsenal she swoops
down on the keys with forte tonic chord
whose overtones subdue the sounding board.

Published in Art Times – Fall, 2014

Ethereal Thoughts

One day I dreamed of Jesus Christ
and the seraphim that sing,
I dreamed of faithful shepherds
and of Herod the cruel king.
I dreamed of Mary Magdalene
anointing Jesus' feet
before he bore the weight of sin
to make his trials complete.
I dreamed that he was crucified
by Pontius Pilate's grim decree,
forgiving those, before he died,
who chafed his wounds with mockery.
Rebuking darkness with my sighs,
I waited for the sun to rise.

Published in Lutheran Digest, Summer 2012

Lauding Laura Dekker

(who circumnavigated the Globe in
her ketch, Guppy, 2010-2012)

While cradling in the cabin of her heart
the landlocked cynics mewling with concern,
she navigates the course her stars would chart
when she was eight years old. And now, astern
at 16 years, she gazes at the blue
horizon like a weathered, salty tar
astride the frothy dragon that she slew.
In just one year this sailor traveled far.
Now piloting her ketch, she scouts the deck,
alert to waves that flow along the hull
of "Guppy" like a doting mom might check
her baby's breathing in the evening lull.
Indeed, her "Gup's" no parent, but a child,
who doesn't cross the skipper he's beguiled.

For sailing having snapped her from her world
of daydreams, grit and fortitude informs
her spirit as she fends off lightning hurled
at her amidst the din of thunderstorms.

Some dozen ports had traffic with the keel
she steers apace. When bird poop drops like dough
on deck, she thinks that it's a worse ordeal
than greasing bearings while the trade winds blow.
And more concerned for troubles left on shore
than for tornadoes mastered with aplomb
she skirts the accolades that lay in store,
when once she disembarks, for trials to come.
For though it's port the gamester in her craves,
she'd just as soon be navigating waves.

Published in The Storyteller OCT/DEC 2012

The Queen of Wards
(or the distaff Zorro)

The proper lady of a house
that radiates domestic charm,
she's meek as a cathedral mouse.
I doubt she'd be inflicting harm
on anyone but naughty boys
that she's enjoined to discipline.
She parries cheek with equipoise
while sloughing off her crinoline
for slacks and patriarchal mask
in black. She dons that gothic guise
to execute her thankless task
on rogues who she will neutralize.
She seems as skillful with the sword
as she is with the diaper pin.
Nor does she date the men she's floored
who cannot take it on the chin.
Yet, she who cuffs them when they're bad
is like the gal who married dad!

Published in Quantum Leap 2012

Fecund Muse

Conceiving a poetic strain,
her forceps waken me from sleep
till germinal impressions peep
as fancies which, like novocaine,
augments the threshold of my pain.
I thus breed sonnets in her keep.
They count my syllables like sheep,
and feed upon my teeming brain
whose metric measures are their bed.
They doff a crumpled dressing gown
for metaphors my verses spread
around them like an eiderdown.
Indelible on sheets I fled,
they mock their weary father's frown.

Published online in Foliate Oak
October 2012

Spinning My Wheels

How cunningly she took me in
by dressing up in simile
the daydream taken for a spin
by my creative fantasy.
I felt imagination soar
while pumping gas inside my tank.
And with a revved up metaphor
I quickly got the mountebank
across the bridge that spans my brain
into the sleazy part of town.
With literate legerdemain
she bilked each adjective and noun,
and then with pentatonic feet
she ran away with my conceit.

Published online in Foliate Oak
October 2012

Writing Shape

As poet, I'm much better when the roar
erupts inside my germinating brain.
I clinch when I get hit, use metaphor
like padded gloves to mitigate the pain
of dealing with a flurry of ideas
that land with combinations from my pen.
Historical conceits are panaceas
for the cuts I suffer when I'm going ten
with fantasies I can't backpedal from.
But otherwise I lean against the ropes
when some unseemly image sticks a thumb
inside my eye. Then I envision tropes
that cushion me from blows before the belle
of fancy. Thus I write my villanelle.

Published in Foliate Oak October 2012

Web Support

Pardon me for savoring my laptop's
responsiveness to your persuasive hands.
But being weaned on lesser moms' and pops'
abortive ministrations and commands
my net connection's naughtiness became
a childish game. And though my manly pride
obliged my passive tendency with shame
to get my internet hooked up astride
resourceful shoulders, riding on your skill
seemed best. Though my PC played hide and seek
with surrogates, your firm, no-nonsense will
transformed its rowdy system to a meek
appendage of authoritative arms.
And I'm enthralled by your arresting charms.

Published online in Foliate Oak, October 2012

Free Enterprise

Some politicians opt to plant the seed
of lenience to cultivate its soil.
As such, constituents are fit to feed
on fruits engendered by another's toil.
Nor do they have to share the husbandry.
Indeed. How often do they spare each weed,
surrounding rosebud, bush and maple tree,
if only for promoting rampant greed
against the prudent farmer's hacking scythe.
What matter if it generates a blight.
They much prefer the forlorn farmer writhe
with grief at harvests lost than that he slight
ambitions that they'd shrewdly bring to fruit.
And should he balk, he's cut off at the root.

Published in Westview, v.33, Issue #2, Sept 2018

Frost Smitten

Despite the fact that I'm not prone to ski,
I love the sultry dalliance of snow.
It makes intense pedestrians walk slow
as though in tribute to God's majesty.
Indeed. It's near impossible to see
beyond the vestments of His ermine show,
still less to counter caustic winds that blow
and make us bend the reverential knee
in abdication to His frigid force.
How humbling to be driven off our course,
though destined for vacation, job or church.
We're steadfast though He leaves us in the lurch,
remembering amidst woolens chosen
that many are cold but few are frozen.

Published in WestWard Quarterly winter 2017

For Prithivi

(thanks for your kindness)

How like a star in a darkening sky,
appears an unexpected friendly deed.
How much more so when storm warnings belie
the growth potential of one's kindling seed.
But though my firmament was overcast
from waiting for a bus to get to work -
which forced me to hop in a van, aghast
at paying more – a kindly girl would perk
me up with navigational finesses.
Assuring me the driver was on course,
she gave me, with additional largesse,
a ticket free of charge. Despite that source
of succor, caring less what it was worth,
I prized it as a token of rebirth.

Published in The Society of Classical Poets

Sick Room

There'll be no more shuffling among the trees
in this deserted garden of Eden.
No footsteps, heavy with expectancy,

from that tender, nocturnal nurse, hourly
materializing in some satin
nightgown, among the rustling of the trees,

to spoon relief like an epiphany.
Love's harvest has already been eaten,
and footsteps, heavy with expectancy

now echo with a hollow litany
of lost comforts I'll never know again
among the autumn rustling of the trees.

This last sickness has brought me to my knees
with grieving. But there's none in time's prison
whose footsteps, heavy with expectancy,

can resurrect those former sympathies;
just rows of scarecrows propped on a frozen
tundra; winds whistling where there once were trees,
and footsteps heavy with expectancy.

Published online in Challenger 2013

Sell Mate

"In that case I'll move in with you," she said,
when I asked her for cut-rate real estate
in Boston – hoping to rattle her head.
Instead I became the fugitive date
of a girl who worked in a clothing store.
Her pat down of the mettle in my sass
was something I was not preparing for,
when preying on this unsuspecting lass.
Arresting thus my sensibility -
like a police detective packing heat -
she all but took me into custody,
along with remnants of my brash conceit.
Thus, rather than awaiting further liens
on me, I purchased bail with Gucci jeans.

Published in Long Story Short
September 2016

Bastard

I scribble to wean fancies from my brain.
For once conceived within my bardic breast
they suckle me till I become insane
ensuring that they're fed till fully dressed
and able to stand up on metric feet.
I diaper stridently impulsive cries
with images dolled up in a conceit
that shows my infant in a pleasing guise.
What irony, that passions in the dark
can spawn a studied, well-proportioned poem
so alien from its creative spark
it could belong in someone else's home.
For lines were each weaned with a measured phrase
that reinforced the separation phase.

Published in Studio 1

Bridled

Two girls are riding rough-shod in my breast.
Sweet Sue, equestrian, with prodding lash,
will play at hurdles, giving me no rest.
The docile Ellen binds me with panache
to service like a lamb roped to the limb
of a strong oak. There's no way to wrest free.
And though I bristle in the interim
to circumvent her, she'll just brush, with glee,
my mane, then harness wagons to my frame.
I champ my bit as Susan cuts me loose,
if only to new-saddle me with shame
of spur and whip till ridden to abuse.
Thus, broken by the mount and worse for wear,
I neigh to stay in Ellen's stable care.

published in Conceit Magazine
February, 2017

Burgeoning Faith

I'm loath to worship gods who hide their art
inside the dusty confines of a church,
or are presumed by mortals to impart
to us the sacred means by which we search
for his divinity. I find my god's
apostolic succession on the field,
and resurrection in the force that sods
the earth which annually shares its yield.
Spring blooms don't hide their glory in a knave,
or castigate their worshippers for sins
that weigh on them for pleasures that they crave
from dancing billows of the bawdy winds.
With catechisms of the new-born day,
I worship where the risen sun holds sway.

Published in Conceit Magazine
February 2017

Freehand

It's hard enough when there's a safety net
beneath the tightrope that you're walking on.
The hexagonal webbing can abet
one's enterprise with lifelines banked upon;
if just to know a failsafe shield is there
when walking soft-soled to the other side.
It gives one opportunities to dare
brash moves which otherwise are scarcely tried.
But going it alone is hazardous,
especially when one is looking down
into a drop, so deep and cavernous,
it draws from most men more than just a frown.
Indeed, it makes their cravens heart afraid
they won't survive trajectories assayed.

Published in Conceit Magazine
February, 2017

Prate Rape

Your honor, she started taking her prose off even before we dated, insinuating she'd like to pay a visit to Shakespeare in the Park. She had already investigated his loft at the Open Air Theater in London's Regent Park. She hankered to see some drama there and, in lieu of that, we flirted with one at Holland Park. My suggestive, "As You Like It" wasn't rebuffed. Nor would I try to intimidate her with a Lear. It also didn't hurt her sensibilities for me to spike her thinking with "A Midsummer Night's Dream" at Richmond Park. But she was wide awake when she lay on the grass. Yes, there was a beam of pleasure in her eyes - for Shakespeare's sake, not mine. But I swear your honor, The Tempest wasn't in my breast, but a downpour that came after the Twelfth Night. And, despite appearances, "A Winter's Tale" was the only one I'd get, when we went together to Harringay's Finsbury Park. It's true, she seemed to yield to my come hither look when I attempted to take her to my treasured "Hamlet". Unfortunately, when later we met, understandably drunk on pentameter, the girl said no. Of course I was disappointed. But when a girl says no, your honor, she means no. And so, I let her go, holding a copy of Love's Labour's Lost, which I'd given her a week before. And that was the extent of it. So it's all so Much Ado About Nothing.

Published in Straylight 2017

Haunted Script

My poems were casements on an eerie house.
They tempted me to slowly look inside
and see what spinning spider there, or mouse,
would publicize the darker side they hide.
Each darting glance produced another verse,
affording me a privileged point of view.
The mist helped me creatively immerse
myself in crevices where fancies flew
like belfry bats inside my bardic brain.
In time, subversive mysteries I'd gleaned
exhorted me to break a window pane
and face the taunting spirits that demeaned
my will. Immobilized by scribbling pen
and metric feet, I couldn't leave again.

Published in The Raven's Perch, April 2017

The Mighty Fallen

I rue those nights I'd slept,
and wakened from a dream
in which I could have wept
from loss of self-esteem.
But I woke up restored
to all I'd left behind
when I - in sleep, unmoored -
sailed seas my fancy mined
with thoughts of ruin and theft.
But pity dreamers docked
at havens they've since left
for quarters where they're mocked
inside the prison cell
they wake up in pell mell.

Published the Raven's Perch
April 2017

Harsh Measures

I tell myself that fancy's not a fact
that merits metaphor or apt conceits
to render it poetically with tact
combining rhyme and soft iambic beats.
It's an indulgent act that no disguise
can hide despite a battery of sounds
and vivid images that mesmerize
the senses to see more than barren nouns.
Nor are you edified by what you write.
But floundering in literary tropes,
you drown in stanzas with perverse delight
before you sense you've written off your hopes
by bolstering what should be fleeting dreams
with metaphors, conceits and metric schemes.

The fact is, rather than construct a poem
to foster thoughts that clutter up the mind
as if it were a metaphoric home,
it's better to pretend you're deaf and blind.
For should you host a wastrel at the door
or furnish scoundrels with a proper suit
of clothes to cover up the rags they wore
when you yourself could end up destitute?

For what? For them to go back on the street
repeating ways you wasted time to mend?
It's better that you learn to be discreet
and choose with care the charities you spend
your labors on. And brothels can't compare
with hospitals dispensing long-term care.

Published in The Raven's Perch 2017

NoBigotsAllowed

(Los Angeles Clippers owner Donald Sterling's banned
for life from the NBA after racist phone comments)

Forget the black man's bitter history
that puts his future prospects in arrears.
America is free from bigotry.

When biased owners get our goat, they see
how quickly an indebted nation veers
away from their disgraceful history -

regarding equal rights and parity
for black Americans. They're making clear
America is free from bigotry.

For didn't we effectively agree
that, as in desert realms of yore that sear
away the sins that stain one's history,

this scapegoat bears the brunt of infamy?
We've managed to dispense with guilt and fears
and free ourselves from claims of bigotry;

not by removing blight and poverty,
but by ensuring that the public hears
the prejudice in one man's history.

Since furthermore it's given currency
amidst recriminations, taunts and jeers,
America's no need of bigotry!

With such pontifical chicanery,
the blight we've put on black men disappears.
And good as Sterling's checkered history,
America is free from bigotry.

Published in Africa vs North America v.1

A Jaundiced Perspective

With tyranny dictators can abuse
the populace who hasn't got a say
in government. But here we get to choose
which representative will take away
our freedoms. And an invisible fence
of finely-tuned decrees our lords enact
to seal free-wheeling backroom deals prevents
the law-abiding in us to react
with pique. For didn't we select those terms
now bristling us when we arranged to vote
our wont in ways that tacitly confirms
the text of what the constitution wrote?
So how can we subversively oppose
de facto servitude we duly chose?

Published in Africa vs North America v.1

Guess Who Come Out the Winner?

(or is it To Dinner)

The Draytons are bigots. So is the maid
who happens to be black. In Hollywood
it's okay to see a black masquerade
as a southern bigot if she's a good
cook. Meanwhile as her guilt accumulates
Mrs. Drayton, in true Christian spirit,
ignores the beam in her eye, and berates -
with displaced hates from this triumvirate -
her white, prejudiced neighbor for the mote
in hers. A perfect solution to sin.
She puts it on the back of a scapegoat
then sends her to the wilderness. Therein
this cast-off is castigated in place
of an out-group. Thus, the Draytons distance
themselves from their working bias, save face
and become paradigms of tolerance
to boot! Forgive my wry hypothesis
while probing where the woman's coming from,
but aren't these the roots of prejudice?
Projecting biases deemed troublesome
onto safe targets may win accolades
from hypocrites, but only love persuades.

Published in Africa vs North America v.1

Ceding Sovereignty

Although my girl's not beautiful,
it's not her looks which turn me on.
It's just that she's so dutiful.
Relentlessly I'm pressed upon
to heed directives she decrees,
until I abdicate my will
to anything it takes to please
Her Highness. Sure, I get a thrill
from being at her beck and call,
if just because by serving her
I'm free from edicts that forestall
indulgent needs. Her force majeure
suffices to grant liberty
from lesser lords oppressing me.

Published in Philadelphia Stories

Blue Collar Blues

(musings of an Army Veteran)

Before you start pointing fingers at me
you first should start to walk inside my shoes.
When they're too tight for comfort you would see
they cause a lot of pain. I doubt you'd choose
to navigate in clogs that blister feet.
Perhaps you had a better pair to wear
or wore them on a smoother floor or street,
and never carried loads I had to bear.
But rather than be grateful for your lot,
and generous to him who still takes joy
in it despite the hard knocks that he got,
you're haughtily committed to deploy
your spleen with liberal ingratitude
for service that allowed you to be rude.

Published in Soul Fountain 8/30/17

Blondie Does a First

A fetching fiddler on the concert stage
methodically resuscitating Brahms!
His strident score was silent on the page
before her learned ear informed her arms
with measures that would make him breathe once more.
With the symphonic members of her crew
her violin made his C voyage soar.
She looked at the conductor for her cue
from time to time, but just to validate
her instrument was answering the bow
she worked to make its body resonate
with fiercely drawn vibrations of a pro.
Nor were the yellow ringlets of her hair -
in sync with oscillations - worse for wear.

Published in Soul Fountain 8/11/17

Bob's Terminal Bay

Wracked by cancer, Bob Marley told his friend,
"It's not me, Camille." No, it's never me
when self-determination's at an end.
For, navigating pain, you cannot see
but knots ahead. And you're preoccupied
with hoisting sails against prevailing winds.
Bravado in your weary crew has died.
A glance into the water shows the fins
of sharks that prey upon engulfing fear.
And battered by the gale you veer off course
until outlying moorings disappear.
Directions lost, mirages reinforce
your desperate quest to cast yourself ashore
where shrieks are muffled by the ocean's roar.

Published in Soul Fountain 8/25/17

Emergent Behavior

She groaned that few men played the hardcore game
with her when she identified her sex.
Were they afraid that she would put a hex
on them, or use her agency to claim
prerogatives when kindling passion's flame?
Yet why else would a winsome woman vex
a guy because of wherewithal to flex
her cyber-muscle toward the modest aim
of demonstrating plastic motor skills?
But if they thought rejection would erode
her competence, it goaded her instead
to juggle out of life related thrills.
"You wanna fight me", she perversely crowed
her budding prowess going to her head.

Published in Bank Street Writers Issue 35

Falstaff Redux

I wanted to impress the woman who arrived from Maine at Shakespeare in the Park in New York City - with her child in tow. I tried conveying to her all I knew of opera while we waited in the dark for lemon tea on the concession line, at intermission. "Which ones do you like?" I challenged her with probing third degrees. "La Traviata, Faust and La Boheme," she answered, with her daughter keeping watch upon her ardently beleaguered mom. The girl assumed Dame Quickly's smarmy mien. "We generally see the tragedies," the 13 year old earnestly averred. "Do you like Madame Butterfly?" I asked, now that I felt the girl was competent
to join the tête-à-tête. "I never saw Madama Butterfly," she fired back. Her glib response would bring into relief my hasty anglicizing of the work, which I construed as a dismissive gibe at my faux pas. With Falstaff looming large as the conclusion of my effort to engage my Mistress Ford, I moved to ask "Dame Quickly" if she saw that masterpiece. She didn't. Neither did her pensive Mom, who rescued her by citing Figaro. But my Dame Quickly drew Gianni Schicchi out of the cache of her aesthetic arms to keep me from the ones her mother had.

And she pronounced the words so perfectly, I dared not echo JAN-nee SKEEK-kee's name in kind - afraid it would entangle my thick tongue. Instead, buoyed by its famous tune, I sang "Ciao Ciao Bambino" - maiden phrase of that dear work's enchanting melody - to operatically precede the siege of my purported Mistress Ford. It seemed that she - my rival's mother - would accede to my presumptuously toned conceit. "O Mio Babbino Caro!" her Dame Quickly rejoined. "My favorite aria in opera." The girl parried once again my bogus thrust into her mother's heart by mouthing the correct Italian words! Dejected by the drubbing I received, I switched my amatory quest to "Meg Page" at the concession stand - as Falstaff might well have done had the occasion rose. She smiled at me, my lemon tea inside her hand while she bemoaned that she had not yet been to the ballet. "The ABT's in town", I crowed, while handing her my cash, content to salvage this presumed romance. Just then I heard the little girl chirp in: "There's also the Australian Ballet," a company that was indeed in town.
"You know it all!" I laughed, in disbelief, amused by her astute intelligence. For he who laughs last, laughs the best", I smiled, recalling Falstaff's final line. And so my nemesis departed with her mom - my fancied conquest - winningly in tow.

Published in Miller's Pond Fall 2017

Sizing Her Up

"I'm five foot nothing," she replied
to cut the conversation short,
when I suggested five foot five
in my endeavor to cavort
with her. She didn't boost her height.
to compromise a connoisseur
of breadth, or whet the appetite
of some 'size matters' amateur.
But like a mother who's fatigued
and more frustrated than beguiled
to grow in tandem with such need,
she'd treat it like a colic child.
'The size you see is what you get,'
she thus proceeded with chagrin.
My babbling brooked a bassinet
with not more than a safety pin
of brash dismissal to foreclose
the argument into repose.

Published in Miller's Pond Fall 2017

Marooned

It's not remuneration which I'll miss
when ceding duties that exacted skill;
nor even losing friends I'll reminisce
about with warmth and feelings of goodwill.
I'd navigate nor'easters many years
when toil and sweat conspired with my pride
to bide the tattered hull that ran my tears
aground, by elbowing the tar inside.
But labor's not a temperate clime for age
to ply its course against the shoals of time
or mediate the turbulence of rage
till docked at piers beside the sledge and slime;
and harbors now are merely a mirage
for battered ships that can't afford portage.

Published in Miller's Pond Fall 2017

Flushing with Anger in a Rest Room

I may as well be hired as his maid,
the way I'm made to clean his toilet seat.
Still worse, the only way I'm getting paid
is that by cleaning the commode I treat
myself to one as dry as that he pissed
upon when targeting the toilet bowl
with urinary fusillades that missed!
But wanting disinfecting alcohol,
I'm wiping dry the saturated seat
with the acidic fluid that resigned
me to redress his penchant to excrete
the stuff without regard for my behind.
If talk concerning urine seems unfit
then pity those who have to sit on it.

**Published online in Society of Classical Poets
August 2007**

Fruitless Outing

Although rejection hurts and hearts can't bide
the agony of unrequited love,
the harshest pain is never to have tried.
Withdrawal hurts as much as any shove
the forward womanizer gets who fails
in his pursuit. How sweet is sleep in war,
or beating a retreat when it avails
combatants in a tattered army corps.
But what remorse Columbus would have felt
to voyage near a hospitable land
whose rolling hills were emerald as veldt,
if docking he did not extend his hand
to natives who seemed bristling with intent
to form a bond he'd happily cement.

Published in Miller's Pond v.16 #2, 2013

Roll Models

What frisky carnivores are these?
Although they target me as prey,
it's less to flay me than to tease
a fellow they'd take straightaway,
apparently - by how I see them play.
They mischievously shoot the breeze
while I slink past in mock dismay.
These gals take down the game they please,
it seems, as one is pushed toward me
in sport. Her friend groans a rebuke;
but not from female modesty,
the fear of getting tagged a kook
or being branded indiscreet,
but, as she purrs: "I need more meat!"

Published in The Poet's Art #60, 2017

Cavalier's Plaint to Damsels

You think I'm being courteous to you
as a preamble to arrange a date?
Although the latter would be welcome too,
I'm bent to prove my manners aren't bait.
And while the painful thought of a rebuff
is not enough to keep myself at bay,
it's partly why I keep on talking fluff.
In any case, I don't care to dismay
milady with the customary tack
my cohorts use as means to meet again,
or setting you up for a drink or snack.
It seems I'm so seduced by gentleman
ideals, I'm scared to more than mingle by
default. As such I'm still a single guy.

published in Barbaric Yawp
November 2017

Nightmare on Elm Street

It seems that Freddie Krueger met his match
when stalking Nancy Thompson for a fight.
Averse to being snatched, she's poised to catch
this culprit of her adolescent plight.
No gender trappings curb her agency
as she sets booby-traps to bag him in
her room from his post-mortem vagrancy.
Nor do they thwart her aptitude to pin
him down before he wrests himself away
from this disgruntled reservoir of pluck.
Indeed, she's clearly equal to the fray.
And even as her fury leaves the schmuck
subdued, she basks with sun-drenched showmanship,
and just a wisp of shadow on her lip.

Published in Star*Line
Vol.41, Issue 1, winter 2018

Culinary Cunning

The way this crafty chef prepares her meal
subserves her partiality to cut
the fatty portion from her beef. She'll peel
beside it, onions. This way she can glut
her taste for spicy bull and still shed tears,
while pieces of the chuck are being stewed.
The dish, accompanied by lighter beers,
has texture, but can easily be chewed.
She renders obsolete the breaded shrimp
the faithful spouse assiduously makes.
And since no housewife likes to scratch and scrimp
remains of mistresses, the former stakes
her worthiness by serving bread and cheese
to someone who she's not inclined to please.

Published in The Helix Spring 2017

Damsel of the Manor

My jousting jest informed your quest
to put on armor like a knight.
In order to redress my plight
I parried your incensed behest,
imagining that I could best
you on love's battlefield. My white
complexion mirrored your delight
when blustering how you'd divest
me of my helmet, shield and lance.
You'd soon be dubbed and doubly blamed
for challenging me to advance
on you, then making me ashamed
at salvaging reverse romance
by riding on the fame you claimed.

Published in The Helix, Spring 2017

Sound Investment

I need a curried diet. What tastes great supplemented by greens, beans and rice, sours when eaten by itself. That's why I prefer being breast man bedding down with sugar chains of wedlock. I wouldn't wing it alone, always needling 4 legs on fables to support my leaden lode of minerals. I also need storied rooms with Persian plumes to mitigate my gin rummy pallor, and living room expanses of tapas for fleet fancies. I feel vested interest coming from somewhere Sundays to warehouses with Coors on the slide. I'm a king of rags and tatters, snappily syncopated. Forget those foursquare harmonies that schmaltz in ¾ time at supper where the courtiers are being smitten by polite perms. I jig from jugs of wining women buttered with winning smiles. Not for me connubial wombats widowed in passion's dense foliage. I need virginal vistas opening high C's of Brunnhildes with tectonic trappings. I tweet Muses for the imagination to hold a staff on, lined though they be with metric markings.

I note by rote that every good Fauntleroy does time in his straight-laced hurdles. I need to play one memory against a zither till each sounds out: "hup, 2, 3, 4, feted to a herbivore!" It's better than marching when you're going nowhere and keeps fops on the beat looking out for date breakers. I need orchestral dissonance to keep me in step with my cleft heart. I crave euphoric warnings in me. Sated by Octavian measures while the Countess marshals on, I'm Joseph with a colorful blazer of sage that cinders its colors. I fade in my age with pallid pastings of the past that blast my paper trappings into ash.

Published in 1-70 Review, summer, fall 2017

Metropolis

What a riot of white corpuscles pass through the arteries of the subway's thruway. Surely, life has cancerous leanings. And I see it metastasizing into the A train, down the stairs, up the platform, sapping energy from my middle age, circumscribing my life with their proliferation. How wonderful it is that these cells
can thrive, albeit at my expense. I grow pale even as I watch them colonize my body's outer extremities, then eat into the heart of the matter. But I get therapy in the doctoring arts of the opera, theater and ballet. Despite such dear expense, life continues through its final stages.

Published in 1-70 Review, September 2017

Finding Turnstiles in Strange Places

Notwithstanding your Medusa-like stare,
I'm sorry for entering your bedroom
at 3 am. I thought it was 8:30 in the morning
and that I was on the Number 4 express train
en route to my office in Bowling Green.
I'm not surprised, as such, at the eviscerating
look you gave me with the crew of MTA
officials standing near your bed. Your glowering
look froze me in my tracks, even as I crossed
the threshold leading to your comfort sofa -
which was apparently made of metal.
Under the circumstances, it was brash of me
to enter your inner sanctum so gingerly,
scarcely aware of the gap between your teeth
and platform shoes. Having stayed there
for 20 minutes, it was generous of you
not to call the cops and have me arrested
before I had a chance to stand clear
of your bedroom's rapidly closing doors.

Published in Poetry with Panache

Scheherazade Redux

Scheherazade could scarcely spin such tales
to keep her interlocutor engaged
like aggravating CNN regales
its viewership until it grows assuaged
by news that is at least a few weeks old.
Not even wide-eyed kings would be seduced
if consorts humored them with tales thrice-told,
that nonetheless consistently help boost
the ratings of its jaded viewership.
No termination of the nuptial knot
with anchors, or its stewardship,
for raking over breaking news once hot.
Oh, they might add a fresh and novel spin
to stagnant summaries to make us get involved.
But shrewd Scheherazade would brook chagrin
from her distrusting spouse till he dissolved
his partner for such antiquated news.
Though he by then dispatched a 1000 wives
another one's still pending his reviews.
For mere Sultanas bargain with their lives
while anchors act like virgin newlyweds
for many years to keep their talking heads.

Published in Poetry with Panache

Harsh Epiphany

Mahler's resurrection bells resounded
a bit prematurely at the concert
I went to the other night. Astounded
by prescient bird calls, I swooned, a convert
to eschatological broodings. Boy,
was I surprised by my awakening -
not to horizons of heavenly joy,
but by godless Verizon forsaking
me with a beeping cell phone! "O believe"
the chorus intoned, imbuing each word
with harmonies to heal wracked souls who grieve.
But how could I believe what I'd just heard?
Was I delivered by chorales that spell
salvation just to heed a bagatelle?

Published in Art Times

Picture Perfect Patronage

Prepare your album in a way that, should
a rogue intrude among the portraits, he'll
appear as someone up to nothing good.
But if the viewers skimming through it feel
he seems to look no different than the lot
of subjects seen before in photographs,
it might be difficult indeed to spot
subversive ones from those promoting laughs.
Of course, we're speaking mindsets here, not looks.
And those who see the former on a page
that's part of socially accepted books,
had better hope that mischief's not the wage
of failing to turn over some new leaf
from it, before their focus comes to grief.

Published in Wild Goose 2018

Back to the Real World, Huh?

Ah, yes! But you misunderstand my friend,
when you contend this workday world is real.
I'll bend to love's embrace at this days' end
and only then will I begin to feel!
The rush of fevered lips that fiercely press
on mine fans flames at dusk though fools inveigh
against diminished light. The meek transgress
harsh edicts of the day when night holds sway
to stay them from their flight. Amour's delight
alone informs. The rest is just a game
that children play to blunt their appetite.
Day's ashen face needs darkness to reclaim
itself. So, in my cradling arms stay curled,
and born to love start dying to the world.

Published in Places in the Heart

Amatory Reprieve

Love's thrall, he starts surrendering his arms
to love's expropriating limbs, both firm
and supple as her armory of charms.
His slackened muscles figuratively squirm
before her cold, excoriating stare.
How fast he fancies being in her charge
before the accusations he must bear,
though he remains a fugitive at large.
If wanting someone starts a fantasy
of summary arrest in her embrace,
without a sign of pending amnesty,
the high court of appeals is in her face.
How fast her smile, dispatching rays of light
into his cell, hence mitigates his plight.

Published in Places in the Heart

Guinevere

I've nothing to offer you on the field
of battle. I who'd vow damsels your age,
when a squire of desire, now gauge
your skills with awe. I feel like some liege kneeled
before a reigning lord whose realm is steeled
against assault. I'm keener to assuage
your moods or play the harmless sage than stage
revolts with javelins I cannot wield.
I serve and yield. For you've become the Sir
who firmly pulled from the sorcerer's stone
the salutary sword, Excalibur.
And I can neither challenge you who've thrown
a gauntlet in my face nor, daunted, stir
in futile flight from where my heart has flown.

Published in Places in the Heart

Death

What do I know of that relentless night
that most men fear? I only grasp the sleep
which every evening grants me some respite
from the astringent harvest which I reap
beneath day's scorching light. And what brief grief
ensues from death to match the ceaseless pain
at watching crimson fade to withered leaf?
In death there isn't either loss or gain
for those whose senses are like slabs of stone
that mark the locus where the grave souls meet
to mourn - aware they've grown still more alone.
Nor need we watch Time's harvester deplete
love's yield cross years that leave a barren field
for us to languish in. The only death
I fear is life enough to feel - congealed
in memory - her pulse and perfumed breath
who gave me rest from Life's harsh regimen;
and knowing that I won't find love again.

Published in Poets' Espresso, volume 13, issue #3

Managerial Waste

This Mother Nature is a spendthrift boss.
She hires many people every year,
Yet runs her corporation at a loss.
Nor does she hold her assets very dear.
For she dispatches young as well as old
to her retirement home beyond the grave
employment plan where they had been enrolled.
The rest may not genetically behave.
But she employs - with sloths - hormonal thieves
who tap into her funds for fiendish ends,
while her own tree of life bears withered leaves,
bereft of fruit and corporate dividends.
And she allots such profitable pay
to lowly messengers of DNA.

Published in Pennine Ink Magazine #39

A Musical Offering

What words obscure, concordance celebrates.
In duple meter or 3-quarter time,
how eloquently it accelerates
the pulse with neither metaphor nor rhyme.
No hackneyed linking of cocoon with June
to harmonize its speechless melody;
it only needs a memorable tune
to function as a gig or threnody.
And though it's deemed a vocal piece or lied
whose text receives the measure of each note,
it's hardly the semantics that we heed
but honeyed sounds the tonal blacksmith wrote.
For notwithstanding each resounding word
it's music's ringing sanction being heard.

Published in Paper Plates V8 #4

Bald Campaign

Now 8 blanched sentinels stand guard
above receding barricades,
while thinning ranks are fighting hard
at reinforcing rear brigades
in light of still retreating lines.
But it's complete futility
to try eradicating signs
which prove the inutility
of using even foreign aid
to bolster a collapsed defense.
And caught up in the windswept raid
of strands whose cover isn't dense
enough to dodge a hostile hand,
they quicken for their final stand.

Published in Long Story Short

The Knight's Lament

There was a time when one could leave armor
with the blacksmith so it could be hammered
back in shape. Those were the days when sober
minded people diligently mastered
their craft. Smithies worked hard, honing their trade
with pride. They worked quickly and did it well.
Now men, skilled at repairing what they made
have been replaced by those who only sell.
What's worn is discarded on the junk heap,
easily replaced by cheaper stuff. Oh!
We'll learn new techniques for uncommon needs
that won't require us to forge or sew.
It all will be disposable, of course.
But who will be around to shoe my horse?

Published in PKA Advocate
April/May 2016

Horseplay

The jockey should have heeded her request.
Instead of jumping over upright planks
with skills that put her in the envied ranks
of men, she'd be content with second best,
while grooming horses at her jock's behest.
She owes the latter, thus, ironic thanks
for steering her astride his filly's flanks
which she now races with commanding zest.
Beyond co-opting his presumptive role
of spurring stallions on their driven course
with dauntless execution and control,
she proves herself to be the potent source
of agency pursuant to a goal
that ultimately may lead to divorce.

Published in PKA Advocate
April/May 2016

For Rebecca

I plodded through the store that you've since left,
remembering when you were working there.
Your absence made me feel somewhat bereft.
The shelves containing goods I'd buy seemed bare
of any meaning that they'd lead to you
when being checked out by a cold cashier.
A grieving mother sadly passing through
the room where just a week before she'd hear
her daughter's voice, it brought into relief
a presence I'm resigned to see no more,
except as sad enforcers of my grief.
Then why should I go back into that store
that's stocked with bitter memories and bile
and you're an absence in each cluttered aisle?

Published in PKA Advocate, April/May 2016

Sleuthing Miss

I never met a girl with spunk and class
like her. Complaining that I lost the book
which I'd once lent to the vivacious lass,
she stared ahead with a forsaken look.
It resonated with a sense of blame
and loss of honor she would hence set right,
if merely to preserve her worthy name.
With only pride to aid her in her fight
I knew the fugitive would soon be caught,
while she investigated every nook
and cranny to uncover what she sought.
Indeed, she'd forge ahead by hook or crook.
And sure enough the suspect would be found,
and hand delivered to me safe and sound.

Published in POETS' ESPRESSO REVIEW, AUTUMN 2016

Misled

I coyly lead you to the dancing floor
presuming to encourage you to swing.
But claiming that my dancing skills are poor,
you move me like a puppet on a string.
You iterate "goladdy dally oop"
intensely. Nonsense syllables to tease
strained rhythms from your thrall. They slyly dupe
my mind like alcohol and put the squeeze
on me. I shrink to fawning ingénue
who you, with deft maneuvers, soon control.
Indeed, with baffling steps and babbled cues,
you overwhelm my body and my soul.
And feeling helpless in your guiding hands,
I cringe imagining your next commands.

Published in Poets' Espresso Review
Summer 2015,vol 12 #3

Condescending Carnie

She warmed to kids I had in tow
while pitching for the vaunted prize
at the amusement park. A wise,
maternal sort, she'd let me throw -
if just to see the children's glow -
more bummers than a dollar buys.
Indeed, she nursed me to their size
by auditing my feeble show
of force - or ineffective aim -
while grooming me to mend my skill
to that suggesting better game.
And thus, inspired to fulfill
her expectations, I'd soon claim
the fancied fruit of her goodwill.

Published in Poets' Espresso Review, Summer 2016, v. 12

Kittens Behind Glass Door

Was ever there a sight more sad?
Three kittens looking for their Mom
and kneading each clawed, fleshy pad
beneath their feet as though for balm
of Mother's milk - which can't be had.
For she sits mewing with alarm
that her fresh litter - pawing mad
behind locked doors of Taco Tom -
might just as well be armor-clad
for all she can give suckle from
her teats. That man must be a cad
who left them thus, without a qualm,
while I look on, a prayerful Dad,
with clasped palms poised as for a psalm.

Published in Poets' Espresso Review
Spring 2016 v12 issue 6

Cat-nipped

How quickly you positioned to attack
me when your feline senses smelled a rat.
And not because I didn't stroke your back,
or offer you a quilted welcome mat.
But sensing hostile vibes, you ceased to purr
while opening your kneading paws to claws.
And I who'd confidently stroked your fur
became a helpless morsel in your jaws.
It gave me pause to think my wounded face
provoked the predator in you to stalk
the dogged intruder of your peaceful place.
And so you forced me to take heed and balk.
Content I was resigned to tow the line,
you stretched for warmth, seductively supine.

Published in PKA's Advocate, August/Sept 2016

Cat Burglar

Domestic felines have nine lives.
But why should they apply to wives?
Aside from those investments made
together, where they should be paid
back what essentially is theirs,
should wives be heirs of millionaires
because they last year married one,
and with the money chose to run?
Of course, where children are concerned,
no matter what each partner's earned,
they have to be provided for
necessities. But nothing more
than what their father's love and means
afford them till they're in their teens.
The rest is generosity
to children and the divorcee.

Published in PKA's ADVOCATE

Der Rosenkavalier

I don't believe in miracles.
I only know the aging Marschallin,
rising before the tabernacle
of the heart-stopping dawn;
slowing up the flow of time
clocked across her puzzled face.
"In God's name", she will grow resigned
to giving up with solemn grace,
the young Octavian who, in her place,
holds Sophie in his arms.
His former love's by younger love, displaced;
her love transformed to that of chaperone.
Out of the bittersweet formality
of stale custom's silver rose,
a blushing fervor crimsons Sophie's
cheek which now, "in Gottes Namen" glows
with young love's golden luster.
Yearning churns the bawdy measures of a waltz
to sparkling clusters of conversant stars.
The stage is paved for the servant boy
to brush away the mist that grows with a hankie's wave,
imparting solace solid as the tonic close.

Published in Congruence Fall 2016

Cribbed Agency

(after a grating entrée)

No matter how I madly strove
to make sense of the garlic clove
the waitress gave me with my plate,
it simply made me more irate.
And thus, like a rambunctious child,
I called her to me, half beguiled
that I could make the gal accede
to claims of my frustrated need.
But rather than impart polite
directives for my addling plight,
she seized the garlic with her hand
and, seemingly to reprimand
me, served it on a piece of bread,
while I bemoaned what lay ahead.

Published in The Society of Classical Poets
June 2016

Turning Tables

"He's being co-operative," she told
her boss, like one interrogating me,
and not a waitress serving casserole.
Perhaps she feared - discerning my esprit-
I'd try to breach the wall of the control
she exercised with an indulgent charm
compatible with her maternal role.
Indeed, how fast she managed to disarm
my cocksure manner, even as she'd shape
my sensibilities till in accord
with hers. Nor was I anxious to escape
the fantasy of being deemed her ward.
I heeded the assessment that she made,
and grew excited that I'd made the grade.

Co-operation didn't feel like much
of an intimidating exercise
concerning someone with that tender touch.
For who's the guy insisting otherwise
who spent his childhood at the mother's breast?
Remembrance of dependence still remains,
and I had neither will nor way to test
resources that she had, or lift my chains.

Indeed, the maître d' attested he
would see me soon while I approached the door
to leave. And pointing at her, I said she
would be the person I'd be looking for;
not as a knight to damsels wooed with sword,
but as a vassal to his feudal lord.

Published in The Society of Classical Poets
June 2016

Julie

Beleaguering her for the kind remark
my fortune cookie said would warm a frost,
I dressed myself in shark skin to embark
on my constrained desire to accost
this waitress. She just purred that I was cute!
No patronizing nod to manly pride
to make me feel like some stud in pursuit
of pleasure she'd indulgently provide.
She made of me a child of her conceit;
a plaything she'd adroitly entertain
until she made maternal whims complete.
In any case, while I played ardent swain
whose courting tactics were somewhat amiss,
she smothered me with eiderdowns of bliss.

Published in The Society of Classical Poets
June 2016

Love Forlorn

How well the seeds of passion taking root
from smatterings of chatter in the brain,
had generated hopes of future fruit.
Propitious memories would serve as rain
to whet the appetite to meet again
for five more weeks. But hence, you weren't there
in your seductive efflorescence when
I'd hoped to pluck the rosebuds from your hair.
Instead the bristly waiters seen were male
who, demonstrating artfully they care,
seemed more evocative of rankling hail
that plunders husbandry, or prickly pear.
Nor was I just content to watch them breed
in spite of me, but stomached them like weed

that strangled my love's garden of delight.
Each kindling sprout became a mockery.
And buds of summer blossomed like a blight
that singed my strangled sensibility.
I huddled in their presence like a fading spray
that lingers haplessly upon a branch
which, pregnant once as any bud in May,
is fated on its withered twig to blanch.

I neither had the will nor way to bloom
beside the dried up season of my dreams.
I just craved room to morbidly exhume
the reasons for my lover's seeming schemes.
My labored steps now trod with rank dismay,
and stomp to dust each rosebud in my way.

Published online in Society of Classical poets with antepenultimate line of first sonnet different and unrhymed.

Lost Quatrain

I'm inconsolable in my remorse.
What matter that I wrote those lines again
by tapping into my creative source?
What's lost is lost. Though pregnant womb or pen
engendered it, its absence sears the brain
with phantom presences whose flesh and bone
remind us they're the progeny of pain.
Resurgent labor spawned a twin or clone.
But rather than replace the child that's lost,
the other only brings into relief
emotional investments and the cost
conceiving it, intensifying grief.
Thus, losing what my muses helped create
I wallow in implacable self-hate.

Published in The Society of Classical Poets
June 2016

Brief Encounter

If you had scorned my overtures
of friendship and, with scathing yawn,
dismissed my amatory lures,
I would have stoically since drawn
the curtain on the show's sole act.
But exiting before the play
concluded made me rue my tact
at walking flippantly away.
Aside from props and scenic dress
ensuing as the dividends
of many dramas that progress
as such, I won't know how mine ends.
I rail thus on an empty stage
where want of closure is my wage.

I'd sooner have performed a scene
with me as suppliant for love,
while you proceeded to demean
my protestations with a shove.
Perhaps an after-theater jaunt -
if only out of courtesy -
that ended in a restaurant
where you were gracious company,

but showed not even slight concern
for friendship or an ardent vow.
What a melodramatic turn
it would have been, in light of how
I thought the drama would play out.
But I'd be spared regret and doubt.

1st verse previously published in Pulsar Poetry Webzine Sept, 2016

Prophylactic Measures

Like any doctor versed in patient care,
the campus carry, gun rights advocate
had listened to the PhD's despair.
For students now bear guns, while poised to get
an education in philosophy.
She heard with empathy the gal's concern
that arguing could spell catastrophe,
should prickly issues make the passions churn
in those who have another point of view.
She then prescribed her Prozac for the soul,
consisting in a sober talking to,
before advising her on arms control:
"Don't just be an ass and don't – bottom line -
assault somebody, and you should be fine."

Published in Antarctica Journal, 8/1/16

Heartless at the Checkout Line

"I'd never take my anger out on you,"
she said, when I remarked she looked so piqued
I had the inclination to skidoo.
As someone who desired her, I freaked
out at the dewdrops missing from her ears,
the stern configuration of her lips,
her strident voice and mortifying leers.
Since these impediments did not eclipse
my longing, they enhanced the rankling sense
of rupture from the ego that seemed dear
to me. Indeed, my zeal had grown intense
enough, she had no reason to cashier
me, or to "take my anger out on you."
A policy position I would rue.

Published in Antarctica Journal, 8/14/16

Strangers Waiting For 2 Different Trains

We both spent hours waiting on the line
for a ticket to Shakespeare in the Park.
I saw her on the blades of grass, supine
while I stood up behind her on a lark
I'd talk to her. "What's the play about,"
she asked, before I knelt on down beside
her to explain, 'The Tempest', and to tout
its virtues. In this way we would ride the tide
of conversation – where we lived and worked –
up to the marble benches to await
the final call for tickets. Fears that lurked
within us proved correct. It was our fate
to leave disconsolate. But still a pair
who, in the subway station, would forswear

our bond. I felt we both were on death row,
with each deliberating who'd go first.
Is she who suffers most the last to go?
The fate of him preceding her is worst.
For he's the one compelled to make a choice
and indirectly tie the hangman's noose.
The other one just heeds the fateful voice
of someone who administers abuse.

I wish it had been she who took the train
that sped off into anonymity,
obliging me to bear love's lesser pain
of dealing with implacability.
Instead, I feel remorse up to the hilt
that I left her to bear survivor's guilt.

Published in Antarctica Journal, 8/22/16

Sponging Up Succor

I'm suffering through vinegary days,
as if I'm Jesus at His Calvary.
Arrested from my customary ways
by modern versions of its harsh decree,
I bend beneath the burden of my cross.
Recalling laurels in Jerusalem,
I'm painfully reminded of my loss
who sport a fool's cap for a diadem.
As I secure my seat at the ballet
amidst the blissful crowd, I yearn for years
of passion, rather than this passion play.
And yet, at intermission, flouting peers,
some Magdalena's kind libations spoil
me at the bar, from which I don't recoil.

Published in Antarctica Journal 8/30/16

Affaires de Coeur

What kind of skirmishes are these?
Us soldiers must surrender arms
we've sheathed, so savvy gals can seize
them in exchange for arms in harm's
way! Even then, while being hard
pressed to besiege their citadel,
our thrust is stopped by flanks that guard
its entrance. Thus, our legions swell
in numbers that cannot retreat
until we forge ahead on terms
that all but guarantee defeat.
For an incursion just affirms
captivity inside a realm
where gals sit at their country's helm.

Published by CC & D
Scars Publication
online February 2016

Mindscapes

When we're together all the flowers fade
before the brilliance of your noonday sun.
But when I walk alone I seem to wade
in blooms that carpet carnivals of fun.
Of course, the daffodils are always there,
along with tulip, buttercup and rose -
receding to the background when your air
of ripeness with its budding leaves dispose
me to the verdant arbor of your arms.
For all the shades and shapes of Nature pale
before the fresh effusions of your charms.
But when I tread a solitary trail,
the field is filled with fumbling bees
that mock me with their revelries.

Published in Miller's Pond Poetry
Sept 2016

Appetizer

Steering me past patrons to my table,
she sets my place. I mull the menu's fare,
riveted by doubt, as though unable
to choose except for her insistent stare.
She beckons for my order as she serves
the bread, then deftly sets the silverware.
Impulsively she hustles husks of hair
round pithy ears as tempting as hors d'oevres.
Arrested, I adopt a thin veneer
of mock sophistication, less to shake
off glares that galvanize her cavalier
demeanor, than to nurse a scrumptious ache
of cribbed volition. I parry for room
from the seductive scent of her perfume -

then realize I must learn to speak again;
not just because my diction isn't clear,
but more so that my sibilants attend
the prodding inclinations of her ear.
Its winsome whorls conspire to cajole
my stunted manhood into waking dreams
predating any vestige of control.
Reduced to a stew of spewing phonemes,

I fancy that she gitchee-gitchee-goos
my coos to romper rooms of infancy,
and shushes restive sighs with peek-a-boos.
And then to consummate this reverie,
cavorting with the tresses of her hair,
I swoon beside her blossoming au pair.

Published in Miller's Pond
September 2016

Dangling Keys

I reel in fish I'd otherwise refuse.
For with the inability to cast
my rod, I've lost the competence to choose.
And so I nibble every chance repast.
Let anglers spurn the muddy riverbed,
or arm themselves to plumb the depths for shark.
I follow passion's tide to where I'm led
by darting trout, a lure or floating bark.
I have a self-consuming appetite
for things that lose distinction in the sea.
And since I'm driven by the need to bite
with indiscriminating gluttony,
I'm apt to chase each ripple in the wave
as if it were the nourishment I crave.

Published in Think Journal

Coffee Klatch

Religions are like rumors promulgated by employees about the nature of their boss. Some say he lives in another country. Others that he's an old man with a stickler for giving orders that he passes down through an intricate chain of command. Financiers say that he gave up the business he started a long time ago to his son who's hip and more accessible than he is. Apparently he has less stringent concerns than his old man. A few say his company's more or less run by a board of directors and that no one's specifically in charge. Still others believe the boss disguises himself as a lowly clerk who patiently brooks being pushed about just to gauge the merits of each of his employees. In this way he'll decide who gets promoted and who'll get the pink slip. Finally there are those who believe he's black or even a woman, mocking the prejudiced minds of his workers. Be it as it may, since no one knows for sure, it's best we do our jobs with respect and diligence.

Published August 2016
Tipton Poetry Journal #31

Giant Grievance
(after Wagner's Ring)

I scarcely understand the gods
for whom Valhalla had been built
by our conscientious clods.
We honored strictures to the hilt
and labored in obedience
to laws and contracts that they made
to spare us inconvenience.
Yet, nonetheless, we weren't paid.
For each injunction we obeyed
that gave them and their peers a boost,
became the fertile eggs we laid
for chickens to. come home to roost.
No apples of eternal youth
that we'd been promised to take hold
of, as our gods grew long in tooth.
Instead, they dazzled us with gold.
And undermining their own laws,
they cheated us to loud guffaws.

They claimed such laws were sacrosanct
that made us pall at drudging toil
for meager benefits. They banked
on craft to use our sweat as oil
to lubricate the gears of state.
Our brothers were the ones who'd grunt
beneath the laws they legislate.
And while we meekly bore the brunt
of service to protect their wealth,
they undermined their very base
of operations, using stealth
to pave our pathway to disgrace.
Then wages that we justly earned
were parlayed into useless gold,
ripped off when Sigmund's son returned
just like those prescient Norns foretold.
We banked on rights that each man craves,
while duty-bound we dug our graves.

Previously Published Blue Collar Review

Lauding Manhattan's Subway Engineers

(during Super Storm Sandy)

Technicians are the lifeblood of the state.
What use are pulmonary financiers
or arteries whose tracks facilitate
mass transit when the plumbing's in arrears?
For networks of essential services
are blocked, along with phones and internet,
that just increases people's nervousness.
We're lost with no technicians to abet
mass transit's underground lymphatic nodes
through tunnels. Filtering salt pathogens,
these experts purge the water that corrodes
electric grids. What saving regimens!
For even concerts, theater, dance and art
need technical resources to impart

their salutary ointment on our wounds.
But how can cultural infusions start
through capillaries when inopportune
disruption of mass transit eats the heart
of our society by hurricanes?

While academics may prescribe the cure,
blue collar doctors, clearing muck from veins,
are needed with a pump and ligature
to siphon off and stay the massive flood
that plagues the state. It's skillful toil, well-spent,
that helps the city's muscles pump the blood
which courses from the heart of government
into the limbs of burdened denizens
that constitutes a nation's benisons.

Previously Published in Blue Collar Review

Supergirl's Down

(but Kara in a single bound)

When clubbing, my wife's super in reverse.
With a cartoonish flair she dons a wig
that's blonde and sports a Valentino purse.
And yet, at home, the born brunette's a prig
who keeps her criminally wayward spouse
in line. She soars, with two kids in her arm,
into the second landing of our house
till they're tucked into bed, secure from harm.
She overpowers prowlers on the run,
though she's in her pajamas half asleep,
with nothing spurring her to brave a gun,
except the spouse and children in her keep.
But Fridays when we dance, the gaudy gush
of red and blue that saturates her cape
becomes mascara. And the facial blush
that brings into relief her sylphlike nape
destroys her competence like Kryptonite,
till home, au naturel, she's braced to fight.

Published in Old Red Kimono, Spring 2016

Cotton Chains

How easily will love enslave.
She humors you with a command.
You heed it since you understand
that this provides the warmth you crave.
You didn't slavishly behave
but ran the errands to expand
your hopes. You took her subtle brand
of force as firewood to pave
a kindling path to passion's flame.
It's easy to be duped like this.
At first it's like a gambler's game
where your reward's a sullen kiss.
And then you wallow in your shame
where pains are gains you sorely miss.

Published in The Pen, July 2016

Chasing Shadows

Foreboding snuffed the twilight of my years,
till I was left with ghosts to entertain
before the setting sun hid scorching tears
and mocked the efflorescence of my pain.
I groped with desperation in the dark
to light my way before the laughter died,
and left me only memories to mark
the remnants of ambition's downward slide.
As such I strayed, a worn, embittered man
who daily finds it harder not to fall
while I pursue life's passing caravan
deriding me with its seductive call.
For love in time will leave me far behind
while I rail at a world that's deaf and blind.

Published in Quantum Leap, #75

Caveat Emptor

Some frauds, espousing liberal views,
endorse a country ruled by laws,
if only so they're free to choose
which ones among a host of flaws
can claim due process; as opposed
to those crimes that they prosecute
when such infractions are disclosed
to trump those of their own pursuit.
Ironically, they use the chance
provided by a trusting state
to foist on us the governance
that they seem predisposed to hate.
And then, when laws they've trampled down
are spurned, they wear a righteous frown.

Published in Quantum Leap #77

Interior Monologue

(Girl with Smart Phone)

Though it's no mace, but cell phone in my hand,
I'd like to favor you. But I've a slew
of messages whose import countermand
desires of my awestruck retinue
who pass me with petitions on the street.
Because of this, I claim the royal right
to read my e-mail following a tweet
to devotees while you keep me in sight.
Indeed, not only are my hands not free,
but texting makes it difficult to turn,
acknowledging those holding doors for me.
Thus, I can't give the gratitude you yearn
for who suppose a royal highness grants
indulgence to her abject sycophants.

Published in Wild Violet 9/25/16

Game 5 of the 2015 World Series

(pitcher perfect through 8 innings)

"Call no man happy till after his death,"
Montaigne wrote. If, Harvey had died before
the ninth and not professed a second breath,
the Kansas City A's might not have scored
the tying runs that helped them win the game
against the Mets. Yet, Harvey's taken out
after he gives up an opening walk,
and the next batter manages to clout
a double. Hence he feels he shouldn't balk
at managers affording him relief
pitching before he's forced to brook the blame.
He seethes inside the dugout wracked with grief.
Instead of sitting out the victory
the pitcher in relief might have secured
to complement his valedictory,
a loss in extra innings was assured.
I watch him as his heart appears to break,
while I'm no less despondent at the wake.

Published in Bryant Literary Review
winter Issue 2016

Ravaged Quilt

The fabric of my life has come apart.
My girlfriend's egress tore into its seam.
A pending hurricane delayed the start
of fireworks the city poised to stream,
like artwork in its weave. But where's my spread
of old - embroidered with a merchant ship
veneered with gold? It lost its figurehead
on weathered cloth that now begins to rip.
The country's debt and job loss punctured holes
inside its battered hull whose disrepair
wants bedding worthiness. Its wrinkled folds
are boarded by a corporate corsair.
Depression takes the wind out of its sails.
And though it veer from keeling, what avails
against the countless launderings it took?
Embellished images began to fade
when sent to banked-on cleaners who forsook
the azure satin where the ship would wade.
The well-knit apertures that served as stores -
astride a lining meant to reinforce
the meshwork - sink beneath its threadbare shores.

There's little left to stay the dismal course
the inlays of my comforter must take.
It soon must be upholstered or replaced
with printed schooners sailing in their wake
on hackneyed patterns; neither stitched nor interlaced.
And I miss jettisoned amenities
so intertwined with its remembered frieze.

Published in Poets' Espresso, v.12, issue #7, summer 2016

Parlor Tricks

"Is that not what the spider told the fly?"
I asked her when she urged me, "Come inside,
and get your box gift-wrapped." It was a tie
in to promotions I was bound to bide.
No sooner did I warm up to the bait,
and she secured her quarry in her hand
than, gossamer-like she began to prate
about a charity I'd understand
she started. And because her words wove silk -
with smiles for spinnerets - I'd not resist
entreaties for donations. Thus, she'd bilk
me, as she snared my box with wrap. A twist
of ribbon tied her captive with a bow.
And bounty bottled, I was good to go.

Published in Haight Ashbury Literary Journal

Ghostwriter

The poem became the key to enter rooms
I otherwise would balk to walk inside.
Therein I found those demons laid in tombs
that years ago had left me sorely tried.
But bedding down where opportunists lie
ensures I wake with Mephistopheles
as mouthpiece to the passions I decry
with honed poetic sensibilities.
They always were a problem to ignore
when I just heard them murmuring within.
But strutting through the halls on metaphor
gave what were haunted words another spin
than when they dressed up as a bugaboo.
And now they pass discreetly in review.

Alas, I didn't have the faintest clue
that there were muses who would badger me
until that evening I would later rue.
For, riding shotgun, my anxiety
advised I detour into their garage.
Along with ghosts I'd grown familiar with,
it introduced a literate ménage
of phantoms dressed in simile and myth.

This made it easy for me to abide
those imps whose once ill-tailored clothes
required me to keep them locked inside.
Now I play host to their poetic pose.
And even as I'm rummaging about
the house, I worry I may not get out.

Published in Pointed Circle 32nd edition
Fall '16 with another couplet to first sonnet.

Getting Tanned

Be wary when subverting rules
to bridge the sexual divide.
For gals possess the basic tools
that tanners use to soften hide.
And once the scraper's in her hand
and she excises flesh from bone,
her industry's a reprimand
to frilly garments she's outgrown.
Soft fingers forfeit past allure
since hardened by the pickling salt.
And with her competence to cure
raw hides, she does them by default.
But once her buckskin's been displayed,
the hidebound mavericks get frayed.

Published in Conceit Magazine September 2017

Breast in Peace

"The average guy likes two things: sports and tits,"
she told me as I stifled reprimands.
For she not just used language that befits
a jock, but stole the thunder from my hands.
Indeed, I'd ceded to that verbal thrust
of phallic potency she dared to wield -
although I'd sheathed my macho blade in trust.
I wondered if I'd soon be forced to yield
to her, whose joust subverted gender terms.
In any case, her breast became a sword
that cut me down to mewling babe who squirms
for placement while he sucks the milky hoard.
And when she broke off half a roll for me
to eat, I scarfed it up with shameless glee.

Published in Conceit Magazine 2017

Shuttering Radio Shack

Like a dying carcass in an electronics jungle, Radio Shack lumbers, exposed to all the elements of economic uplift and decline. Since corporate giants swallowed up their peers, it lies there with finances in arrears. And its body's an open sesame to avaricious shoppers. An invading army of consumer ants starts picking on its cut-rate inventory till the shelving supporting it starts slanting forward. Its armature begins protruding through the merchandise like meatless bones. Stop motion photography could not have done a better job displaying the swiftness of its decomposition. Today I see the shelves are bare. Their bones stare back at me with a spare, metallic glare. The musculature that bore so much inventory bears witness to the Shack's once bristling business. I see nothing on the store's painted concrete plain but skeletal remains, and a gaping note of closure on its door.

PUBLISHED IN ASCENT ASPIRATIONS 2/11/17

Prophylactic Encounter

I scarcely thought her bedroom was smack in the heart of the pharmacy. But the way she glared at me, it could have grown out of her heckling hide, or else she wore peripatetic bedding to bide what was bugging her. Anodynes - seemingly secreted in crevices of her salutary skin at the express check-out counter - it's not surprising she locked horns with mine in the safe of her incubating mindset. Bedded near proscriptive drugs, she wore Rx pants like sackcloth for the bulldog barter. Her lethal looks infected me like a syringe inoculating a viral glance. With clinical duress, she measured passion's pulse, poised to fend off a lubricious encounter. Was I a druggy, rummaging through the philter of her medicine cabinet looking for an angry fix? Ginseng notwithstanding, there's no hospice in this supreme deceit of courtship. And so armed with my doctored addiction I pay for my Pillsbury mixture like a flattened doughboy kneaded to leavened flour rising. With the salubrious jewels in my hand, I paid Miss Glam Puss with a post-transactional "Thank you, ma'am."

Published in poetry and Prose with Panache, February 2017

The Blessed Virgin Chastises the Infant Jesus

(after the painting by Max Ernst)

Although the child possesses rank
when swanked by saints in Heaven's sphere,
He swallows pride astride her shank
while she raps penance on his rear -
despite presumptive blasphemy.
Albeit not of woman born,
and sworn to bear the cross for me,
He's not above a woman's scorn
when matters turn to discipline.
For no one is above her law
who's swaddled with a diaper pin -
regardless of prophetic awe.
And since He suffers every man's
development at woman's hands

His kingly crown has tumbled down
beside her. She, with feet apart,
imparts with unforgiving frown
harsh blessings from an anguished heart.
For though He's God's anointed son,

He's spared no trials while on her knee
who, faithfully, has just begun
to trod the road to Calvary.
Indeed. If he'd redeem His flock
He needs ambassadors on earth
who lovingly make us take stock
of life before our second birth.
As such, He raises from the tomb
the blistered fruit of woman's womb.

Published in Bindweed Magazine, February 2017

Mourning Sickness

(the day after losing to Donald Trump)

How like a mother poised to bring to term
what would have been the distaff side's first born,
must Hillary appear amidst the sturm
und drang development. Her fans are torn
to hear gestation periods so long
could bring to bear such inauspicious fruit.
They're gathering to find out what went wrong
with a delivery that seemed astute.
Forget a baby shower's diaper packs,
as Secretaries line her cabinet
with Treasurer, Defense, and State - like cracks
inside a ceiling made of glass. Regrets
alone inform her mortuary mood,
like hens on hatches that they failed to brood.

Published in Bindweed Magazine Feb 2017

Free Throw

Imagine if Dan Sterling's senile rants
were not made public to the autocrats
who smugly dictate what we can and can't
communicate to girlfriends in our flats?
Our black Americans would still be riled
by fruits of their oppressed ancestors' plight.
and street gangs would be running wild,
ensuring that their neighbors heed their might.
But now that Sterling's forced to sell his share
of ownership by Teflon corporate shirts,
the black community will get a fair
proportion of the wealth for all the hurts
inflicted on them. Poverty's passé
when knights in mail that shine like silver slay

with magic dragons those who scarcely puff.
Forget a hundred years of slavery.
A sacrificial goat appears enough
to show the world belated bravery.
Who cares if it's 200 years too late
to fight the battle when it mattered most?

They also serve the cause who sit and wait
self-righteously to trumpet a riposte
against offenses in an old man's brains.
Instead of reparations to oppressed
descendants of those victimized by gains
acquired thus, those presently obsessed
to compensate the loss of photo ops
to jocks, insist this worse injustice stops.

PUBLISHED IN BINDWEED MAGAZINE FEBRUARY 2017

Relay Race

We're all destinies waiting to unfold.
Oh, moral pundits say we're free to choose.
But what we do already was foretold
by options and desires that infuse
our sensibilities. And each, in turn,
upon Life's fast, deterministic track,
is factored in the road map where we'll learn
about a future that was programmed back
millennia ago. We're left to reap
the harvest of our own and other deeds.
Their fruits - before we're on the rubbish heap -
themselves possess the germinating seeds
informing generations still to come
believing they're the whereto and wherefrom.

Published in Poetic Diversity November 2016

Inflammatory Verse

Why would you entertain a renegade
to compromise your enterprising mind?
Although a foursquare sonnet's to be made
his rebel bent will put you in a bind.
For now you'll either have to let him in
and brook the consequence of broken law,
or keep him out with his subversive grin
revealing an incendiary flaw.
And yet, your verbal finery conceals
his mischievous intent behind a set
of quatrains and a couplet. This appeals
to sensibilities that will abet
the fugitive to snuggle in your breast,
while you, unwitting host, will scarcely rest.

Published in Westview v.33, issue 2, Sept. '18

After Terrorist Bombings

(9/11/01 in NYC)

Today everybody is my brother.
Today, the slit throat of a stewardess
afflicts me like the death of my mother.
Tonight, an orphan's cries kindle my distress;
a hijacked airplane shapes a patriot,
as if invaders stormed my brother's house
with guns. My language is our polyglot
of tongues, and every woman is my spouse
who seeks out solace for the loss of hers.
I'm shaken, blasted out of comfort zones
in the safety of my bed. Saboteurs
break my bones, and beams fall like ten ton stones
thrown at me. From my scorched fireplace, I reap
the ash interring friends I've lost, and weep.

Published in "Time of Singing" Fall 2014

Customer Support

What retrogressive interchange is this?
Locked out of access to the internet,
I must petition a maternal miss
to authorize a password that will let
me navigate it safely for a day,
till trusted to select one of my choice.
She even called my mobile, on the way,
to lend an ear should I have qualms to voice
concerning the instructions that she gave.
Her motherly solicitude made sure
that I could access roads she helped me pave.
Chagrined at first at her divestiture
of my autonomy, now left alone,
I wax nostalgic at the cradled phone.

Published in The Stray Branch
Spring, Summer 2014

Ardent Caveat

For those obsessed with women, I can show
you that the wiser thing is letting go.
She may be just a one night stand or, oh!
the woman of those dreams that sandmen blow
into the bunk bed of one's bungalow.
But clinging men must reap the fruits they sow
when they refuse to heed a woman's "No".
Yes! Sadly, there might be those women – though
I may seem paranoid - who let buds grow
dependent on their jutting branches so
that they could feel the warming afterglow
of cutting striplings from their kindling bough.
But that's why it's important to bestow
upon one's world an infinite tableau.
Though tempest-tossed, become a Prospero
whose magic power is a quid pro quo
of finding happiness in what you know.
For love becomes a constant curio
to those who just sit back and let it flow.

Published in Miller's Pond, winter 2015

Housebroken

Since he's already learned each trick
she otherwise would have to teach
him, his response is double quick
to facial gesturing or speech.
Thus she'd be daft to have him chained
and make him wonder what's beyond
her sphere of influence. For trained
with doting love, he's grown so fond
of her. He happily retrieves
her slippers when she comes home bushed,
and gets assurance when she leaves.
him for her office, once she's shushed
him with a kiss. And rain or fog,
he isn't loath to walk her dog.

Published in Miller's Pond
Winter 2015

An Actor's Lament

It was in the middle of my famous soliloquy.
The one that brought the house down
in my prime. But not anymore.
I must have muffed my lines,
slurred the words, or teased them
to a tedium. Perhaps there was an edge
of desperation in my voice, or it lacked
conviction; full of empty gestures
and posturing. I should have let the words
speak for themselves, and put aside
the throbbing, sobbing theatrics.
Maybe they saw puffing under my bleary eyes,
surmised I'd seen better days, or were just
damned tired of listening to the blasted thing
for the umpteenth time! Who knows? If I did,
I would have done better, whatever that means
in a world where being good is gall enough.
It's enough they're leaving in droves,
for whatever reason, and it'll get worse
before the season ends, and only closest friends
go scrambling at the box office, like vultures
swooping down on a mangled carcass.

The rest are leaving with all sorts of excuses:
wives, husbands, mistresses, children to feed,
foodstuffs on the stove. And most of them
will not return. Divorced, widowed, tired of living,
they move away, or stay and age in furnished rooms,
and die, sooner or later. I can't hold them all,
passing through the world like sand
in an hourglass. What do they want from me?
To hold them by the wrist, feel their pulse,
and tell them which way their blood flows?
It's enough that we don't drop dead.
That we can still wonder if it's any use
to have blood flowing through our veins
rather than water, air, fire, or just the muck
of the earth where the worms keep fucking us.

But I'll resist complaining. All change is for the better in the crazed turnings of this ever-changing world. So if fair weather turns foul and the howling wind begins its bulldog reckoning, I know it could always be worse than what it is. So I never die to one dissipation without celebrating another. And when God's henchman appears, advancing like a prancing cavalier, with his chalk-white mask and a fatal diagnosis, I'll dance my changes. Not like a blushing school-girl waiting to be asked, but like Shiva, brandishing cataclysmic fire on the edge of the next universe. I'll laugh in his face if it's a man, kiss it if it's a woman, and piss on everything that doesn't sing its changes. I fart for the joy of passing wind.

Published in Red River Review, winter/Feb '15

Elephantiasis

To ignore the thorns of virtue's rose is
like trying not to think of that hidebound
elephant. The more I'd quit the mammoth,
the surer is it that I can't. The more
I'd free my horny brain of pachyderm,
the larger looms his big and burly frame.
As long as purging woodland fires burn,
I'm sure to find him foraging the plain.
And though, at last, he's caged and blocked from view
outside the bedroom door, his proboscis
tickles my nose until I smell a zoo.
Buried in this jungle of neurosis,
I lie in bed with sackcloth for my pants,
stampeded by a herd of elephants.

Published in Red River Review
winter Feb '15

Vespers

Withdrawing to the anteroom, I lay
disconsolate before its gilded shrine,
and bowed my head in folded arms to pray.
I importuned God for redemptive signs
confirming that he heard my plea for grace.
But learned-by-rote invocatory lines,
which I'd been taught from childhood to embrace,
seemed futile next to closed Venetian blinds.
With sun-conversant eyes, I pulled them up
and slung my parched petition at the sky.
There, torch-lit congregations hung my cup
of grief which scaled the heavens for reply.
Night's shroud then flared,
as though my prayers were heard
by pulsing stars that never said a word.

Published in Stepping Stones

Beleaguered

Odysseus could barely make the grade
when battered by an unrelenting storm.
Then temptress sirens cunningly parlayed
their parlous straits to let mirages form.
For since he brooked slim chance of reaching shore,
still less of entertaining nuptial thrills,
what use was steadfast steering anymore,
or plying vaunted navigating skills?
Arresting music made him veer off course
while he was left to rail against the wind
in lieu of finding its demonic source.
For piqued Poseidon, not his sailors, pinned
him to the mast that devastated hope
and shrank horizons to his fancy's scope.

Published in Quantum Leap Poetry Magazine
February 2013

Hot Chocolate with Attitude

I tell her not to cap the cup
she's blithely topped with frothy cream,
that I'm prepared to gobble up
before it starts to melt in steam.
No toddler could exert less sway
than I do. For she snaps the lid
in place, gainsaying my dismay
with no more than a "god forbid
you sue me if you burn your hand."
She neither listens nor demurs
with reasons I would understand.
But like I'm just a ward of hers,
whose predilections grate her nerves,
I drink the bitter cup she serves.

Published in SEEMS #50 2016

Mother Superior

For you who doubt the species has a will
that contravenes the individual,
you've never had to feel the caustic chill
of being haplessly residual
to children that a mother holds in tow
as she parades them down the city streets.
These mothers think their procreative feat's
a civic virtue worthy of a show
that stops the city traffic in its tracks.
Forget the ambulance, the parish priest
or workers bearing steel beams on their backs.
The first among us are considered least
before those ladies heeding Nature's call
to harness teeming traffic to a crawl.

Published in Gemini 2015

On Foreign Shores

The flashing amber of your eyes
rouses me from sleep.
Ferocious hounds gnash at my loins
as I stumble into custody.
You whisper strange worlds
In the cochlea of my ear
as I scrutinize your face.
I map out its intricate topography
like a mariner in a strange land.
The air is humid, filled with the pungent
exhalations of your sultry breath.
I sway to the rhythm of your seething pulse.
You smile, hover over me,
hair cascading like fragrant
folds of drapery. I buckle under
the sweet duress of insistent kisses,
searching secret places.
Your probing fingers breach
me. My wide-eyed stare
seems fixed into the gaping visage
of a vanquished knight.

Pinned by rapid firings
of your body, I brace myself
against its incendiary siege,
taste the tartness
of invasively spastic breath.

Your cocksure manner
jostles my nerves
like a prison guard
rattles bars of confinement.
You won't let me sleep
despite amorous promises.

Constrained within the borders
of your smoldering world,
I ride waves of whimsy
on its perfumed fringes,
surfing your face
for safe, familiar spaces.
Stoking enchantment with insistent sighs,
I shed skins of desire
on the highlands of reconnaissance.

Images multiply in my brain
like a virulent virus.

Your scrutinizing eyes are everywhere,
like ubiquitous portraits
of tyrants whose minions
blandish what they fear.
And I feel throbbing
in my veins, uncertain
if I'm living or dead
in this half-life of desiring you.

Roaring commandos storm
safe havens of habit.
Couched in scented corridors,
the coiled persistence
of your striking visage
preys like a snake
on my puffed-up purpose,
infiltrates languid flesh.
Caresses scale the citadel
of my heated brain,
traversing creeks of blood
boiling with insurgency.

You ask me for my name and,
brainwashed by your skin's
soft-limbed prison
I chant yours, over and over,
like a magic mantra.

Provisional lips whisper resistance
in guarded terms of surrender.
My tongue's an olive branch,
hung with slavish importunings
at the portals of your ear.
Crouched at the outpost
of your woodland's brushed clearing,
I trace the promise
of its porcelain peace.

You slip seditious arms
under the cover of blankets,
gathering burgeoning life
like a rich harvest in your hand.

I understand that the pathway
to release is through the winding
road of love's trajectory,
out of safe houses of reason
into the unswept byways
of your body. Your white-breasted
beacons of light tender refuge
from life's impending storms.
I plow across open spaces
toward your furrowed field,

follow its meanderings
to clandestine recesses.
And you buttress
my precipitate descent
into welcoming caverns
of a far-reaching peace.

Published in The Stray Branch 2016

Aborted Love

Not only can't we salvage what is past,
but subsequent encounters mock our loss
with effigies whose tawdriness contrast
with scenes which previously bore a gloss.
Indeed. The blossoms blanketing the earth
emerge as midwives of the ghostly air,
foreshadowing an inauspicious birth.
For now - the operating theater's bare
that flushed love's fetus from its teeming womb.
The fragrant flowers stretched across the field
forlornly, loom like markers on a tomb
and presages a mortuary yield.
Thus vain regret's the progeny we reap
like lilies for the wake we're doomed to keep.

Published in Samsara Magazine

Frankenstein

How well you shaped the monster I'd become.
For first you left me prostrate on the bench,
immobilized by shame, both deaf and dumb
to your maneuvers. Then you'd deftly wrench
me from the affability I'd known,
along with all my budding social ties.
At last, calumnious assaults would hone
me into someone good folk ostracize.
Indeed. High voltage threats would jolt my nerves
with well-timed doses of electric fear.
And then addressing what a brute deserves,
I'd see revulsion lurking in my peers.
For they'd react to my affront in turn,
confirming what your cunning made them learn.

Published in Handshake #90. 2015

Tech Support

She certainly did not accord me slack,
when she tapped into my computer files
with all of the autonomy I'd lack -
while subject to the technologic wiles
she flashed. For her apparent probing hand
brushed over them so she could take a look.
It seemed my documents served her command,
and all its content was an open book,
while I just sat in silence starry-eyed.
Her ranging finger stroked my mirrored face
when, pausing at my journal in its stride,
she engineered to get into my space.
But I protested with a feeble laugh
that I did not want private files explored.
Nor were they guardians on my behalf
that I consented to have thus aboard
as tech support. But loath to give her guff,
I pondered that sometimes a parent's rough.

Published in Antarctica Journal 4/18/15

Titania on the Couch

(the fairy queen in A Midsummer Night's Dream)

Could magic cause midsummer ecstasy?
It's true, perhaps that asses traumatized
me in the past. But fantasy reprised
the scene in order to claim mastery
of it. Indeed. Besides recovery
it's been agreeably eroticized;
a saving facelift to what I despised.
Thus, compromising my propriety
has not just rendered Bottom sweet, but stirs
the very embers of my heart's delight!
A floral juice applied by Oberon
could not have rendered me obsessed with fur's
embellishment. The castigating slight
to my conceit caused this phenomenon

of pining after paws and "fair large ears!"
But it's the very coinage of the mind
which rendered me emotionally blind.
Embarrassed by primeval scenes and fears,
how fast an ardent inclination rears
up like a turncoat realigned
to troops to whom he'd been resigned

as captive. "Either brook the jeers
of Oberon or savor Bottom's voice",
I mused. How economic is this ploy.
Constrained by shame at Oberon's behest,
I bide this forced alliance as a choice.
And a repulsive beast that should annoy
me looms as ardent object of my quest.

Published by **CaveaLLector, vol. 27, 1**

Dear John

(the Sophie to Der Rosenkavalier)

Just like the Marschallin had been resigned
to cede her lover to the ingénue
to whom his heart would later be inclined,
so Marietta's mistress bade adieu
to her so that her "Quinquin" could pursue
no younger woman but a different sex
than formerly she'd been accustomed to.
Perhaps she needed someone who could flex
the muscles firmer than an aging shrew
could do; was confident she'd circumvent
his manhood, or perceived her ex's shoe
would fit what seemed to be his passive bent.
In any case as their concessions grew
the marriage that ensued felt heaven-sent.

Published in Soul Fountain 6/9/15

Summery Summation

Heat wave, my jazz! Would you prefer a tepid mistress stroke your brow, and breezy exhalations from her breath that promise Autumn's in the offing? I want a steamy bed with heated vapors coming from a south that's scented with the harems of Arabia. Seasoned by the sun, I want her breathing charcoal silhouettes, whispering gusts of shibboleths that pass muster in the misty morning. I need a chain of solar rays around her neck, sunbeams in her eyes and scorching fingers on a face swarming with perspiring streets. I want her searing with warmth. I'd as soon smell roseate odors in the swooning torpor of arms unblemished by a branching armistice of trees that tout domesticity. I want fractious heat waves of sultry soldiers parching in a war of nerves. I seek surrender in sheets soaked with jamming pajamas exhaling saxophones of snazzy riffs. I'll sniff her smarmy dew from steamy grasses. And chilled by cruciform rays of Fall, I'll savor streaming lashes fluttering with godsend suns.

Published in Common Ground Review pub spr/summer 2015

Sorceress

Bizarre things happened by the sultry strand.
While I'd as soon my steadfast Anne beguile
me with her sweet, ingratiating smile,
a Lorelei extended me her hand.
Her grip felt like I'd sunk into the sand
or otherwise had drunk a potent vial
containing soporific herbs. The trial
disarmed my former altruistic stand.
As though I'd passed through some magnetic field,
I lost all interest in my faithful girl
friend. Slowly, I could feel affection yield
to this coquette who set my mind awhirl.
Yet soon as she felt strong enough to wield
control, she morphed from water sprite to churl.

And after I'd been haplessly traduced,
she sidled near the lass that I betrayed
while I stood by, disgruntled and dismayed.
I sensed the plethora of vibes unloosed
on her were gleaned from qualities she sluiced
from me. My energy had been parlayed
into her prowess, flagrantly displayed
like wattles on the cock who rules the roost.

But, since she strutted with a part of me,
I felt somehow emotionally bound
to her, if just to salvage dignity.
For, having plucked my image from the sound
I stared into while fixed by reverie,
she mirrored me as stag before her hound.

1st verse published in Handshake #91, 2015 in England

Satie's Gnossiennes

Stop probing open wounds with slinky treble keys. High-strung tones cluster like bones on your forlorn keyboard. Their ivories are skeletons in my heart's closet. Those are suicidal notes, salt to sores. They're hushed conversations drawn from a dying patient. How can you be so sweetly clinical? Or is it cold outside, and droplets of rain freeze your saccharine prescriptions to frost? My lesions sting while they're cauterized by wide harmonic spaces that hide poor prognoses. Their hushed petitions sweeten even as I swoon. And I'm in love with caustic loneliness.

Published in The Homestead Review, September 2015

Serviceable Duo in a Restaurant

Once Angela was docile and demure.
She waited on the tables, poised to brook
my culinary cravings to ensure
that I'd be deftly served. How fast she took
away the plates and bottles left behind
my meal! Now that Patricia waits with glee
and au pair leanings, Angie's not inclined
to spend as much time looking over me,
but seems determined that her child be raised
to independence. Pat's now motherly
instead. And since her understudy phased
her out and seems intent to smother me
in love, poor Angie has the thankless role
of parents forced to exercise control.

Published in The Homestead Review September, 2015

Ode to Olympia

(in The Tales of Hoffman)

I'd love a mechanical doll
that's readily wound as I please.
She's neither tyrannical moll,
seductress, curmudgeon nor tease.
Though placing footsteps gingerly
she rhapsodizes stilted moves
by liberally chiming "oui"
before she vigorously grooves.
Yet should her mechanism fail
and she collapses on the floor,
the winding of her springs avail
to help her rusty spirits soar.
She even bounces on her feet
when her recovery's complete.

And no component gives her pause
to entertain us with her song
and cybernetic dance. She draws
applause as soaring trills prolong
the demonstration of her skill.

Her florid vocals are enough
to make the most complacent thrill
when she adroitly flaunts her stuff.
Oh, let me bask in the display
of the impeccable technique
behind her color-laden lay.
And note, those weary of her squeak.
Beyond the turn-on of her trill
are means to turn her off at will.

Published LPEZING MAGAZINE

Song of the Night

However much we fret
it will always come to this:
battalions of regret
for the lips we didn't kiss.

For the love that's unrequited
fans imagined flames of bliss.
And its fire once ignited
will remind us what we miss.

And it doesn't really matter
if autumnal fruits resist
relentless winds that scatter
leaves that garishly insist.

For whatever love we lavish
in the early morning mist,
by the evening we will languish
for the lips we never kissed.

Published in:
Lyrical Passion Poetry E-Zine 2015

Breaching Godiva

Displaying shades of dishabille,
she glides her hand through auburn hair
whose parted strands look willowy
enough to make me gawk and stare.
A pretty gal who's slovenly
informs us that she doesn't care
to chide or send to Coventry
some guy content to see laid bare
a brow in lieu of nudity.
Though tresses glimpsed in disrepair
suggests degrees of fancy-free
beyond which she'd be loath to share
with my specific company
my gaze won't leave her worse for wear.

Published in The Poet's Art 2016

Ties that Bind

Desire is a loaded gun.
But once the suspect's been disarmed
his fugitive obsessions run
from the pursued one he's alarmed.
It helps his case when caught, unnerved
by this complainant whom he wooed,
to plead 'no contest' to time served,
once outlawed passion's been subdued.
Indeed, it constitutes a chain
around him hard as doing time
unless he, wresting heart from brain,
confesses to a lesser crime.
Thus he wakes from a sleep that's sound
beside her to whom laws have bound.

Published in The Poet's Art 2016

Odysseus Bound

Amazing how Calypso teased my brain
with bawdy fantasies once I'd lost hope
of ever wresting free from her domain.
For having neither liberty nor scope
to exercise my will, what might have reeked
of shameful manacles on those ideals
that guided me in former times, now piqued
my sensibilities to thunder peals
of bliss. Dejected by the lonely shore
while contemplating loss of loving wife,
I garnered pleasure from the ocean's roar,
anesthetizing servitude and strife.
And what first left me overwhelmed with grief
afforded me new sources of relief.

Published in Ship of Fools #74 Fall, 2016

The Apple Game

(offshoot of Chytilova's film)

Although he's propped against the wall, stone drunk,
and might have been inclined to sleep alone;
as amorous as she's infused with spunk,
she shoulders him so that her collarbone
provides a point of leverage for the hunk
whose protestations peter out to moan,
in counterpoint to his resounding funk.
Thus flowering from fertile seeds he'd sown,
she hauls the hulk upstairs into her bed
where he sleeps soundly, till the breaking dawn
illuminates her lush, disheveled head
of hair whose strands frame her complacent yawn.
He then boasts intimacies that he'd dread
to contemplate were they supposed her spawn.

**Published in The Storyteller,
July, August, September 2015**

Christmiffs

$200 worth of gifts
and the stuffed turkey's gone. The rifts
at home won't heal with silken shifts,
electric trains or handkerchiefs
brought by this despondent spendthrift's
common cause with Santa's airlifts.
I tried to stay love's wayward drifts
from falling off suburban cliffs
of Dover. There my sister sifts
through Xmas cards as Snoopy sniffs
the family, reprising tiffs –
amidst intoxicating whiffs
of coffee – fueled by whats and ifs
at supper. Forget the Pontiff's
prayer for peace, but don't give short shrift
to that piece on holstered sheriffs
receiving mortuary stiffs.

Published in The Story Teller Oct-Dec 2015

Noblesse Oblige

It isn't strange that some sweet girl who's charmed
a male combatant in the sexes' war
should, seeing that her former foe's disarmed
by awe, forgo hostilities she swore.
For, after all, a man thus smitten cedes
his prowess to exigencies of love.
His heart is focused on romantic deeds
and gallantry instead of duelist's glove.
As such, why should the conqueror accord
her doting captive less diplomacy
than that which foreign diplomats afford?
And thus, with all the proud propriety
of delegations in a subject state,
she cedes her cheek for him to osculate.

Published in Soul Fountain 8/18/15

Lay Figure

A woman's like a full form mannequin
some tailors utilize to make a dress.
For well-stitched fabric needs a frame to pin
itself on to ensure that points of stress
are placed to maximize a proper fit.
But fantasy's a pattern that demands
deft needlework if guys are to acquit
themselves with more than merely needling strands.
They need to lay their whimsical designs
upon a prop. If not, the garment's sewn
according to the undulating lines
configured out of fancy's overblown
conceit. It's fashioned out of whole cloth shapes,
where bodies are more substantive than drapes.

Published in Soul Fountain 8/18/15

Fast Food Service

The one girl commandeers my frothy shake.
Another, wary of the method used
to garner it, starts probing in her wake -
in the event due process was abused.
Perhaps she feels there's basis for appeal
from violating sanitary laws,
that would entitle me to get a meal
for free, that prompted her to serve my cause.
Or maybe the competitor in her,
resentful of the gal who's serving me,
maneuvered to ensure that we don't stir
too far from her presumed hegemony.
In any case, she's certainly adept
at seeing that proprieties are kept.

Or else, suspecting I've been served up dregs
from the container, she exerts control
from pride, who'd blithely take me down some pegs -
did I not play for her a minor role.
Still I feel safer by the measured means
she musters to make certain of fair play.

But having validated the machine's
efficiency, I bristle with dismay
at just how well the girls together work
at keeping their unwitting ward in check.
I mark what fugitive desires lurk
within my breast to have them at my beck
and call. But seeing how those two take charge,
I just feel lucky that I'm still at large.

Published in Soul Fountain 5/23/15

Disarming Germans

Though I move courteously to the side
of the street to let the family pass,
they seem with cool impertinence to bide
the patient demonstration of my class.
As one by one the children make their way
ahead of cell-phone toting Herr und Frau
ignoring me, I scarcely can display
more than a stern-faced arching of my brow.
This look, brooked by the eldest of their brood -
a dashing Fraulein flanking the brigade -
is parried by her with such fortitude,
my outflanked pansy yields before her blade.
I understand, as I resume my pace,
that self-examination is in place.

Published in The Homestead Review
September '15

The Emperor of Yen

I spent so much time staring at the ice-cream cone in the cool whip of desire that its double dip started dripping to the floor. Rushing to scarf up what remained, I was left with nothing but regret at letting candy-coated moments pass.

Previously Published in Star *82

Collector

She grappled with his hypothetical lapels,
then shook his image, railing in his face
with heated words that worked like potent spells.
She not just dramatized the man's disgrace
but mounted, like a butterfly, his soul,
before the rapt inspection of her friend.
And while she made her fractured showcase whole,
he'd shrunk to wings that hobbyists append
to pins. My throttled senses shook beside
the honeyed trappings of her flailing arms,
if only to vicariously bide
the striking charge of her impressive charms.
And there I fluttered, fixed in fancy's flight,
the heir apparent to her shadow fight.

Previously Published in Poets' Espresso Review
Spring 2015, V.12, Issue 2 (a few lines different)

Quisling

He thought his gruff demeanor was enough
to trigger an advisory alarm
in her that would summarily disarm
her tiff with peers. But braced against his bluff,
she counteracted with a stern rebuff
that all but leveled the reserve of charm
he'd flaunt to emphasize he meant no harm.
Instead it was the formidable stuff
she demonstrated that would override
his pride and make him acquiesce to terms
that she mandated to secure the peace.
How quickly he retreated to her side,
to play the turncoat warrior who firms
up flanks he follows to secure release.

Published in The Eclectic Muse
v.20/21, Christmas 2015

The Spider's Stratagem

There's no defense against your skeins of hate.
You stealthily disseminate rumors
like spools of silken twine that bind, then wait
until their rank legions spread like tumors
across the frozen confines of my fate.
Spidery, you spin your myriad threads
of innuendos that in time mutate
to crowns of thorns, or bounties on my head.
Resist? I'm held tight by your web of past
intrigues. Submit? You knit across the net's
lattice new snares. Thus, paralyzed, at last,
by fear, I'm mincemeat for your spinnerets.
And predigested by consuming rage,
I'm stewed in juices sucking up my age.

Published in The Eclectic Music
v.20/21, Christmas 2015

The Love Bug

Desire's like a soporific drug
whereby the patient loses self-control,
reducing him to an enfeebled lug.
The object of his interest takes the role
of prophylactic nurse who guides him through
successive stages of his slow demise.
She chastens him ensuring he'll pursue
the healthy regimen that she'll advise
him of before he gets the medicine
prescribed for mitigating his disease.
Regrettably increased adrenaline
will leave the patient still more ill at ease.
Indeed, beside himself, he seeks a cure
that only love's transfusion can ensure.

Published in The Eclectic Music
v.20/21, Christmas 2015

The Father of Her Child

(sits across from her in a subway car)

She greets his fleeting glance with scorn.
For nurturing the still unborn,
she deems the guy completely hers
or useless where desire stirs
concern for her prospective brood.
So lest the both of them get screwed
by dumbing down the mating call,
they'll be her terms or none at all.
And since he'll help to spawn her son
or daughter, breeding's lost or won
through him. So, if he's acting glib
she must remand him to a crib.
What drives her will to play au pair
and monitor this subway fare?

The apple of her eye sits there,
in lieu of him who'll help her bear
to term the seeds of happiness.
She frowns, content to let him guess
how he shapes up in her esteem.

Indeed. She doesn't want to seem
impressed by how her charge behaves,
and thus withholds the nod he craves.
For she's concerned with nursery,
not wedding anniversary.
And so, although she beams - beguiled
by his engaging mien - lest wild
assumptions foster his conceit,
she acts disarmingly discreet.

**Published in The Eclectic Muse
v.20/21, Christmas 2015**

Bewitched, Smothered and Gored

"I'm not a witch," Christine O'Donnell demurred with maternal solicitude - and smidgens of smug conceit - to those enchanted by her Circean sorcery. Bewitched, indeed, and swept away - not by broomsticks but by charming naiveté, puritanical pundits cackled anxiously for the removal of her hex on their submissively parochial psyches.

The nerve of her for wheeler-dealing with such craft! Never mind Chucky, Lord of the Rings, Witchmaster, the ubiquitous Ouija board, the Exorcist and Holy Roller healers. She had the nerve to roll up her sleeves, probing inside the rattling backdrop of superstitious mischief despite the shadow of muckraking trials that loomed centuries behind her. Never mind the transformative magic in Extreme Makeover and the iconography of Gothic Rock! Witches are too bitchy for their britches.

She should apologize for having corrupted all those Salem sensibilities into gathering kindle for the high stakes burning of her senatorial pursuits; for making her swim from channel to channel protesting her innocence on Cspan, CNN. NBC and their coven of affiliates, who hoped she would drown in tell-tale tales of sorcery only to find out she'd been lying through her dimples, and would finally declare her innocence through comedic familiars on Sabbath Night, Live.

There's more Osmond than Oz in this indulgently maternal media matron who'd smarmily persuade gullible grown-ups that the skeletons in her collegiate closet were not real. "I'm not a witch," she smiled with an air of condescension, assuring a jittery electorate who'd been peeking under cover of enchantment. She really gave Delaware townsfolk the scare of their suburban wives. Sorry that she refused to stay in middle America. But she's not a witch! She never even stirred brew in a pot, still less smoked it. In fact, she loathes ministering to the same lubricious members whose uprising hexed adjudicators of her ancestors. And indeed, witches don't write hysterical laws; legislators do.

Previously Published in Abbreviate, December 2015

Tiger

Like the Phoenix, I rise out of the ash
from the chastening fire of your rage.
How sweet the sting of your linguistic lash
confining my wild tiger to its cage.
Fleet-footed carnivores prowling the plain
must seem no fiercer stalking helpless prey
than I, smoldering, making you maintain
control of me. I doggedly obey
your every whim, as though your verbal whip
exacts my shamed submission to your rule.
And I'm afraid to move for fear your grip
will lose its feral hold on me. I drool,
while you keep pacing – following my rout –
like you're inside the cage and looking out.

Published online in The Poet's Haven 2015

Remembering Ali

I'm standing on line. Boxing's ringmaster
is about to autograph copies of
his book. In his prime no one was faster
with either dancing feet or jabbing glove
than this gentle man who now emerges,
tied to apron strings of celebrity.
Drones of "oohs" and "aahs", as the crowd surges.
Invocations begin: "Ali! Ali!"
as if to exorcise demonic time
and resurrect together with the chant,
the lightning fists and tantalizing rhyme.
They chuckle at his jibes like sycophants
at the court of a king. "You blocks! You stones!
You worse than senseless things," a cashier groans,

echoing Shakespeare. And I start to think.
Isn't this the Caesar of the 60's
Olympics? The Pax Romana who'd link
legions of imperial victories
to the farthest reaches of the world, while
civilizing the pugilistic mind
with grace and humor? He coaxes a smile
from a black woman who's standing behind

a row of books. She exults: “You’re the champ,
Ali! You’re the champ!” Ali sets the bait.
“I’m a tramp?” he mugs. “You called me a tramp!”
“No, I didn’t!” she cries, less to placate
his mimic rage, than to admonish him,
who served the disenfranchised from a gym,

like some pastoral priest ministering
to his congregation. But Ali was
no paschal lamb sacrificed to the ring.
His two-handed offering gloved the cause
of underdogs. Knightly deeds looked easy.
Twin-fisted monsters dispatched with aplomb
made guardians of the grail feel queasy.
Their forked dragon was just another bum
who preyed on fear left over from youthful
nightmares. With gaping mouth and mocking frown,
he’d comb its lair with regulation tooth
and nail, then cut the puffed-up monster down.
In storybook style, he battled and won;
forging greatness in a spirit of fun.

Published in THE CHALLENGER
Summer 2013

Shooting From the Hip

How quickly she rides over from the wings
when she's enlisted to take center stage.
Corralling retrograde imaginings
of macho men she's eager to engage
in cowboy antics on a movie set.
With pistol, lasso, chaps, and riding boots,
how dauntlessly she takes control to whet
my appetite before she coolly shoots
some varmint in a face-off. Neither shame
nor awkwardness at sporting rowel spurs,
bandana or a Stetson stays her game
for blurring lines dividing his and hers.
And since she's peerless in her dustup part,
I quicken at her unaccustomed art.

Published in the Poet's Haven, January 2016

Divine Ordinance

If we believe in God, we must believe
accounting books are balanced in the end.
Retainers who work earnestly, but grieve
that for such hardship they've scant cash to spend,
will gain admittance to the better schools
from which head hunters pluck the qualified.
And those who sneer at them or bend the rules,
move down the corporate ladder's other side.
Thus, rogues who mock our labors with disdain,
while profiting in firms that workers build,
are not the lot God's secretaries train
for better paid positions to be filled.
But those whose virtue doesn't have a price
this day will be with us in Paradise.

Published by Ancient Paths
online February 2016

Civil Blights

The ones who troubled me the most
in life were not mere criminals
in line for a condign riposte,
but those who bank on principles
to keep unlawfulness at bay.
For those I served - at their behest -
to shield their interests, so that they
can live their lives as they deem best
were quick to flippantly betray
agreements I was drafted for.
What worth a contract that will pay
men back as if it can ignore
the basic rights for which they served,
while it gives shirkers undeserved

amenities? Accordingly,
the contract void, I want returned -
since it has ceased rewarding me -
the time in service that they spurned.
To these I add the other years
my mother had to sacrifice
to see her kids as volunteers
who subsidized another's spice.

Why feather someone else's nest
when our wings are singed in flight,
and anomie can't be redressed?
So let them send their sons to fight
for civil rights at their expense
while I mend, pending recompense.

First sonnet published in The Potomac

Same Old Story

Our modern times are High Noon in reverse.
While Marshal Kane fought Miller's gang alone,
as craven townsfolk hid behind his hearse,
today they'd make a movement to disown
him, fortified by laws they've etched in stone.
What matter if a demagogue holds sway,
should custom bring to fruit the seeds they'd sown?
They're heady from the perfume of the fray.
For notwithstanding all that we have learned
regarding lawlessness and civil rights,
where subjugating others are concerned
a threat of violence works like plebiscites.
It's fun, if what's been tabled isn't turned
around so that its architects get burned.
Then trials without a jury are adjourned
and rogues who promulgated them are spurned
by those same citizens who gave them range
to begin with. For only seasons change.

Published in "The Potomac" Summer 2016

Saint-Saëns' 2nd Piano Concerto

Like a bystander at a barroom brawl,
while focused instrumentalists play on,
I watch the keyed-up concertizer maul
the Baldwin like a pint-sized Amazon.
What use are catcalls from the whining winds,
resounding supplications from the brass
or svelte sonorities from violins?
She counters with the tarantella's sass.
Combining strident bass and treble chords,
she overwhelms glissando-rattled bones,
then looms suspended till the sounding board's
subdued. The last of dying overtones
will fade before trombone fortissimos
can shield the keys from her explosive blows.

Published in The Eclectic Muse
v.19/Xmas 2013

Winehouse Elegy

Like acolytes of prophets doomed
to be redeemed by history,
I rifle artifacts exhumed
to ferret out the mystery
that trails behind your troubled life.
You were the sun who warmed my days,
my fellow traveler in strife,
my friend in exile from mores
that keep Life's prisoners constrained
from tugging free of mortal bonds.
Since you no longer are contained,
you're spared distress, while I despond
at ever hearing you again
uplift me in my psychic pen.

Indeed, your music serves as toys
a mother finds inside a room
that resonates like choirboys
amidst the empty, silent gloom
confirming that her child is dead.
I tuck your album in its sleeve
right after liner notes I've read
belie the news for which I grieve.

For in my heart you're still alive.
I wait for your renowned return,
like moms whose college kids arrive
enriched by wisdom that they learn.
And with your posthumous release,
I fancy you'll at last find peace.

**Published online in Pulsar Magazine
September 2013**

Union Dues

We're here to pass on DNA.
For that's what we've been hired for.
We still can whittle time away
until the boss knocks on our door
to ask us how much work we've done.
But smart employees turn the trick
of managing to have some fun
and still show the arithmetic
which tells employers they're clocked in
and diligently did the work.
And how can he be docked who's been
industrious and doesn't shirk
the load he's been assigned to bear
because no children needs his care?

Resourceful workers use the phone
and other office products to
amuse themselves and thus postpone
the task they've been assigned to do.
And since they get a weekly check
that lets them educate themselves
to be a doctor or exec
and read the textbooks on their shelves,

it's easy for them to forget
that there's a tougher job in store
for them than how they can abet
advancement, whether rich or poor.
And though they might deceive the boss
they'll bear his losses like a cross.

**Published in The Eclectic Muse
v.19, Xmas, 2013**

Gestating to Beethoven's Fifth Symphony

(as performed by an all-female orchestra)

How sweet that women in the prime of life
should choose to carry on the lineage
of someone lacking progeny or wife.
For, evidently grumpy personage,
he'd scarcely win from one of them a date.
Yet, now they're bowing strings in unison,
infatuated by his fertile fate
motif as though he were a paragon
of every virtue that a girl could hope
for in a man. His love notes are the score
they look at as they amorously grope
through bars, delivering the spawn they bore
for many months before it's brought to term,
a godsend from the partner they affirm.

Published in The Eclectic Muse
v.19, Xmas, 2013

Tacit Camouflage

A girl is like a Venus flytrap plant.
This wasn't Nature's devious design.
Nor is it just because some women can't
give up the fruit that's budding on their vine.
They simply simulate the ones that can.
As such, a guy who's fly will take the bait
regardless of a gal's hair trigger plan.
And all the man trap has to do is wait.
It doesn't matter whether men just smile
at some coquette who smugly starts to text.
What if she's granted access down an aisle,
before she scowls - as if she had been vexed
by sexists with insidious intent?
Deft mimicry is hard to circumvent.

Published in Eye on Life Magazine
Spring 2014

Sister George

(in the movie: "Where Angels Go, Trouble Follows")

The girl stares down a biker with a knife.
And chucking habits, nuns could bank upon
to smugly separate themselves from life,
she lets her gumption overpower brawn.
For even though he's well-armed for a fight,
we never doubt it mitigates the fear
he has of doing more than sitting tight,
in the event her pluck will persevere.
It seems, as she implies, his biker clothes
do more than her black habit, to sustain
the substance that's behind their steadfast pose.
A half-clad strumpet scarcely would constrain
the brash intentions of this macho male
with more allure than she does in a veil.

Published online in: Eye on Life 3/20/14

Tancred to Clorinda

(who fought him in mail)

It's not as though I sued your swordsmanship,
or that your brutish tactics wouldn't hurt
my pride, if you were burly as your grip.
Nor were you ever dangerously curt,
as when we fought while donning cuirassiers.
But incognito in the mail you'd worn
to skirt convention, troubadours and peers,
you opened dormant passions when I'd shorn
the armor that concealed your lithesome sex.
Accordingly my putative disgrace
before your pluck was checked. For you'd annex
with flair, a bent I ardently embrace
which, if you were a burly Amazon,
would make me keep my body armor on.

But what use breastplate I was wont to wear
against the darts of Cupid in a fray?
For brazenly you utilized my dare
as grist, till your impassioned will held sway
and stormed the portals of my heart's divide.

And though I'm apprehensive of romance,
you forced me to dismount the steed I ride,
then pricked my sluggish passion with your lance.
Yet, though a bashful bridegroom, I'd be healed
had not a shroud replaced your bride's trousseau,
when you were borne from battlefield with shield
that failed to block my frantic counterblow.
And so you die a warrior at peace
while my conflicted yearnings never cease.

Published in Eye on Life. Spring, 2014

Fudging Origins

I don't believe you physicists
who don't think we need catalysts
preceding an effective cause.
And even that must give us pause.
For catalysts need parentage
like babies inside carriages.
It's not enough to cry "Big Bang!"
unless somebody puts the dang
contraption into outer space.
But what's the latter without place
contingent on what put it there.
Thus howsoever, when or where
the universe dispelled the dark
it must be from a godlike spark.

Published in Soul Fountain Spring 2014

Conscript

I wrote those taxing lines a thousand times
and flirted with a similar conceit,
as though obsession could be masked with rhymes
and self-indulgence with iambic beat.
Forget that they exploit my verbal skill
and dupe me into serving noxious ends.
A rhyming quatrain infiltrates my will
until I think I write for dividends.
Of course my words are enemy brigades
seductively dressed up in metaphor
to camouflage incendiary raids
that draft my metric measures into war.
But it's a war of words I cannot win,
the more so since it leads me far afield
into a poem that saps resources thin
until it hurts to press on or to yield.
Of course this serves the interests of the foe
who, keeping me entrenched behind the lines,
insures I sow poetic seeds that grow
to turncoat tropes which further his designs.
And thus, this misadventure doesn't cease
while I compose entangling terms of peace.

Published in Soul Fountain, Spring 2014

Cosmic Musings

Concerning that belabored, bearded sage,
we need a newer model for an age
where He's a walk-on part upon our stage,
content to earn a piddling Sunday wage.
We need a mythos able to engage
the senses better than the printed page
delineating prophet, saint or mage.
Perhaps we're felons in a cosmic cage
that's watched to see how each of us engage
the rest. The good die young, the sinful age
until their good deeds manage to assuage
their keeper, or malicious acts outrage
Him. Then the world's consumed in a rampage
of stellar catalysts turned macrophage.

Published in Soul Fountain, Spring 2014

Stood Up

I'd never buy a costly suit of clothes,
but for believing you'd go out with me.
The wise would wait till the occasion rose
before investing in such finery.
But getting dressed before my fancied date
in garments suited more for formal wear
than play, I only could procrastinate
resolves, while wondering if you'd be there.
Indeed, you never came. And thus arrayed,
I scarcely could pursue productive ends.
But still I wonder how you could persuade
me into wearing clothing effort rends
in ways that force me to play mannequin
while you, sweet seamstress, take my trousers in.

Published in Blast Furnace, v. 3, #3

Following in His Footsteps

Restraint becomes the cross I have to bear,
and city streets are my Gethsemane.
The jeers are crowns of thorns I have to wear
for abdicating self-sufficiency
to scriptures that state emissaries write.
They guarantee that sheep may safely raze
my garden with perfidious delight.
For I lie prostrate, even as I gaze
dismayed – as conscientious citizen –
at liberties self-righteous shepherds take
by scourging me. And wherewithal or when
to rise again so that my shackles break
depends on scruples; each a devotee
of prickly paths that lead to Calvary.

Both poems published online in
Miller's Pond Poetry, Spring 2014

On a String

My life's a balloon filled with the air of prior days. It rises like a ghost amidst the blue haze of memories. It floats over high-rise presumptions, and bounding off a pane of glassy rejection, gets tangled in branching reveries. As such, its airy confidence slowly dissipates into the noxious cocktail of smog and exhaust fumes that I breathlessly imbibe.

Previously published online in Stride Magazine

Before Dawn

The night rises from your lips.
Mountains of desire flank your arms.
My eyes are a 1000 stars
infiltrating wooly blankets
closing your eyelids.
I'm memory's Ferris Wheel
spinning in your carnival
of dreams. A stop sign opens
on the road of precipitous longing.
A barrel of heat in a coldwater flat,
I swerve around the flatiron
district of your curves and park Cupid's
chariot in the backwaters of sleep.

Published in Miller's Pond Poetry, Spring 2014

Tough Customer

Compliance is a t-bone steak
dished up to whet the appetite
of someone it can barely slake
before he takes another bite.
Accommodation is the sauce
poured on the fear that seasons meat,
while pleas are lettuce that you toss
at him to make his meal complete.
And seeing you serve his behest
with such ingratiating mien,
he's quick to gobble up the rest
of it, until his plate is clean.
As tip, you'll find this patron's thrown
at you the masticated bone.

Previously Published in Able Muse 2014

Complexions

The queen of colors
fleshes out with flashy tones
the sallow stretch of skin on bones

to spread her glow on ashen men.
She plies the pigments Nature owns
with brushes used like magic wands

while sitting on her throne,
deciding who she'll touch
and who will groan

beneath the grays of love postponed.
Fine bristles gleam on chin and cheek
of budding boys who, green and meek,

start growing toward the light we seek.
Thus, canvas stretched to skyward blues,
we blossom in full-bodied hues,

hearts throbbing for her finger tips
to squeeze out oils from sanguine tubes,
and with rapid strokes, to finish us.

Published in The Same, v.12, #1

Cowgirl Kate

Cavorting in her native state,
with jutting chest and strutting gait,
a cowboy hat upon her pate
is all she wears to decorate
a body that men celebrate
till they find she's a candidate
for sheriff who can pull her weight
when there's a job to consummate.

And though a gun is excess freight
to her, who doesn't wear ornate
attire, nor delineate
a macho attitude or trait,
if she can't rehabilitate,
she bares enough to captivate
the libertine and reprobate
and make the renegade go straight.

Published in Writer's Bloc

Skirting Bankruptcy

(by promoting a female rival for
her boyfriend's affections)

His pride of masculinity foreclosed
when he drew from the interests of her sex,
how fast he suffered sanctions she imposed
on him. For he'd crossed gender lines to vex
her sensibilities when he extolled
the assets of a rival for her guy's
affections. Notwithstanding having sold
her on his skill at managing high-rise
apartments, he lost credibility.
As broker targeting her boyfriend's heart,
his banked-on manhood traded solvency
for her estate's devalued counterpart.
And though backed-up by vaunted financiers,
what he'd expended put him in arrears.

Published in Writer's Bloc

Online Service Chat

My straight-laced carriage furnished her the cue
to coo asides as a precursory
move. "Gotcha, baby!" was designed to woo
me to her metaphoric nursery.
Indeed, her texting left me tickled pink,
while pampering my antic 'soul mate' gibe
with 'salt and pepper' and a scripted 'wink'.
Pert patronage seduced me to subscribe
to her conceit that she maintain control.
She'd soon translate my quote from Cymbeline
into Norwegian to complete the role
of neophyte I'd play until she'd wean
me off her prophylactic tête-à-tête.
She left emoticons to contemplate.

Published in The Stray Branch
Spring/Summer 2014

Sweet Siege

Parading on the stage with show of arms
as she maneuvers the piano off,
her exercise insidiously charms
him. Leery this admirer might scoff
at her unearned incursion, she performs
with expertise, self-consciously aware
that such adept athleticism storms
his heartland like a conquering corsair.
Rapt captive to her militant advance,
he settles for a compromising peace,
whose terms afford him the defector's chance
of bartering allegiance for release.
But though he's pledged desired dividends,
concerning seizures she won't make amends.

Published in The Poet's Art
Issue #52, 2014 Spring

Swept Away

A perky cog in the machinery of appetite, she swishes her broom in the fast food eatery to gather the day's residue. She's stirring the pot of a witch's brew. I'm less a customer waiting to be served by one of her familiars than acolyte of her domestic sorcery. Her corporate cap twists the tips of her ears like a summons to bend before the tasks at hand. She gathers sweepings from beneath appliances, then reaches over to capture coins fleeing penal pockets. Having mapped my position from the start of her broomstick's raid, she looks up, less piqued object of my gaze, than guardian. Nor does she offer more than a glance at her earnestly observant charge.

Published in Feelings of the Heart
Dec/Jan 2015

Hung Over

How like the aftermath of crime
are pains we bear that we induce
ourselves. We know we'll do the time
while making efforts to hang loose.
Of course, the pretense doesn't work
and we proceed in cuffs and stripes,
remembering that we were jerks.
And how relentless are our gripes
when, like a felon since discharged,
distress still seethes inside our breast.
For then our bodies, still at large,
are reconciled to the arrest.
And although free, we seek release
from sanctions to somatic peace.

Published in Feelings of the Heart
Dec/Jan 2015

Philosophical Rant

Let ravages of sickness lay me low,
while I endure it with a sober mind.
Let all the fickle fates and furies know
that tense encounters scarcely will unwind
me. Able to maintain a steadfast heart,
I shall consider I'm a lucky man
if self-destructive urges don't impart
far worse than any act of Nature can.
If I secure integrity intact,
should all society impugn my name
or taunt my steps, their venom won't distract
me, or extinguish my ambition's flame.
But woe to those who, lucky or bereft,
abandon self-restraint, till nothing's left.

Let every girl I dote upon rebuff
my amorous advances as a key
I'll stand before life's sterner stuff.
For unrequited love may sadden me,
but not destroy the fabric of the clothes
my biologic nature dressed me with.
Nor will I rend them with a caustic pose.
Let storms be metal for my bustling smith

to forge into a more effective sword
that I can wield against adversity.
Let tribulation be my treasure hoard,
and I'll brook shame and poverty with glee.
But woe to those who use their privileged birth
to wallow in the entrails of the earth.

Published in Feelings of the Heart, Dec/Jan 2015

Chinese Squeeze

If I'd been spotted compound nouns,
where language was a boxing ring,
I'd tire after seven rounds
of her linguistic pummeling
when speaking in my native tongue.
Employing phrases off the cuff,
she left me dazed from words she flung
before me like a sound rebuff
to verbal assets I might boast.
Not hesitant or insecure
with western ways, a cool riposte
was all she needed to ensure
her breezy use of English tropes
would keep me tongue-tied on the ropes.

Published in Feelings of the Heart
Dec/Jan 2015

Moral Outlaws

Much worse than men committing crime,
are those who give them currency.
At least the former does the time
that mocks their sense of sovereignty.
But what of those who claiming rights
protecting them from theft and harm
play fast and easy with the plights
of others? Do they think their charm
secured those laws that play a part
protecting them? Forget the fact
they're callous souls without a heart.
Since privileges that they contract
from us they've withheld from their peers,
their social contract's in arrears.

Published in Feelings of the Heart
Dec/Jan 2015

Gal Trucker

You're neither an enforcer nor a cop
serving summonses. But I'm arrested
by the dry rejoinder of your dewdrop
nose pin when the call tags are contested.
You apprehend the boxes that I hand
to you and stack them snugly on your cart.
Your sweating strikes me as a reprimand
that prompts this deadbeat laborer to smart.
The hallway's an interrogation room
where I accept collusion in the crime
to dodge the warrant of your strong perfume.
In any case I'm forced to serve the time,
until you confiscate the final piece
and leave receipts that furnish my release.

Published in Magnolia Quarterly

Circe

She doesn't need to rifle through a book
of witchcraft for incantatory spells.
She just accords him a come-hither look
to notice how the guy she's hexing swells
into the porcine visage of a pig.
No sorcery's required to annex
repressive inclinations in a prig,
or stimulate the appetites that vex
his sensibilities. She'll only need
assume the role of farmer in the field
of love and plant the germinating seed
of sensuality to make him yield.
Thus, coupled with her headstrong husbandry,
she'll reap the fruit of his fertility.

Published in Ship of Fools Fall, 2014 #21

Reflections on a Surf Board

Today I woke up happy
after finishing my tax returns.
Once you start on anything,
the most quotidian of duties
becomes pleasurable. The different
looms like a new horizon.
Then I went to the dentist
because my temporary
cap fell off for the third time.
In jurisprudence, three strikes
means you're out. In commerce, you get
another chance to screw up again.
But even the dentist is a spring break
in the winter of routine.
And I basked in her dental chair
as if it were a chaise longue.
I didn't see the fluorescent light
in her office, but the noonday
sun on a beach in the Caribbean.
And while there weren't any bathing beauties
lounging about, at least I didn't get burnt.

Published in Avalon Literary Review
Fall 2014

The Wren Goes To ’t
(Lear Blasts His Daughters)

In the image of God? Hello?
No friendly, effervescent glow
is seen on them to show they know
the skyward branch on which they grow
from seed divining planters sow.
Not even a creative flow
of energies to humbly toe
the line and sideswipe Cupid’s bow.
Instead, they passionately go
wherever Nature’s currents blow,
like Juliet and Romeo
or any lovesick Jill and Joe,
to reproduce, as deer the doe,
successive souls in utero.

Published in Art Times 2015

Glass Ceilings

he opera with Satyagraha)

While Philip's music boasts impressive craft,
because I have a penchant to get bored
I sometimes wish his music lines were staffed
with more than an arpeggiated chord.
Though rehashed passages can mesmerize
us to a point, an unremitting strain's
like water torture that can traumatize
the musical receptors in our brains.
At least I felt that way when at the Met
I heard his Satyagraha songsters sing
descants that, though hypnotic as the set,
when finished summoned words of Dr. King -
whose modulated tones held listeners fast:
"Thank God almighty I am free at last!"

Published in Art Times 2014

Doctor's Visit

They treat me like a criminal.
"Take off your clothes!" I must appeal.
But to whom? Regan? Goneril?
Goneril says I need three meals
daily. No more than four ounces
of wine each day! Hear Regan sneer:
"Why four? Why two? Why - " She pounces
on my needs like a raptor. Lear
would not endure such insolence.
I'd just made peace with losing hair,
turning grey, diminishing sense
of sound and sight. It isn't fair,
I brood. Goneril: "And don't eat
greasy foods, liver, fats. Limit
coffee intake!" Ye Gods! They'll cheat
me out of living, bit by bit,
these harbingers of death who tease
me out of groceries that please.

Published in The Pavilion 2014

Gender Games

Constrained behind your girlish masquerade
you draft me as a soldier bearing arms
of war as I prepare an ambuscade
to seize your heart. If brave, I'll put your charms
with triumph, on parade. You watch me storm
your silken locks in lieu of an assault
on those strategic sites where I should form
a militarily more apt gestalt.
But tangled in the tresses of your hair,
I fruitlessly attempt to disengage
myself while you triumphantly declare
me captive in the war you made me wage.
For while real conflict offers terms of peace,
in amorous campaigns there's no release.

Published in Barbaric Yawp, v.17 #3

Library Check

Delinquent suspect she's obliged to frisk,
I'm patted down on her computer screen.
As if Security thinks I'm a risk,
my name, address, and e-mail's overseen
by her. Though I survive her scrutiny,
she keeps me subject to her beck and call.
My ruffled pride prepares for mutiny
against this bailiff holding me in thrall.
But since I'm cross-examined with such flair
and she exudes the bored official's bliss
at having me remanded in her care,
my captive passion's more inclined to miss
the charm of her procedural control
than stiffer terms imposed on my parole.

PUBLISHED IN TRINACRIA
SPRING 2014

Voyager

When stormy waves of life befuddle you
and threaten to engulf your battered skiff,
recall past perils that you've padded through,
near promontory, reef and rocky cliff.
Veer windward, take in sail, and brace yourself
to navigate disgruntled Neptune's might,
through rain and gale force winds. Beware the shelf
of shallow waters promising respite
beside seductive banks where moonlight gleams.
Though harbors seem to flicker in the mist,
you'd best maintain your course near lighthouse beams.
This is no place for a nocturnal tryst
with treacherous sirens. For time is short
that stars permit to steer your boat to port.

Published in Slate and Style, Summer 2014

Tight Jersey

Domesticating garden state!
Though wedded to your floral bed,
when I wake up to allocate
discretionary time, my head
is filled with high-rise reveries
of Gotham town's décolletage.
It burgeons into dishabille
with skyline vistas by the barge
along the Hudson's rusty edge.
For though in sickness and in health
I've benefited from your pledge
to bide me till I die, the wealth
and glamour city life contrives
exceeds that of suburban wives.

Published in Gulf Coast Writers Assn
July 2014

For the Girl Skimming through Hitchcock's "Psycho"

I see you think that scanning stuff's okay.
That scenes included on the DVD
are boring fluff that just get in the way.
They're merely there for dilettantes to see,
instead of what the movie needs to say.
Then why in hell grow up and get engaged?
Why plan to celebrate your wedding day
and have romantic fantasies assuaged,
if afterwards you'll simply reproduce
at Mother Nature's ultimate behest?
Start scanning till your child's in a papoose
or, further, to those years when you've addressed
old age. But if you haven't time to spend
on narrative, fast forward to the end.

Published in Gulf Coast Writer's Assn
July 2014

Ardent Hostage

While biked by you through regions near your birth,
I fancied kindling for desire's flame.
The village bustle brought me down to earth
as captive to your own preemptive claim
on me. For coasting through routine terrain -
while greeting strangers in your native tongue -
you turned advantage into a campaign
for sovereignty. How feebly I soon hung
my head upon your shoulder for the ride
to your ancestral home. Unnerved by fear
of unfamiliar spots, I swallowed pride
and shrewdly waxed loquacious in your ear.
My missive was a mixture of complaint
and passion framed in terms of shamed constraint.

Published in Magnolia Quarterly, Fall 2014

Talisman

So what if some men opt to hedge
their bets? Some dabblers crave the hue
of sea, and the horizon's view.
They'd rather skirt the river's edge
with navigating sortilege,
while sailing in a snug canoe,
than dive into the ocean blue,
where they'd come up with weed and sedge.
The rest prefer a souvenir
the ocean coughs up from the deep;
a seashell placed upon the ear
with echoes of the sonic sweep
of waves above which gulls appear
in fancies lulling them to sleep.

Published in Magnolia Quarterly, Fall, 2014

Bitter Harvest

Like a man in prison awaiting trial
remembers blissful days when he was free,
I probe the barren landscape of my vile
deed with a prosecutor's scrutiny;
seal the crime scene, where graveyards of my grief
have done tormenting me, and sow the seeds
of healing that will spring the new-born leaf.
I walk love's path before it fell to weeds.
Forget since garnered crops that distance me
from knowledge of the rot my chill would yield.
I seed with torturing consistency
the fertile furrows of that fateful field,
then comb for nectar honeybees had sucked
from blossoms which I subsequently plucked.

Published in Dirty Chai, winter 2014, Issue 4

Brackish Blue

My life's receding further from the shore
where I'd cast anchor in my better days.
The enterprising outpost is no more
that functioned as a thoroughfare to phase
me into some compelling port of call.
And each quay seems more barren than the last.
Indeed my memories begin to pall
along with faded banners on each mast
that used to wave their vibrant hues with pride.
But they've been long since folded up and cased
as I prepare to face the rising tide
and navigate a world that's been erased
by time. And what few precious sites are left
just bring into relief Poseidon's theft.

Published in Soul Fountain, Spring 2013

Structural Damage

A building whose foundation starts to mold
infects the very basis of its strength,
and in due course exerts a stranglehold
on its interiors. Indeed. At length,
the mold pervades the books a thinker delves
into, then compromises where we keep
the dinnerware that fills our kitchen shelves.
It infiltrates the sanctum where we sleep
at night to seek out some relief from stress.
At last, we wake up in an amber light
that barely makes us able to assess
the damage done by such oppressive blight.
It mandates that for safety we abort
the very wellspring of our Life's support.

Published in Soul Fountain
Spring 2013

The Cat's Meow

Whenever I get a high standby number for a free theatrical presentation, I ponder aloud if those waiting with me were aware that some luminous heartthrob was outside; as though culture vultures would care. This time it was a platinum songstress, as appetizing to sophisticates as uncooked fish. While casting my line to cause ripples of laughter I was surprised to see a young girl stalking the frothy shore of my humor, imploring me to confirm the alluring tale she'd just heard. The stage manager assured her not to believe anything I said. There I was, peddling fish, unaware there was a kitten in the house.

Published in The Poet's Art 2013

Mighty Aphrodite

It's easier to throw a punch
than have the will to weather it.
And while I'd mercilessly bunch
my combinations, you were fit
enough to parry them in stride.
But I in turn began to lose,
along with confidence and pride,
the stamina to even cruise
with someone who displayed such verve.
Your countering depleted me
of both resourcefulness and nerve
to challenge such a battery.
And even as I stood bereft,
I clinched to stay what you had left.

Published in Trinacria Fall 2013

Linguistic Fray

How nice to flounder in a foreign tongue.
The more so when a lass has mastered mine.
For from my verbal arsenal she's wrung
enough to storm across the language line
of my defense. Thus, verbally disarmed,
I field dispatches from her motherland.
She soon escorts me, less alarmed than charmed
by my attempts to make her understand
a syntax that I lack the skill to use.
Now she who, so to speak, holds down the fort,
protects me from vernacular abuse
across its minefields. Such pronounced support
just reinforces her discreet behest
that I progress from where I've acquiesced.

Published in Trinacria Fall 2013

Madrigals

I worship at the Juilliard.
For there my music god resides
amidst allegro and retard,
Fidelio and Bartered Brides,
in a community of saints.
I visit there to warm my heart
and not to cleanse my soul of taints
which lore says devil's trills impart.
Therein the maestro's acolytes
can play along as he says mass,
while music-loving anchorites
submit to blessing from the brass.
And better than to be evolved
from sin, is dissonance resolved.

Published in Chrysalis Reader
Patterns 2013

Spirited Advance

Forget the bossa nova, galliard,
or women led by partners in a dance.
It's more exciting when a gal, en garde
while fencing, chooses a proactive stance.
For then a guy's not forced to press his suit,
or feint and parry to secure a match.
He just need raise his blade up in salute
in order to be privy to a snatch
of agency from her who'll brave the fray.
And while most men prefer a solid hit
with penetrating thrusts of their epee,
I revel in her moves to counter it.
For fencers who would rather coast than boast,
score better with a woman's strong riposte.

Published in River and South Review
winter 2013

Love's Gauntlet

It's wise to don a shield and basinet
when crossing lances with a daunting knight.
Yet when my lady's edicts aren't met,
I cede before her challenge with delight.
It doesn't matter if, astride her horse,
I'm stripped of both my armor and my pride
while being forced along her headstrong course.
For soon I grow enamored of the ride
that shows how well she handles spurs and reins,
although no long-eared grains will ever rise
to grace the trek across such sterile plains.
And thus I husband my estate with sighs
and, under pretense of noblesse oblige,
essay the feudal farmer to her liege.

Published August 2013 in Quantum Leap

Capital Loss

If once upon a time I told
myself adventures that were bold,
I learned to settle down in life.
I bartered violent storms and strife
for sober worlds that compensate
frustrated longing for a mate
with social ties I stood to gain
in time. Now that my fortunes wane
I find no reason to withhold
those fancies which, though grey and old,
resume their stranglehold on me.
With an inflated currency
they drain the pittance I have left
and leave me with its sum, bereft.

Published in Convergence December 2013

Clothes Call

A cancelled date's like a garment
that's too large. I hate loose-fitting clothes.
Laundered habits keep me warm.
They fit snugly around my small frame. No need
for a sales pitch. But discount prices
make me want to try on something new.
I walk with shoulders back - stomach in,
chest out! - so I'm not swimming
in outsized clothes. But I take
a liking to them. I benefit
from the change of fashion. I preen about
in things I never would have considered wearing.
And then the phone rings. Last minute
alterations. Date's cancelled.
So much for the hard sell - being sold
on merchandise I didn't want in the first place.
So I draw from my old wardrobe.
Now once perfectly good clothes seem
drab-looking. They begin to feel too tight
for my puffed-up pride. I promise
I'll never go shopping again.
At least not in the same store.

Published in The Avalon Literary Review
Summer, 2013

Foraging the Green

A tiger doesn't change his stripes.
For should he wander from the woods,
no matter how some pundit hypes
the value of domestic goods,
there's nothing like the wild life prey.
It keeps him focused on the course
that stimulates his will to play
the game in ways the times endorse.
And though his game be under par,
concerning black or white-tailed deer,
survival instincts take him far
afield to dodge the hunter's spear.
And thus a birdie, doe or yoke
of oxen yields before his stroke.

Previously Published in The Lyric 2013

Sweet Tooth

Sometimes, if I begin to pout
beside a waitress who rebuffs
me, I imagine pigging out
on apple pie and creamy puffs.
She serves banana splits so rife
with caramel topping I forget
that there's a use for fork and knife.
And after eating crêpe suzette
with apple sauce for the entrée,
I haven't room for the dessert.
I wish for fish and chardonnay,
or that my stomach wouldn't hurt.
Thus, when my beaming waitress comes
with sweetbread smiles, I'm pleased with crumbs.

Published in SEEMS, Issue #49, winter 2015

Courting Bonded Men

Why should a woman choose to be pursued
by the advances of a faithless man
who, being satisfied, leaves her subdued
by an arresting need which he outran?
Why should she let the fellow call the shots,
deciding when to love her or to wed,
when being tied with more than nuptial knots
ensures he doesn't take her maidenhead
for less than his commitment to be bound
before more than a coterie of friends?
If he resists constraints he should be crowned -
though not with a tiara - for amends.
Why should she settle for his post-sex snores
when hunting him for bounty settles scores?

It's just like sex when women are on top
of this intense, exhilarating game.
No need to woo a guy she's got the drop
on, acting sensuous to stoke the flame
of lust. And after the climactic chase,
she sits in bliss beside her charge, content
he'll neither split nor have another place
to go to that precludes her loath consent.

Though intercourse here isn't perfect sex,
post-coital ennui affords no more
reward, and hurts when romping with an ex
who nestles near her body just to score.
And while she sleeps in consummated peace,
her worked-up thrall is still denied release

while chafing in her sybaritic snares.
But palpitating like a blushing bride
before a host of uninvited stares,
how fast his independence is belied
as soon as she secures his hand to hers.
And though he once was deemed a worthy match
for belles, she's heedless that resentment stirs
within them that she's made this vaunted catch.
For even if she hasn't won his heart
whose pride insists on keeping her at bay,
she did succeed in capturing that part
of him which gives her power to hold sway,
despite his fugitive, distracted eye.
And carnal bonds are hardest to untie.

**Published in Talking River Review,
Issue #39, autumn, 2015.**

Schopenhauer in Love

(addressing his beloved)

Although I found the woman of my dreams,
who's to my Romeo a Juliet,
I know that true love isn't what it seems.
For those romantic trappings just abet
the species at the cost of me and you.
And just before our true love ardor fades,
we'll find we should have heeded Montague
who gave short shrift to Cupid's masquerades.
For they concealed a treacherous intent
that contravened the interest of the self.
As such, my cynic's bent must circumvent
this marriage for the books that line my shelf.
And lest we die in marital duress,
we'll live apart in single happiness.

And why should we become the species' dupes,
promoting Nature's procreative urge
like circus mammals jumping through the hoops,
when I can use that elemental surge
of energy to write The World as Will
and Representation, and you're spared schnooks.
I feel a nobler, independent thrill

when having mental congress with my books.
Okay, I guess the future of the race,
for better or for worse, is your concern,
and that instinctively we both must face
our fate. But reason gives us means to learn
and turn desire for the nuptial bed
into Nirvana's mystic bliss instead.

Published in Jerry Jazz Musician, 2013

Rogue's Gallery

"Goya!", I crowed. His name became a ram
that I would wield to batter down her door,
or show her that her learning was a sham
that didn't have a window to explore
beyond the cherry blossoms in her yard.
"Ah, yes. He was a grim, embittered guy,"
she pondered, as if putting me on guard
against my puerile urge to glorify
grotesqueries that issued from his brush.
My brash, enfant terrible she's parlayed
into a painted gamin with a blush
that Fragonard or Renoir might have made.
Thus rendered, I waxed innocent and dumb
beside the prudent artist she'd become.

Published in Plainsongs
v. 34, No. 2, winter, 2014

Mugging Amiss

"You have to think big" I boasted to the coffee-counter
girl after telling her I wanted a cappuccino grande.
I was standing in the line-up of patrons waiting
to give my order, when my billet missed its mark.
My wayward shot must have triggered her fight
or flight reflex that fixed me in her sights. I was being
playfully amorous only to be served the summons
of her piercing, police cruising blue eyes impaling
me with dilating third degrees. Their interrogatory
glare seemed to be frisking me for heat that would
have been hard to find in the purblind pockets
of desire. Even so I stood summarily disarmed
by her ocular pat down, palpable even from
where I paled, under passionate arrest.

Published as "Creamed" in HQ Poetry Magazine
#42 Oct 2013

Frau Direktor

You made believe I'd won a leading part
in a movie you were making. Though geared
for fame, I'd find you had more craft than art.
For just as the first day of filming neared
you made some drastic changes to the script.
I found the romance angle redlined out
as I became a fallen angel, clipped
of wings. Indeed, a villain who'd soon sprout
horns. I was given unsavory traits
to complement your screenplay's new-spun theme:
a story where the gal repudiates
her beau. That I'm now outcast is a scream
to cineastes who've studied in advance
your twists and turns to gothic from romance.

I'd have been better served if arrogance
had stoppered up my lips and I'd been mean.
My entertaining you with song and dance
gave you the opportunity to screen
me like night rushes. First takes yielded scenes
your craft adapted to subversive ends.
For my concerns are celluloid routines
to piece together, flattering the lens

of that projector running in your mind.
You highlight parts that make you look the star,
while my impressive turns are left behind
on your cutting room floor. It feels bizarre
to find I play the heavy in this flick;
my role changed by some post-production trick.

Published in HQ Poetry Magazine, #42, Oct 2013

Inflammatory Thoughts

Rife fantasies are toxins in the blood
which mobilize the white cells in my brain
to thus articulate a surging flood
of mental images. They form a strain
of poetry intended to contain
the progress of the virulent disease.
In fact such mental processes inflame
the very system they're presumed to ease
from torment with a regimen of verse.
For these engender more diseased conceits
and fantasies that make the sickness worse
until contagion rides iambic beats.
Thus, lest the virus run its fatal course,
it must be extirpated at its source.

Published in WESTVIEW

Disclaimer

I want to leave this world before my time;
before the mocking maladies of age
and self-inflicted ravages of rage
become the rumored consequence of crime,
in which I'd squandered precious years of prime.
I want to die upon life's bustling stage
as though too soon upended in my climb
to fame; not stumbling in a musty cage
that duly functions as some scoundrel's wage.
I want to die before the smoky slime
that plagued men slither through, implies that I'm
to blame. Distress won't pluck my bearded sage
or wrack my brain, confounding who I am.
I'll stop the dealings of this crooked game
that makes me butt of random wrath and shame;
before, too agonized to give a damn,
I add hate's sore contagion to my lot
and make it seem God's justice that I rot.

Published in WESTVIEW

Jersey Blues

New Jersey! Thanks for standing by my side
when I was growing up and still at home.
You introduced me to my future bride
when my heart's fancy later on would roam
beyond the confines of the city mile
where it would take its customary walk.
But moonstruck by the Hudson skyline's smile,
effulgent with Manhattan's lights, I'd balk
at tumbling down beside your river's bed.
For New York flashed me that come hither look
that in the end persuaded me to wed
the broad expanse that opened like a book
with thousands of adventures to be had.
And still I sleep beside you like a cad.

Published in River Poets Journal
Autumn/Winter 2013

Pastry

"You need to think in bigger terms,"
I blustered when she said she sold
just small cannolis. Fireflies
were flashing in her azure eyes
as though to warn predacious me
she'd leave a bitter aftertaste
if my intentions weren't good.
Indeed, I crimsoned where I stood,
until I felt her wings enfold
me with an amber livery
appropriate for spineless worms.
Thus zapped, like insects liquefied,
my ego melted into paste
to fill cannolis just her size.

Published online in *82 Review March 2014
as CREAMED

Fighting Erosion

If sensuality's the H20
and fantasy's the sodden hole it makes,
then sublimation's soil helps us to sow
creative seeds once mental prowess rakes
it so its suitable to bring forth fruit.
Detritus won't find refuge if no hole
is there for random fancy to take root.
Let every inch of earth support a knoll
that branches out like canopies entwined.
For even with desire's wind and rain,
there'll still remain sufficient earth to bind
the sandy grains together and to drain
the excess runoff that would waterlog
the ego and reduce it to a bog.

Published in The Magnolia Quarterly, Fall, 2013

Choice Roles

It isn't just the tawny pants
and fearsome glance that now enchants
him. Nor the way she casts a spell
personifying Ariel
in Shakespeare's Tempest. These just show
the potency of Prospero.
The fact she's sporting bat-like wings
while riding sprightly underlings -
who shoulder her about the stage
while she exacts a fearsome wage
on captives of the shipwrecked crew -
make rascals rue what spirits do.
But he does not boast rude intent
that she would have to circumvent

until his head is hung in shame
near embers of his ardent flame.
He's moved more by the art and heart
she puts into her perky part.
Forget the cap and tights she wore
in "As You Like It" weeks before,
or that she smartly effloresced
thus, from how Rosalind was dressed

to blossom in a young man's clothes,
with Ganymede's presumptive pose.
It's her progressing from that state
to strong arm of a potentate
with such insidious delight
that makes his daunted heart take flight.

Published in The Magnolia Quarterly, Fall 2013

Stirring it Up

She thought a meal by candlelight,
combined with an exotic fare
that's served in costly chinaware,
would whet his sluggish appetite.
But fancy schmancy wasn't quite
inviting as a beef steak rare,
embellished with vin ordinaire.
Nor would he take another bite
till, having gotten in her hair,
he saw his mistress brusquely clear
off silver, plates and coffee cup.
Her grim, unappetizing glare
would make the beans served next, appear
like haute cuisine he'd soon scarf up.

Published in The Magnolia Quarterly, Fall 2013

Airborne

Why squish a laugh
through pursing lips
unless my quips
(which missed, by half,
your landing strips)
played on a graph
of sinking blips
that tracked my trip's
regressive gaffe.

Your radar knew
this airman flew
love's wayward course
around your force
of gravity,
and not to rent
that firmament
which vouchsafed me
such smooth ascent.

Posted online on a Scandinavian
board in 2000

Mordant Melody

Unlike composers whose indifferent tune
might bloom into a dulcet melody,
seductive strains that I began to croon
developed as a threnody
for want of the composer's solid craft.
Not only did I lose my major key,
but tumbled in a tailspin from the staff
into a castigating minor G
that even now pervades my tonal hues.
Nor can I silence that staccato chord
reminding me that loneliness ensues
for those with dampers on love's sounding board.
For strings succumb to tympani and drum
which sets the tone for dissonance to come.

Published in Storyteller magazine

Death Watch

A dying man who's in and out of sleep,
my life's sustained by cronies who pass by
me; mirrors of the memories I keep.
But I must wait till dawn to fortify
my temperament. My friends are specialists
who know my needs and wonts. Their drugs, prescribed
by trial and error, serve as catalysts
of visions, lost as fast as they're described.
No sooner do I recognize a face
to be an ally who could care for me
then it dissolves into that misty space
where dreams rub shoulders with reality.
And thus I live life on a bed of wheels,
delirious between my sleep and meals.

Published online in Drown in My Own Fears
April 2013

Bewitched

Though not Leucippus, dressed in woman's clothes -
offending nymphs who found out he was male -
apparently she read a catty pose
behind my guileless effort to regale
her boyfriend with the photo of a girl
arrestingly risqué in bathing suit.
My hair might just as well have been a swirl
of bouncy curls, and my demeanor cute
as peaches, for what filtered through the eyes
of her who challenged me with prickly scorn.
I felt like some gal rival in disguise.
And even as she managed to suborn
my sensibilities, I'd cede to her
entrenched positions that had caused the stir.

Published in Talking River Spring/Summer 2014

Picking Up Slack

Though well-proportioned and extremely buff,
you chose more to offend than tantalize
when you walked by with odor strong enough
to trump a man and cut him down to size,
were body smells a sign of being tough.
You certainly refused to patronize
my sex with any mark of girlish fluff.
Indeed, no stud's sweet-scented, passive prize,
you tacitly seemed keen to strut your stuff
with cockiness analogous to guys.
And though most men loathe women they deem gruff,
and are impervious to compromise,
relieved of rival males and proud rebuff
of prissy gals afraid to fraternize -
and thus, of my subversive macho bluff -
how fast I found my flagging prospects rise.

Published in Talking River Spring/Summer 2014

Thorny Blossoms

You came in drag. But thistles in the rose
cannot gainsay its redolent bouquet
or compromise the freshness of a spray
exuding fragrance when the rude wind blows.
Just so, your strutting, autocratic pose
in captain's suit, adopted to dismay
me, just parlayed the bosomy display
that firmly effloresced beneath your clothes
into a posy on a prickly branch.
Forget the headiness of your perfume
which testified to vitalizing roots,
and crimsoned cheeks which had begun to blanch.
When I saw your protected shoots in bloom
on layered bark, I reveled in its fruits.

Published in Talking River, Spring/Summer 2014

Staged Encounter

Though he prefers his mistress in a dress,
it doesn't bother him if she wears pants,
as long as he can see her effloresce
with assets that are suited for romance.
And when she's on the stage in man's attire;
if her seductive contours are implied,
he anxiously expresses male desire,
enchanted that a woman blooms inside.
But when she covers up her native fruit
and plays the virile sex with fervent game,
though he'll suppress his amorous pursuit
while she enfolds her histrionic flame,
it piques his passive bent to know she can
accost her bashful lover like a man.

Published in Talking River, Spring/Summer 2014

Passing Muster

You glowed in Shakespeare's Measure play with art
enough to make me wish you were my wife.
And yet you parlayed Isabella's part,
as supplicant to save your brother's life,
to Caesar's Antony. How fast you'd slough
off femininity in your pursuit
of leadership. Nor would I give you guff
if I'd been Brutus poised to prosecute
his doomed campaign. Was Isabella's meek
demeanor cauldron for such sterner stuff?
Or did conceit afford you means to pique
my sensibilities, thus, off the cuff,
as Antony? And no more than your bluff
in simulating prowess seemed enough.

Published (with different lines 9 and 10)
in River and South Review winter, 2013

Aphra Behn's

unlike the Stratford bard, Will, forgotten.
And justly so, based on the play I saw -
"The Patient Fancy". Weak, ill-begotten,
it's less an adult body in the raw,
than a child posing in her mother's dress.
There isn't even jewelry and rouge
in lieu of verbal glitter and finesse.
The hoops that gird her petticoat are huge
enough to fill the stage with sweeping airs
and gestures of the grown-up world. But terse
mimicry with a purse hardly compares
with shapely contours of accomplished verse.
Despite the borrowed trappings of her speech,
real poetry is just beyond her reach.

Published in The Homestead Review, spring 2014

Man, Woman and Child

She wears the fruit of his loom astride the firm frame of her shoulders. Head rollers in her hair serve as handles for the warp and weft of his needling fingers. They thread her silken tresses while she shuttles him along to ratchet up the taut aspect of her high-strung lover, as he dawdles with her ear. The latter, seeing her court-appointed hand-me-down in knots and stitches as she weaves her yarn, fast becomes unwound.

Published online in Stride Magazine

Revision

The demolition phase has run
its course. Emotions have been spent
and, after building has begun,
I casually use cement
to reinforce a brick or two.
I smile to think of the distress
I suffered weeks before when new
to that dread project I would dress
myself in denim workman clothes.
Recalling dust that loomed before
my poetry relaxed to prose
adjustments of a metaphor
that seemed about to topple down,
I doff my hard hat with my frown.

Published online in Stride Magazine

Going Gaga at Juilliard

I stormed their heartland, made their senses smart,
when asking female ushers if the rock
star was to be performing to jumpstart
the show. I'd hoped to give them aural shock
as they dug in their trenches for the siege.
Assailing their aesthetic barricades,
I trusted they'd surrender to my liege
lord's musically incendiary raids.
Just 3 weeks later at its concert hall
I show my ticket to an usher ette.
Awaiting a symphonic Pastoral
by Beethoven, my straitlaced senses get
cacophony instead. For in détente
with rapt artistes, a phalanx of their peers
exult in jest that GaGa's next, then daunt
my sensibilities with martial jeers
and laughter. Having crossed the Rubicon
successfully, my conquerors march on.

Published online in Stride Magazine

Early Bird Taxi

A bit perturbed because I made her wait,
she chastens me with her forbidding mien,
as if I had been tardy for a date
with some despotic, promenading queen.
I scramble toward the back seat of her cab
to catch an airplane to the Philippines.
I feel as vital as a frozen slab
of beef. She shifts gears as the car careens
into the highway. No safe sights abut
my mental wilderness to mitigate
the stark rebuke of her ducktail haircut.
I just see roads unfolding toward a fate
which I, dismayed, submit to by default
before her subtle, sensory assault.

Published online in Stride Magazine

Grave Markers

I dread those fleeting harbingers of death.
A vendor's gone. A friendly colleague leaves.
The gal behind the deli counter left,
I heard, sometime ago, and no one grieves.
Do they wax blissfully beside a wake
who when they're at a wedding shed no tears?
Indeed, such emblematic ruptures break
the hearts of those who nurse bereavement fears
when neighbors move into another house.
For they're aware the Johnsons' dying child
made moves as bold as that. And Sam's sick spouse
passed on into a region rife with wild
expanses farther than another town.
Just so, however friends depart, I frown.

Published in The Stray Branch
Spring/Summer 2015

Birthday Wishes

Though serial birthdays have plundered your years
with breaking and entering tempests of grief
that tarnished your quicksilver youth with their tears,
may today's celebration collar the thief.
Use high-flying kicks and an amorous hold
that scuttle his fugitive progress in flight
and empty his pilfering pockets of gold.
Let sly indiscretion squeal out with delight
then pin with new trappings the treasure he stole,
exchanging his jagged-edge latchkey with smiles
and raggedy coat with a fresh camisole.
Now powder his scowl with insouciant wiles
till his silently quivering lips draw near
with whispered confections of love in your ear.

Published in Mature Years, Fall 2013

Shifty as Charged

The springtime peppers holes in my conceit.
For memory is masked in woolen clothes
at winter when I trudged through snow and sleet.
I still insist on fancy's youthful pose
when there are few infractions to recall
that aren't cloaked in muffling masquerade.
But bare-all spring commemorates with gall
the life of each post-mortem escapade,
like crimes ticked off from my contested years.
And how can I ignore a rap sheet flung
accusingly with evidence from peers
who many years before this charge I'd hung
around with. Hostile witnesses to age,
they seal Time's verdict at the judgment stage.

Published in The Stray Branch Fall 2013

Clockwise

I owe it to myself to be on time
or not accept its challenge to compete.
Since celebrated as a paradigm
of knighthood, I won't grumble in defeat.
Nor will I implement my whip and spurs
to keep my hurtling charger on its course
until the inevitable occurs,
with shameful tumbles, and a voice that's hoarse.
I won't besiege Time's chariot in flight,
as though I were a coward in reverse
by tilting at a windmill that can't fight.
For reeling in its aftermath is worse.
So either I'm positioned for the fray
or bide my time, lest there be grief to pay.

Published in The Straybranch Fall 2013

Sea Mist

My crew's asleep in the cabin. I guide
my ship on its parlous course into port.
But the gleaming beacon of your eyes glide
my steerage where sirenic waves disport.
I'm queasy in the quayage of your arms,
astride that salty scent which I resist
while soaking up your coastline's shifting charms.
Though shouldering the shore, your thighs insist
I lie beyond the placid sailing lane
I've grown accustomed to. Strong undertows
of passion open corridors of pain
to torrid crossings where the gale wind blows
my kingfish halcyon to turbulence.
Bereft of navigating instruments

I take the plunge in billowy waters
where the foundered spellbound of folklore sleep
in liquefied arms of Neptune's daughters.
And there I brave submersion in the deep.
Disruptive motions of its surging tide
convince me that it's easier to lie
transported by the current that I ride
than try to fix my bearings to some guy

in distant keys. Thus, wind-tossed, I enter
your gulf like seamen during the deluge
that tempers drought. Refuge and tormentor,
you spread safe harbor as a subterfuge,
until I come. Relieved of my command,
I lie exhausted on your brackish strand.

Published in Sandy River Review
Spring 2013

Scholastic Arms

No well-developed muscles in a bout
to demonstrate tenacity and skill
has the advantage of cerebral clout.
The wise diminishes her rival's will
by studying the drama of the past
and what led to a character's demise.
Perhaps it's being fancifully cast
as knights in shining armor in the guise
of Ajax, Galahad and Lohengrin.
It could be mimicking adaptive styles
conveyed by Hamlet, Beowulf, Harlequin,
or to adopt Ulysses' cunning wiles.
But muscles scarcely pin opponents down
with such finesse, amazement or renown.

Published by Hawai'i Pacific v. 27/2013

As the World Turns

I'm wondering if light years hence
some Martians - thawed into rebirth
with hydrogen peroxide - sense
elusive signs of life on earth?
For once its frozen landscape warms
and starts emerging from its shroud
of freezing gusts and dusty storms,
its carbon just might fuel a cloud
of oxygen. It'll kindle life
that hibernated underground
when pressured to avoid the strife
of gravitating round and round
its thermo-challenged star, which sun,
since scorching earth, makes Mars well-done.

Published in The Martian Wave
August 2013

In the Woods

While waiting in the car to get my ride
back home, the woman I'd been flirting with
was demonstrating sporty skills outside.
I aped Actaeon in the Grecian myth,
while she became the goddess Artemis.
For she began to bathe my tired eyes
as I espied her metamorphosis
from gymnast to a more balletic guise.
But when she spotted me inside the car
my voyeurism quickly hit a snag.
With Kung Fu moves she now began to spar
with air. Thus dogged, I morphed into a stag.
Indeed. I felt like any hunted prey,
until my driver quickly sped away.

Published in Ship of Fools, winter 2012

In a Doctor's Office

As if she had the key to my house -
along with private access to my heart -
she didn't play the doc's assistant anymore,
but started talking down to me
as if I were her boyfriend or a tot.
The surgeon's mask she wore would not
constrain the salutary license of her sex.
For she addressed receptive signals
that I must have flashed for her.
Even rudeness in her tone of voice
might well have put her in a different zone
than mine, and spared me her egress
into my sensible abode. But barring this
I settled for exploratory intercourse -
with scarcely options to invite her on a date,
or wait for some more opportune occasion
to expose myself. Neither would the gal disrobe
while lying near my palpitating smarts.
But shorn of courtliness applied when one
anaesthetizes transplants from a single's bar -
while prepping them for nuptial bliss -
there were no pre-ops here. Instead a humdrum

nurse engaged in wifely chores,
she waxed romantic as a weary mother
after tucking in her child. Intimate procedures
having grown domestic, her concession
to a facial mask disconsolately dangled from her neck.
And I woke from my fancies happily sedated.

Published in Ardent, Spring/Summer 2013

Concerto in A Flat

I think I'm composing a concerto
for piano and orchestra. In fact,
cowed by the public, I'm improvising
the keyboard part. My halting snippet
of a tune progressed sotto voce,
muffled by the beat of ominous drums
which I oppose with harsh, staccato chords.
Where once I sought the broad, romantic line
now I settle for melodic patches.
Soon I lose the key I'd been working in
amidst the thunderous cacophony
unleashed by the rush of blustery winds.
I won't mention the surprising stridence
of once civil strings marshaled by the din.
I press on the pedal to hear the notes
resound, start losing my cool. Never mind
the audience marking my performance!
It's not the piece that I started to write
before I had to heed market constraints
and the stern baton of the conductor.
But I don't care. Experts fathom the plight
of creators; the rest suffer the just

measure of their ignorance. I compose
in order to be faithful to the piece.
Still, my metric muse senses something's wrong.

What happened to rapt motives I began
with? Do fans recall such lush harmonies
when I hammer the keyboard in response
to that percussive swell? Or will they think
I'm mad? Indeed. Habit deadens my nerves
along with raising my auditory
threshold, till I'm addicted to fortes,
not to speak of mind-benumbing interludes.
Oh! Nasty critics love to disparage
what they're slow to understand. They protest
such clamorous discord. Some of them hissed
me off stages promoting philistines.
But connoisseurs know that real artists forge
their handiwork amidst severe hardship.
And they acknowledge the difficulty
of our craft even if they don't laud it.
Meanwhile, I'm left with a brief cadenza
nearing the end of the second movement.
For the rest, I hope I salvage something
before my instrument's banged completely
out of tune. And then I can only guess
at the criticism awaiting me.

That's why I'm leaving out my signature
and cede responsibility or claims
that I'm the author of this potboiler.

Published online in Nth Position December 2012

Poetic Circe

As soon as you start musing in her cove
she jumpstarts first your heart and then your brain,
constraining them to cede your treasure trove
of cerebrating seamen she can train
to populate the fauna of her realm.
With rhythmic incantations she can change
a journeyman in ways that overwhelm
his senses till his porcine needs estrange
him from his reason. Snorting at the trough,
he digs for truffles filled with reverie.
Nor will the sorceress exact enough
until she consummates her revelry
in physical translations of conceits
begun with measured, metabolic beats.

Published online in Nth Position
December 2012

Opera Bluffs

Are patrons who watch opera at the Met
enthralled by music or by curtain calls?
Why else applaud the curtain as it falls,
when chordal resolutions haven't yet
achieved the main part of that grand duet
of sight and sound? No tom who caterwauls
will purr until the cat's mew that enthralls
him stops. He heeds no backdrop sun that's set.
Then why do fans erupt into applause
before the tonic chord concludes an act?
The tone deaf see the visual as cause
of all that made their viscera react.
In fact, I wish their tract contractions pause
just long enough to keep the work intact.

Does one applaud medieval trumpet calls
mid-scene in an Elizabethan play
before the dramatist has had his say?
Of course, the theater curtain never falls
before the closing dialogue enthralls
enraptured listeners. In such a way,
expecting a catharsis, fans delay
their dispatch of enthusiastic squalls.

Then why not give Puccini the respect
accorded playwrights and the written word?
Don't unresolved tonalities affect
rapt listeners much more than words not heard?
In Europe, fans sit frozen to collect
themselves - with bliss, instead of chords, inferred.

Then why can't they aesthetically hang tough
who rudely clap before the music ends.
What ardent lover indiscreetly spends
his manhood for a woman in the buff
before - midst love's embrace - she shows her stuff?
What matter if the curtained night descends
on them, and atmospheric quiet lends
to their rapt nakedness its sable muff?
The substance of their argument's not done
until the ardent music that they make
resolves itself in harmony hard-won.
Love's tonal rush won't brook a screeching brake.
Yet they break us who interrupt the fun
of spells thus spun, and thirsts we're poised to slake.

Published in Nth Position, 2012

Around Dawn

At times, when Morpheus delivers me
from sleep - before Aurora brushes earth
with the roseate colors of dawn - I rise,
surprised as Maya lifts illusion's veil
from my eyes. Having bared life's rank
malignancy, she makes it wrap about me
like a musty shroud. Hostage of incarcerating
tombs I pray for the muscling contractions
of Thanatos to ferry me across undulating
Acheron and Styx into Hades. But Morpheus
mercifully sedates me with resurgent sleep.
Soon I waken - after Maya (Nature's Prozac)
works her mesmerizing magic - to pastoral
harmonies. These combine with chimes
in homes and squeals on enterprising streets,
where the screeching of careening cars
resonates like choirs of spirited children
hollering hosannas at the newly minted day.

Published in Epiphany February 2013

Shrewd Investment

The channeling of impulses that press
on us into more cultivated aims
is like the blossoming of consciousness
out of the wayward thrust of childish games.
The loss is only felt when, thus engaged,
we're driven to indulge life's pleasure source
until our basic cravings are assuaged.
But once we're on a more productive course
and parlay Nature into dividends,
instead of money spent at her behest,
we benefit from self-enhancing ends,
forgoing fun and games for what works best.
And if forbearance blinkers disco lights,
it scans illustrious, if sober, heights.

Published in Long Story Short, 2013

Honda Xmas Commercial, 2012

What matter if she's only 4 ft tall,
too small for older peers to more than hear
her interrupt her selling spiel to call
out "Shotgun!" to their disregarding ears?
She settles for the backseat of the car
as they talk teenage shop among themselves.
For she's now an adept recording star.
Hippolyta ensconced among the elves,
the Honda Civic lets the child take stock
of what they plan to do when not around
their parents. Parodying how they rock,
her flailing arms kinetically rebound
up toward the ceiling as her mien assumes
a province all but presaging their doom.

For she's decided that the interchange
is interesting, if just as reportage.
She doesn't worry how it might estrange
her wary sister's female entourage
from sharing teenage secrets openly,
while she plays scribbling scribe inside the car.

Indeed. The 'shotgun' passenger's esprit,
deflated when the girl has gone too far,
has registered with evident dismay,
her disapproval of the sneaky snitch
to be. It's clear this patsy won't betray -
without a more precautionary hitch -
another surreptitious enterprise
till she has cut the gadfly down to size.

And who'd opt being in her custody,
for all the telltale secrets in the world?
See how the enterprising bonhomie
of her conversant, smiling lips have curled
into a frown at the presumptive threat
to her inveterate hegemony.
For she's astutely managed thus, to vet
the comments of this inauspiciously
intrusive tween musing in the back seat
of her car. It's true our nosy scribe finds
her flanking party-goers' indiscreet
downtime disclosures 'interesting' signs
of pending teenage disobedience!
But she won't hear much more from this time hence.

first 2 sonnets published in Long Story Short Dec. 2013

Character Disorder

It's not enough that gals should wear my drawers
and steal my parts! For years I plied my trade
by playing soldiers, cops, suave troubadours
who courted damsel, courtesan and maid.
No longer paid to please the stalwart male
who tuned me in to see my saber's thrust,
I now delight in Lord Fauntleroys and flail
in impotence before an ample bust.
And being soft in defense and attack,
I'm game for feminists whose flailing fists
make obsolescent their once genteel smack.
For film patrons who are masochists,
love is not enough. They trade temptresses
for androgynes who, braving me with scorn,
join brainy broads and brawny empresses
contesting me till potency's forsworn.
Thus, I'm transported to the passive track,
upstaged by Amazonian campaigns
or, animated, on a horse's back,
astride which feisty Mulan holds the reins.
I thrash about like some defenseless slut
while cute, seductive buccaneers kick butt.

Published in Quantum Leap Poetry Mag
February 2013

Sweet Service Provider

What salubrious psychology she used
when dealing with this guy who was upset
at not connecting to the internet.
As though he were a toddler who'd been bruised,
she boasted that if she had been abused
like him she probably would also get
annoyed, and put aside the etiquette.
With hints she'd otherwise be not amused,
she said she didn't take it personal -
since she was proxy for the firm reviled.
At such a turn, he grew emotional,
as to a mother who might well be riled
by conduct close to confrontational.
But she consoled her disconcerted child.

Published in Quantum Leap Poetry Mag,
February 2013 as Serviced Provider

Snowsuit

While her children are asleep,
Mother Nature, sporting white
plush puppies, steps stealthily
through the night and leaves
behind her, Christmas drifts
that decorate her trees.
In the darkness these are lit
by street lamps that snuff
their amber glow
before her children's
hushed awakening.

Published in Quantum Leap Poetry Mag
February 2013

Beleaguered

Odysseus could barely make the grade
when battered by an unrelenting storm.
Then temptress sirens cunningly parlayed
their parlous straits to let mirages form.
For since he brooked slim chance of reaching shore,
still less of entertaining nuptial thrills,
what use was steadfast steering anymore,
or plying vaunted navigating skills?
Arresting music made him veer off course
while he was left to rail against the wind
in lieu of finding its demonic source.
For piqued Poseidon, not his sailors, pinned
him to the mast that devastated hope
and shrank horizons to his fancy's scope.

Published in Quantum Leap Poetry Magazine
February 2013

Fifth Column

Like someone who's intent on sabotage,
you infiltrate me with linguistic skill.
Your playful jargon sounds a soft massage
on jaded senses. Rather than just kill
your adversary, you adopt my land
as yours. You master complex routes of train
and bus until I lose the upper hand
and waver in retreat. What strange terrain
of styles and manners you adroitly map.
Precise coordinates inform the mask
you wear to patronize and then entrap
me. Lax defenses! Weary from the task
of holding down my fort against love's siege,
I hail you, foreign agent, as my liege.

Published in Challenger, Summer 2013

Ill-Seasoned

It's tough to live outside the loop.
I'd warm to tiller of the land,
and clean the barn or chicken coop.
Or I could be a farming hand,
haul bags of wheat with wiry arms,
be liable to blight and sere -
as well as to a lady's charms.
I'd sweat in heat to toil and shear
on soil where the cicadas hum.
But they must miss the monsoon rain
before which vital crops succumb
(or otherwise supply us grain)
who, though exempt from winter's rage,
endure the harvest of their age.

Published in Challenger, Summer 2013

Where's the Beef?

How trace the reasons for Mad Cow Disease?
Does it begin with runny nose and wheeze
that put afflicted bovines ill at ease?
Perhaps, instead of giving milk, they sneeze
in England wishing they were overseas -
sunbathing on blue beaches in Belize -
instead of being tethered till men seize
them for the steak that ends up in deep freeze?

If Elsie chewed the cud in Broolynese
she'd soon conclude: "da problem's dem and dese
beefeaters who, averse to greens and cheese,
give bulls just time to let us cows reprise
conception, det and rebirt fantasies.
What should we do when brutal breeders tease
us with da hanging sword of Damocles?
It wud be nice if gods wud hear our pleas
when cowed "how now brown cows" kowtow their knees."

But butcher shops are not church dioceses,
and if they were, would these please devotees
who serve God less than slaughter industries?

Published in Challenger, summer 2013

In the Wings

How nice it'd be if Life let us rehearse
a play the dramatist has yet to write.
The prose we speak so poorly will be verse.
Such words delight when we don't have to sight
read our lines. God knows it takes a lifetime
for each of us to master our part;
and getting panned by destiny's a crime,
that can be rectified when actors start
in earnest. Thus, Life would be a run through
for accomplished readings on the proper stage
that's waiting for us when we're paid to do
our stellar presentation for a wage.
And much is due this weighty enterprise
where the protagonist each evening dies.

Published in Challenger, summer 2013

Life Sentence

No prisoner, whose daily regimen's
restricted to a life constrained by bars,
regrets the loss of recreation time
inside the prison yard when once his sentence ends.
It certainly was great to venture from his cell
and walk outside unshackled into open air
to stretch his limbs, enjoy the chirping birds
and feel the incandescent warming of the sun.
But such an exercise could scarcely override
his feeling of constraint so that he wishes he were there
when once he's served his time. Just so, will we,
incarcerated by this life of flesh and bone -
though periodically relieved by those amenities
we cherish now as precious reprieves from life's stress -
regret their loss when we have served our term.

Published in Challenger, summer 2013

Cartwheeling Gal

Like Arthur brandishing a sword at fed
up nobles who declared him déclassé,
she offered us a cavalier display -
her legs thrust skyward, arms uplifting head,
gyrating - neither seeming, thus, ill-bred,
nor fearing such athletics might dismay
presumptive nobles of our present day,
or jealous fops she'd scarcely care to wed.
She slipped off gravitation's forceful grip
and, more like Arthur pulling sword from stone
than lancers going on an ego trip,
she demonstrated hardy muscle tone
with flippant, unintended showmanship
suggesting prowess she'd as soon disown.

Published in CHALLENGER Summer 2013

An Extraterrestrial Affair

“So you boast you’re on top of it,” she said,
before she pinned her husband to his bed-
rock theory of there being life on Mars.
But all the guy could see was clustered stars
when hearing her affirm, “Now I’m on top
of my initiative to put a stop
to your relentless probe. In lieu of his
attempt at playing astronomic whiz
with wild hypotheses and telescopes,
she took the basic steps to learn the ropes
of scientific sleuthing. Lunar probes
gave way to her beleaguered gynophobe’s
decision to bring science down to earth
and help his life-supporting wife give birth.

Published in Italian American 2014

Jane and the Dragon

It's not enough the dragon be subdued.
He must relinquish his potential threat,
acknowledging his lady's fortitude
in getting him to happily abet
the exercise of her emergent skill.
Accordingly he cedes to her the sword
affording her a weapon that can kill
her captive if he ceases playing ward.
It also serves to penetrate his scales
and make him acquiescent to the ride
that he unhesitatingly avails
her. Pandering to passive bents inside
him, he's content to serve at her behest,
supportive adjunct to her knightly quest.

Published in Italian American, Winter 2014

For Therese

(the dedicatee of Beethoven's Fur Elise)

I hope your beauty was well-spent,
considering you'd not consent
to take poor Ludwig as your spouse.
For although not the powerhouse
you'd choose to live with all your life
behind the honorific, "wife",
at least you'd have your namesake piece
not misconstrued as For Elise!
You'd claim your just posterity
along with some celebrity.
For since few novelists or bards
can serenade like music cards,
when you snubbed Ludwig's score with name
misspelled on it, you'd forfeit fame.

Published in Poet's Haven, March 2013

Couples

Of all life's oddities, it seems most strange,
that couples treat as if they had the mange,
fellow travelers searching for that love
the paired are shamelessly partaking of.
Would they plant smooches on their woolen gloves
then snuggle to them like they're turtle doves
because they saw some bloke whose hands were cold
or jump with youthful joy to mock the old?
And would they, teasing, dangle from a fork
in bistros, appetizing chunks of pork
at vagabonds who can't afford to eat?
Just so they play with amatory meat
beside starved men who only have a bone
to soothe themselves while journeying alone.
Do gourmets gorge with smacking emphasis
near dietary fare like lovers kiss,
as if filet mignon and Peking Roast
taste better next to tuna fish on toast?
Then pity those who living on the dole,
are treated like they didn't have a soul.

Published online in Miller's Pond

Fruitless Outing

Although rejection hurts and hearts can't bide
the agony of unrequited love,
the harshest pain is never to have tried.
Withdrawal hurts as much as any shove
the forward womanizer gets who fails
in his pursuit. How sweet is sleep in war,
or beating a retreat when it avails
combatants in a tattered army corps.
But what remorse Columbus would have felt
to voyage near a hospitable land
whose rolling hills were emerald as veldt,
if docking he did not extend his hand
to natives who seemed bristling with intent
to form a bond he'd happily cement.

Published in Miller's Pond v.16 #2, 2013

Making Waves

She seemed unworthy of my heart's pursuit
when I first chatted with her on a lark.
I pondered that she wasn't one I'd toot
my horn about or otherwise embark
upon romantic journeys with. Then she,
describing sea adventures with aplomb,
regaled me with her sailing odyssey.
She might have boasted crossbones, swigging rum,
and piracy, while buttonholing me
with all the savvy of a weathered tar.
I stood engulfed by waves of fantasy
as she enumerated rigging, spar,
topgallant, mizzenmast, and sloping slip,
till I became a hostage on her ship.

Published in Write On! & Talking River

Poetic Bondage

My poems were bonds of friendship that I'd seal
with any fancy posing as my friend.
And in the sense of loyalty I'd feel,
whatever thoughts were vouchsafed me I penned.
Ideas I scribbled soon became my own
which I explored with a creative bent
that followed leanings where my heart had flown
until my mental currency was spent.
Conceits that I'd committed to the page
to dissipate anxiety and fear,
became the bitter pittance of a wage
I'd glean, precisely as in yesteryear
I profited from money that was clean.
And thus each dividend became a lien.

Published in Write On! & Talking River

Battling Beethoven's Emperor

(piano concerto #5)

How brilliantly she parlays every note
into an aural sortie with her hands.
There's nothing this astute composer wrote
that's not transmuted by her firm command
of fingering and instrumental skill.
She cannily assays the cryptic score,
advancing with finesse through furtive trills
and short, explosive chords whose fortes soar
resoundingly. A pro with 32
sonatas up his sleeve should temper her
commendatory mission to subdue
his battery of notes with force majeure.
And yet with fingers as artillery
she surges forward toward the tonic key.

Published in Westward Quarterly, 2014

Diphthong

I touched you in your native tongue
by scaling syntax, rung by rung,
as though my words were rapt arms hung
with handy idioms that flung
their ribboned sentences among
your tresses. Clauses were beads, strung
together with your hair and slung
across your shoulders where they clung
with fervent ardor, till they wrung
responses which from you seemed sung.
Then you expelled your petalled lung
like honey bees had sweetly sprung
from fragrant hyacinths and stung
my senses with an artful tongue.

Published in POETZ online, Spring '06

The Verdict

(in Simi Valley, 4/29/92)

What dissension, rampant within themselves;
what troubling sin thought transgression needed
atonement far beyond the pale for twelve,
just to retain - what riot in their blood?
What devilish brew blistered compassion,
hexed fairness to a toad of ridicule,
sapped wronged manhood to a sluggish motion,
dwarfed courthouse jurors into circus fools?
What fear lurked behind the mask of fairness
with its charade of deliberations,
while the shadowy mind pitched carelessness
into the reckoning eye of reason?
For even cities quaked with a result
that Justice, blind, would find for those at fault.

Published in Danger magazine, summer '93

Wages

How nice when I had money still to spare.
Big deal if I passed up a meal or two.
A more nutritious dish was always there.
I wore drab clothes. Nor did I need a new
wardrobe every spring. Now, with diminished
funds, I've developed an impulse to buy
items that I'd not previously wished
for. Approaching financial ruin, I sigh
for days when there were still dozens of doors
to open, packages to be unwrapped.
Appliances had graced the shelves of stores
in shopping districts which I'd hardly mapped
amidst the bustling crossroads of my mind.
Now tawdry goods sit marked-up in a mall
that with the best directions I won't find,
despite the fact that I now want it all.
And trapped in backroads of my penury,
I seek less sustenance than shopping spree.

Published in Words of Wisdom
December '05

Terra Mater Indeed

Corona must be a parental vent
for sure. She's sent millions of us to bed,
and billions of her wards brook discontent
at home, or otherwise ponder and dread
what other punishment she has in store
for us. While God can forgive, it's not nice
to fool Mother Nature! Those who foreswore
masks probably will pay a stiffer price
than those who hide behind a masquerade
of obedience. For Gaia's not blind,
like Justice is, and thus must be dismayed
when seeing us not only leave behind
earth's warming, but its consequence, the plague!
What more of Mother Earth shall we renege?

Published in Jerry Jazz Musician 2020

Barnes and Noble Closing

(at Manhattan's Lincoln Triangle)

He was scarcely 15 years old; a patient with a poor prognosis after being mugged by an Amazon. All the caffeinated smoothies in Starbucks couldn't keep him up till midnight. Ordered to bed no later than 10 pm, a cordial crew of concert attendees kept a vocal vigil around the percolating brew that succored him. A once vibrant child pulsing with corporate corpuscles coursing through artsy arteries, his bed's now a mortuary slab. He stares vacantly at the city street's circulating capillaries. For with a steady diet of well-fed patrons wanting purchasing fiber he waxed sclerotic. Fiscal physicians cut his visiting hours to stave off staff infections. And now he's dead. A steady regimen of health books on the second story couldn't help him. Neither could an intravenous stream of Juilliard students or doses of celebrity speakers.

Bypass surgery linking him to Lincoln's triangle proved fruitless. Overhead stress and the spendthrift ways of internet consumers caught up with him. Web-scammed, wishy-washy well-wishers massed by his bedside resting in pieces of prose from books they didn't buy while tendering solace to his waning pulse. No wonder he died at such a young age. And now this bleached decedent serves sad notice of absences that people my brain with pleasant pastimes spent in his spirited presence. And decibels of silence remain to fill the hollow chambers of my fibrillating heart.

Published in Orbis December 2020

Snow Job

Where are you Persephone? Your mother is freezing and taking the rap for you while you're cavorting with Hades or God knows who in the netherworld. Or maybe you're enjoying your stint as Queen in the land of the dead. Maybe it's Demeter, your resentful mother who hasn't called you back yet from your winter recess to start the process of Spring awakening. Too busy bickering about your abduction. Maybe she forgot to turn the page, as it were, or seething with resentment at Zeus, she's reluctant to. She more determined to nurse her bitterness in the cold while the rest of us freeze than in welcoming her daughter for the season of renewal. I heard that Zeus had his hand in your abduction. Be it as it may, it's getting cold up here and it's the middle of March.

Meanwhile, I'll tell your mother to check her calendar. If you're not exactly in her house by this time, you certainly should be on your way. Remember Zeus has already sent Hermes to tell Hades to let you go. I know he made you eat that stupid Pomegranate fruit but he ain't kidding nobody. Zeus wants you back! I want you back. We all want you back, especially in New York City where we're not used to this kind of weather so late into the month. Are you so whipped by gusts of wintry venom that you forgot the date of your return? Okay. So you're not yet home. Maybe you got lost, can't afford a Metro card because Hades is stingy. But your mother and most of the eastern coast is waiting for you. Please give us some of that warmth you're famous for.

Published in Home Planet News 2020

Budding Friendship

Now this former face in the crowd's a voice with a distinctive tone structure. My casual asides are sentences she pins on me like subliminal charges. Her interrogatory air gathers fingerprints from the hand she'll shake me down with for hormonal glands. I've hidden histories with discreet misdemeanors. Disjunctive idioms are beau conspirators she polygraphs for future use. Conversational exchanges give continuity to disparate measures. We're a work in progress, a symphony in see where it goes from here, after she removes the slip from her sash register. I'm an unstrung gift box, flashing its contents, my house undress tailored to her surmise. My cup runneth over and she drinks deep or tastes not reverberating strings of my heart's unsung measures. My furtive thoughts morph into phonemes, words and phrases, culminating in self-incriminating surrender. I've finished my sentence and, pigeonholed, I'm remanded to her cell, where I get time off for food behavior till her discernment ends.

Published in Home Planet News 2020

Post Rosenkavalier

The Marschallin - guess what? She kicked the bucket! See how they like that, those fat cat aristocrats purring in ermine furs. Octavian - cock, dead as the proverbial doornail - shudders; too distressed over the loss of his erstwhile mistress to caterwaul duets with Sophie, his bride of so many years.

Besides, he's saddled with debts. Forget past sonorities! Sopranos scaling solar heights morph as veiled encomiums at disconsolate rites. Tears add tepid grains of rice to Sophie's disingenuous blush - her girth wide enough to fill the Met with raucous laughter. And ravages of arthritis make it easy to forget the virgin fuss that cluttered up the stage she's soon about to exit with Octavian - sullen witness to her age. See youth's orchestral swoon glean shards from a cloud-disheveled moon that nearly hides from sight the stumbling footman, his livery a little frayed from use. No high-spirited dive for his mistress' handkerchief to bring the curtain down with crowning ceremony, but his frown suggests: "Why the fuck am I schlepping this?"

Published in Home Planet News 2020

Ministrations

(of Christine O'Donnell, former
Republican Senatorial candidate)

"If he can nurture himself, I mean then why am I here for?" the winsome woman hoots through the wide-eyed gap in her toothsome smile. Poor little thing. She feels left out of the ball game, put on the sidelines, a benched fielder pounding an empty mitt, as it were; a spectator in a play conceived without her. "Give me something to do," she seems to pine, pondering the conundrum of self-indulgent men.

I mused: "What about standing by him in sickness and in health; till wealth do you smart and ask for a divestment of his assets. Okay let's not get encyclical here. Actually, you're there like gaudy blossoms pillowing the earth, so foragers on a beeline for your honey can pollinate your pistils. There you go! You mutated to a true evolutionary biologist. How unwittingly Darwinian, so adaptively proactive: we're here to reproduce. Never mind puritanical prescripts. Even Jehovah instinctively grasped the full scope of that anachronistic monkey business adjudicating in the courtship rooms of Tennessee. Be fruitful and multiply.

Put aside your right-wing leaning dictates on the one hand, or right winging left-wingers who leave Freud on the burner of their percolating concoctions: we're here to reproduce. You grow, girl! You've the right of way into his heart, albeit wrong roots of reason. Poor little seething cauldron of a pressure cooker. You're leery of being outsourced by resourceful minds; displaced by the machinery at hand. Look at the blight side. It affords only a small penchant of stock images with minimal interest. It yields no crops, no returns for future generations to profit from. Indeed, no generation. Their consummate executors resignedly bequeath our sun no burgeoning patrimony. Their antsy handiwork's passively produced, as it were, on fanciful copiers; digital transfers of synthetic pictures on disposal CD's in a cut and dried rubber plant.

Indeed. What are you there for? You're Hush Puppies as he toes the line, plush carpeting in his homebody, blooming tulips on the table of his membranes, a noodling bowl of soup to spoon with; a hot cup of meme sweetened with honey, a dash of lemon crossing his T with an eye on his doting sensibilities to aid his misconception. You're there to keep hm aligned with the species and to mind the p's and q's of your suffragette set. You're the picturesque window opening up to spin the loom of his woolly imagination, clear eyes in stormy weather and the belle's tether that draws him out of his caged complacency to stalk your wild side."

Published in Home Planet News 2020

Street Wise

The Drilling Company moved from Ludlow Street's Parking Lot and I forgot to bring their new address with me. Walking out of the F train down Essex Street, the burly guy I'd marked for assistance walked across the street when he saw me stopping beside him. But I got more than I bargained for when I saw 5 girls conversing on the corner and decided to interdict them to ask for directions. My eyes fixed on one of the 4 white girls while asking for assistance, though my heart was with the black chick who seemed too hip to give me the slip. "She'll help you, the white girl said as they all continued talking. Then, "What are you looking for?" my Nubian princess asked me as the others dispersed, leaving me in her custody. Maybe they were asking for directions too? "I'm looking for Orkard Street," I said phonetically. "Orkard Street? You mean Orchard Street," she corrected me, like a teacher in grade school. I did the same thing earlier with an Asian girl who got me there in the first place. I had to repeat the street I was looking for 5 times before she maneuvered through the thickets of my mispronunciation. "Yeah, Shakespeare in the Park. Yeah, I know it!" she said with cocky insouciance as she rummaged through the options on her cell phone. I was afraid to take too close a look at her, but she was breezily gritty with looks to match.

“Shakespeare in the Parking Lot,” I corrected her, while biting my lip, lest I usurped the agency I banked on. It was the only time she fell silent. “Yeah, I know Shakespeare in the Parking lot,” she countered in defense, “They used to be on Ludlow Street.” My affected shyness complemented the surging interest I took in her. There were bars all over the place, so my guardian and her cohorts must have been of age.

But I don’t like subverting the kindness of strangers, so I barely looked at her. Yet, though I saw a chic chick, I heard a teamster. For she was cavalier using a popular 4 letter word, and it wasn’t love! “Okay, this is what you need to do. And if somebody tells you something else, they’re fucking lying!” Her cavalier cusses were filtered through her genial, rough-hewn personality. She tossed them about like dressing on a table salad. Hell, she was Rosie Perez in the body of Zoe Kravitz. “I tried small talk to ease my nervousness as she hustled to get me on my way while 2 of the other girls were signaling for her to join them across the street.

She nodded impatiently, as I played up to her. "Yeah they're doing a play there tonight," I assured her to allay any concern she might have had about me. "I know Shakespeare in the Parking Lot," she insisted. "Well, you should come,' I half jested, knowing she was en route to probably bar hopping. "Maybe tomorrow," I added to cover my footsteps. She laughed, perhaps surmising that I was rising to the occasion. Or maybe she felt I was easy! "Okay, it's 112 Orchard St. I don't know where, but it must be a few blocks down from here and if you ask someone and they tell you somewhere else, they're fuckin lying! Don't listen to them. See I can't get a map with this phone here," she continued as I made to leave - against my wishes - not wanting to try her patience. But patience she had as she now proceeded to map out the address and pointed it out to me on her Smart phone, while advising me what I needed to do. My mind was set to go but my heart was fixed on this pert custodian who was being pestered by her white sisters across the street to cede custody of her witless ward. I reluctantly eased myself from her spell. Was ever captive set free boasting less enthusiasm? I don't think so.

Published in Home Planet News 2020

Piquant Aftertaste

"Poetry is passion recollected
in tranquility," a versifier said.
Then why's my tasteless past resurrected
as passionate delicacies instead.
Pert Ana Lisa patronizing me
as rival to Vanessa for my love.
The bread I wrested from the latter teed
her off enough to force me with a shove
to come to her when I'd be checking out
at the Deli - where she worked as cashier.
She'd roast her peer. who simmered with a pout,
while I froze in their headlights like a deer.
Of course, I'd be arrested, baggage searched,
until she found the culprit that besmirched

her reputation. Perpetrator found,
she looked at it with scorn and brash
demeanor as she threw it to the ground
while castigating it as being merely trash.
Their tease was a soufflé, quotidian
enough. Two females stir-frying favors

I'd accord them at the meridian
of my life. An added spicy flavor
to my nutritious, creamy mushroom soup.
But now, the after dinner of my years,
when lettuce in my garden start to droop,
the memory of their concoction smears
its steamy condiments inside my brain
like a rotisserie that starts to drain.

Published in Nomad's Choir

Soccer Mom

Like the Moon goddess
she waxes with its orbit's
monthly rotations.
And, like the chameleon,
her shape-shifting fascinates.

Published in Sci Fi magazine

Daybreak

Wakening from sleep,
mortality unwraps me
from its cold cocoon.
Kindled by the morning air,
I start fluttering my wings.

Published in The Aurorean
Fall, Winter 2012/2013

Ardent Overtures

The hound keeps braying
at the lascivious moon,
which beams in tandem
with its serenade of love;
the dog reciprocating.

Published in Raw Dog Press
July 2013

Haydn Quartet

Velveteen voices
intermesh like branching leaves
rustling in the dark;
fresh blossoms, bunched together
for a redolent bouquet.

Published in Bear Creek Haiku Sept '06

2 Haiku and a tanka

On fire with love;
how garish the fireworks
by the maiden moon.

The Casanova
lies tangled in love's vineyard –
a thousand green eyes.

Lips sweet with honey;
love's fresh, opening flower
dripping morning dew.
Your kisses light my forest,
like night-infiltrating stars.

all of the above Published in:
Bear Creek Haiku #136

Autumn Colors

With an unseasonable warmth
coming on the heels of a cold spell,
your leaving brings into relief
the fruitful days of summer
that now begin to fade.
Nor is it odd that your departure
leaves me bent with grief,
as if I were a sapless tree
in winter, and you its last green leaf.

Previously published in Shemom Spring 2014

String Serenade

The lady in love
bows submissively to her
cello, practicing.

published in Bear Creek Haiku, Sept '06

Pale Male, Full of Grace

(hawks facing nest divestment)

Though pacifists prefer the dove
in wartime to the tomahawk
and guided missiles from above,
in times of peace it's safe to chalk
one up for birds clutched with a glove.
And though the pious weep and gawk
at saints professing selfless love,
and deign, with righteous mien, to talk
the talk when it's a question of
beneficence, how fast they balk
when it comes down to push and shove,
and they're enjoined to walk the walk.
For then they show a lesser love
for those whom storms of winter stalk,
poor beggars without coat or glove,
and homeless folk than for the hawk.

Published in Ceremony

Elegy on the Death of Little Children

Though mourners weep and reminisce
with silver-tongued solemnity,
the first buds of a sobbing kiss
will strew a precious elegy
of pursing lips upon your grave.

Nor shall I murmur lullabies,
anointing with my salty tears,
the soil in which your body lies
with vestiges of prior years
ascending from your somber grave.

The bearing of a kindred grace
will mirror stellar sympathy
like glowing embers in that space
sequestered from my agony,
and radiating from your grave.

Though men cannot endure the truth
and fruitless meaning of their birth,
I'll seed the promise of your youth
and sanctify this barren earth
with flowers on your fallow grave.

Oh God! Sustain this fervent rage
that beggars tears from ancient men;
the budding buttress of our age
lies withered in the dust within
the fragrance of her youngest grave!

Lie softly in the firm-set earth,
the settled sweetness of your youth;
the buried meaning of your birth,
the passing of your gospel truth
will follow in your floral grave.

Published in Nomad's Choir
December 2012

After Schopenhauer

The perceptible world's a stop-off point
for the Will before its homecoming.
Everyone's a tourist here in this huge
bazaar where metropolitan buses lumber
like circus elephants trumpeting trunks
filled with gas instead of air. Here, city clowns
perform economic juggling
acts, balancing budgets atop beams
that gird high-rise stories materializing
like sandcastles out of the river's mouth.
Such impressive spectacles to write home about
with beautified clichés before the tides
of time engulf receding shores.
Many leave their footprints trailing behind
ribbons of nucleic acid. In this vast amusement
park, most pay for short thrills, others get tickets
that seem to let them ride for free,
at least until the winter season.
Then the doors are shut for rich and poor
alike, the props dismantled and the tent
is folded till the harbingers of Spring.

Published online in "nth Position"

Ebenezer's Christmas Card

So what the dickens! Calling me a scrooge
for thrift and working like an honest man?
Do I employ a shameless subterfuge
to outsource Cratchit's job so that I can
secure myself obscene amounts of wealth?
The money that I have is what I earned
by honest enterprise and not by stealth.
In fact, it's from your ethics that I learned
that no one gives you anything in life.
Isn't that what industry's about?
I ceded pleasure and potential wife
to earn not near the money that you flout
conspicuously with transparent pride,
while most in your constituency bide

privations that would make this miser blush
from shame. You like to fabricate straw dogs
to pummel while you unctuously gush
out festive carols by your yuletide logs!
Yet all the time you're feathering your nest
and leave it to the poorer of your peers
to borrow funds from their retirement chest
in order to partake of Christmas cheer.

And so what if I loathe commercialized
indulgences that lure us into stores
so credit unions can be subsidized
with interest rates that annually soar?
It's true I didn't have to be a scrooge.
But, being so, prevented a deluge

of bailouts jeopardizing all you banked
upon to comfort you in future years.
That caring sprit you deem sacrosanct,
and Dickens touts when Marley's ghost appears?
I didn't see too much of it when I
was left alone to scramble for myself,
beset with longings most folk satisfy.
Nor did my stocking on a mantelshelf
solicit Christmas cheer and merriment
that you could ill afford. For you denied
me love who, even now with smug content,
berate me for my bitterness and snide
behavior. You ignored a sad youth's plight
that would have cost you nothing to set right

beyond that Christian charity you boast
about when reading my creator's book.
What's more, no grouch can entertain a ghost
unless he has the empathy to look

inside himself. For ghosts just haunt a heart
receptive to the warmth that lies within.
And after all I played my paltry part
in emulating Him who's free from sin.
But I still get a table in the rear
when I set out at night to eat my meal.
Alone, I add! For it's just once a year
that relatives emotionally feel
some kinship with a grump set in his ways.
This notwithstanding, Happy Holidays!

briefly published online as second place contest winner in 'Eye on Life'. Dec 2011.

Charu Turns Lovelorn Shrew

(in Satyajit Ray's Charulata)

How slowly the eternal feminine
dissolves behind the sari Charu wears,
as she's empowered by adrenaline
to entertain her amatory cares.
Like some frustrated voyeur on the prowl,
she peers at life behind her window pane,
with opera glasses poised above the scowl
domestic mores force her to maintain.
She uses them to bring into relief
her distant husband's cousin, as he lies
unmindful on the grass, of any grief
he's causing her. But we can see her size
him up as prey for predatory bents
that hold her reservations in suspense.

While reconnoitering the prison cell
that cossets her, she entertains her spite,
as much as love, to storm the citadel
of her beloved's pride. She starts to write.
With pen in hand and pulverizing beam
in studied eyes, she edits what she reads,
then starts again with energizing steam

until she musters images whose fruit precedes
the words that mirror windmills in her head.
They populate the piece she will complete
and publish. It should put her in good stead
to trump her lover's literary feats.
At least it'll serve as prelude to the paan
she'll stuff into his mouth to lead him on.

For not content to see herself in print,
she bolts to where her author in-law's
playing the piano. With searing glints
of victory - in lieu of soft guffaws -
she beats him with the magazine to show
him just how much he'd underrated her.
Not that he did, but she's resolved to blow
her horn with literary force majeure.
He might have been a child she'd toilet train
to clean the inky scribblings left on sheets
of paper so he'll boast a cleaner strain
of writing for the poesy trained elites.
I'm sure in future, chastened pen in hand,
he'll pamper himself with her reprimand.

Published in India-USA
Punjabi English Magazine 2019

Sound Rearing

While waiting for the train one night
he met this gal from Pakistan
whose native hue was burnished tan.
Her raven hair beamed marble bright
as she began to shed a light
on honor that she owed her man.
Nor did she preen as women can
who demonstrate from pride or spite
the need to make a fellow smart
to show that they're a privileged breed.
He eulogized her fiery eyes,
which wheedling praise she didn't heed
as she proceeded to apprise
him of an honest woman's heart.

Respectable as she was sweet
her values served as guiding jewel,
refracting any indiscreet
propensity to ridicule
he might have harbored in his breast.
"You have to understand, sweetheart"
she chastened him when he'd protest
that she was now a world apart

from the traditions she had known.
She mesmerized him with the phrase
as though, instead of fully grown,
he were a ward she poised to raise.
Indeed. So much was he beguiled,
he eagerly became her child,

and readily grew reconciled
to her polite, arresting airs.
Her mien was pleasant, manner mild.
Subordinating all his cares
to this maternal surrogate,
adopting him as ersatz ward,
now seemed a reasonable bet.
Forget her giving room and board
to him while in her custody.
He found a place within her heart.
It functioned for the fuss she'd be
creating to parlay his part,
commemorating her mores,
into his separation phase.

Published in India-USA
Punjabi English Magazine 2019

Breaching Mrs. Peachum

(in a school staging of The Threepenny Opera

Perhaps because she seemed an easy mark -
as someone pleasantly demure offstage -
the fact that she assumed a role as stark
as Mrs. Peachum scarcely disengaged
his amatory sensibilities.
As such, he'd fancifully take the part
of daughter Polly so that he could squeeze
indulgences from her, despite the tart
exchanges that ensued. The bickering
between the mother and her child went back
and forth while his enamored heart took wing
to see his Polly give his heartthrob cracks
at playing loving mom. Alas, a right
cross landing on her daughter's jaw, before
she's swept across her shoulder out of sight,
was not the way he entertained rapport.
with her. Nor did it whet his appetite
to fancy himself scandalously slung
across the torso of a girl as slight
as any fragile beauty he had sung.
Indeed, his ego trip, unwisely tried,
did not accord him such a pleasant ride.

Published in Art Times, October 2020

Chef-d'oeuvre

Die Meistersinger's like a 5-course meal
that well-nigh's too delectable to eat
in just one sitting. Never mind the veal
fillet that garnishes the trio treat
in Act 3 with polyphony to whet
the appetite for more. This chef has craft
sufficient for the table to be set
for 6 including me, with one more draught
of intermission. That would make me stout
enough to gobble up the final act.
And though I don't have operatic gout,
regaling clogs my gastronomic tract.
Thus, lest such music dishes make me gag
on riches, I'd prefer a doggie bag.

Published in Art Times 8/14/19

Rumors

Forget the slanders of a wicked tongue.
For foolish people think what they will think.
It's when their vile effluvia have wrung
from you approval that your feelings sink
in ways that reinforce their sick conceit.
You have too many measures still to sing
to let some madcap make you skip a beat.
Nor should you waste your time considering
what people say who are so far obtuse
that they can't tell the difference between fact
and being hijacked for another's use.
Your mission is to keep your mind intact,
and heart and soul courageously at odds
with those who are opinionated frauds.

Published in The Society of Classical Poets
11/4/20

Retired

I've lost the ship I banked upon
to shield me from this stormy world.
For I've since crossed the Rubicon
and sails no longer loom unfurled
that marked my navigating days.
My schooner scarcely can escort
me from my maritime malaise.
The stalwart craft I'd bring to port,
with either treasures to unload
and share with members of my crew,
or tales of some rough episode
that they would help me travel through,
is lost. Now stranded on the shore,
I'm tortured by the ocean's roar.

For it implores me to embark
on journeys that meant much to me
against the backdrop of my stark
environs. Now a memory
of bustling lands I once explored
with enterprising waves of bliss,
it mocks a heart forlornly moored.
It's social industry I miss.

The camaraderie of hands
engaging in a common chore
that seemed to stay the flowing sands
of time's disbanded. Stevedore
of stored-up cargo from the past,
my body's anchor has been cast.

Published in The Society of Classical Poets
11/4/20

Wham! Bam! Thank You Ma'am!

They blundered again, those Lotharios at the Met!
The rakes did Cio-Cio San for almost 3 hours
then left without a parting kiss.
Right after Pinkerton's terminal cry
of "Butterfly!", before the shattering
dissonance of her wake-up call
could chill the death pall in her cheeks
and prompt bestowals of a post-chordal kiss -
never mind the salutary effect
of smoked silence on strained sensibilities -
these opera oafs applauded. Impulsive ingénues!
Clock watchers, marking time rather than feeling
the pulsating music emanating from her body,
and cradling it in protective arms!

Did they forget the chopstick patter
of her dainty feet, choral kimonos,
the broad arches of ethereal song
through which she entered their hearts
and blushingly undressed? Let them be fickle
in the ways of love, play fast and easy
with harmonic suspensions, the rising ardor
of her perfumed voice, floating airs
crowned with chrysanthemums, and the scented
raptures of scattered cherry blossoms.
Were they weary of such lush fragrances,
cloyed with the varnish and lacquered
tenderness on discreet silk screens,
startled by the rustling currents
of her plaintive melodies? They had to be.
For they rushed from the moon goddess
and then from Cio-Cio's petal-strewn home
after the emotionally charged climax
left her heartbroken and fatally spent.
No lingering excesses to comfort her
before the curtain pinned the clipped
wings of her porcelain dreams.

Published in Red Rock Review
Spring 2020

Desperate Measures

To win back love's embezzled stash,
I played at blackjack and roulette,
then turned my chips in for hard cash,
which only got me into debt.
For after hitting all the slots,
I withdrew savings from my bank
and patronized the hotter spots,
imbibing liquor till I stank.
And as each tavern closed its doors,
I wandered soused and penniless,
my spirit where the eagle soars
and heart in search of love's caress.
Thus, driven to regain my wealth,
I lost what still remained of health.

Published in Poets' Espresso Review
v.14, Issue 1, 2020

Fighting Aphrodite
(outdoors)

She watched with glee Love's Labor's Lost
beside the Sailor's Monument.
Herself, star-crossed, was her hat tossed
into the ringing argument
of nobles sabotaged by love's
commands? For she robustly clapped
as though she sported boxing gloves
and had vicariously trapped
Amor's opponents on the ropes
once they'd been cornered by their beaus.
She seemed to thrash the lovelorn mopes
with brash guffaws in lieu of blows.
Between rounds she sustained with food
her quest to have these lords subdued.

Published in Poets' Espresso Review
v.14, Issue 1, 2020

Political Caveat

Be careful with the social seeds you plant.
For liberal, pontificating rants
may make the world safe for democracy,
but otherwise it breeds autocracy.
Then hearsay functions for the rule of law,
where growing pains become a fatal flaw,
and visceral respect for basic rights
is compromised by making free speech slights
against unwritten rules. A flip remark
that resonates like Pekinese dogs bark -
without a bite - are bellowed in the court
of Cable News where one's defense falls short
of an acquittal by the talk police,
whose smug reverberations never cease.
For they project in other people's hearts
the remnants of their own internal warts.
It's somewhat like the Salem trials of yore
where witches drowned on charges they foreswore.
For no defense can satisfy demands
of smug, self-righteous demagogues who stand
in tandem with the people who they judge,
because the mote that's in their eyes won't budge.

Nor do I miss the bitter irony
that one can't hurl an ethnic slur at me,
but someone threatening to kick one's butt
gets points for this dehumanizing juggernaut.
I don't mind liberals with bleeding hearts
if we all donate when the bleeding starts.
Nor do I mind alleviating grief,
as long as mine is not brought in relief.
Beware politicos cum autocrats
who purge our interests in the laundromat
of CNN and some such cable news
outlets. They brainwash us with slanted views -
according the foundation that they built
on backs of slaves, a plush veneer of gilt.
And though I certainly do not endorse
self-centered people who are acting coarse,
I really see no reason to complain
when decent people go against the grain,
expressing valid views. For if no one
defends those dudes who liberally run
their mouths affirming rights and liberty,
I'll be defenseless when they come for me.

Previously Published in Dissident Voice 12/6/20

Lightning Source UK Ltd.
Milton Keynes UK
UKHW040711191220
375534UK00008BA/369/J

9 781664 146457